AF886338

A Practitioner's Guide to

Test Automation using

Selenium

A Practitioner's Guide to

Test Automation using Selenium

Ashish Mishra *and* **Aditya Garg**

Co-founders of QAAgility Technologies

Tata McGraw Hill Education Private Limited

NEW DELHI

McGraw-Hill Offices

New Delhi New York St Louis San Francisco Auckland Bogotá Caracas
Kuala Lumpur Lisbon London Madrid Mexico City Milan Montreal
San Juan Santiago Singapore Sydney Tokyo Toronto

Tata McGraw-Hill

Published by Tata McGraw Hill Education Private Limited,
7 West Patel Nagar, New Delhi 110 008

ISBN (13): 978-1-25-906382-4
ISBN (10): 1-25-906382-8

Vice President and Managing Director—Asia-Pacific Region: *Ajay Shukla*
Publishing Manager—Professional: *Praveen Tiwari*
Editorial Researcher—Science, Technology & Computing: *Sushil Gupta*
Sr. Copy Editor: *Neha Sharma*
Manager—Production: *Sohan Gaur*
Asst. General Manager—Sales and Business Development—Professional: *S Girish*
Deputy Marketing Manager—Science, Technology & Computing: *Rekha Dhyani*
General Manager—Production: *Rajender P Ghansela*
Manager—Production: *Reji Kumar*

Typeset at Text-o-Graphics, B-1/56 Arawali Apartment, Sector 34, Noida 201 301 and printed at Rajkamal Electric Press, Plot No. 2, Phase IV, HSIIDC, Kundli, Sonepat, Haryana - 131028

Cover Printer: Rajkamal Electric Press

Cover Designer: Kapil Gupta

RCCLCRXHRBBLY

The McGraw·Hill Companies

To

I would like to offer gratitude to the God Almighty and my parents Dr. R.K. Mishra and Mrs. Sudha Mishra. I specially thank my wife Rashmi in making this book a possibility by her unconditional support in all my endeavors and misadventures. I would like to dedicate this book to my adorable sons Rishabh and Devansh.

Ashish Mishra

I would like to thank Almighty for giving me this opportunity. I would like to dedicate this book to my parents Dr. S P Garg, and Mrs. Madhur Mohini Garg and to my entire family including my brother who has been a constant source of inspiration. I would also like to specially thank my wife Prachi who has stood by me, most importantly during our difficult times and my three loving daughters.

Aditya Garg

Foreword

The appetite for open-source test-execution automation tools is increasing at a rapid pace. More and more organizations are shifting their automation from commercial tools to open-source and effect of this is seen in the Job market where the demand for skills in these tools has increased rapidly.

There is a gap in the market between what is demanded and what exists. The skills required to become an expert in any of these tools can't be acquired in a few weeks nor can it be acquired by just reading a book. Acquiring any skill requires substantial amount of practice. It is said that to know a subject you need to spend a few hundred hours but to become an expert you need to spend thousands of hours practising and honing your skills. I sincerely hope that the present book will be able to guide a practitioner of the craft in an appropriate direction with its emphasis on examples, samples and hands-on exercises.

Vipul Kocher
President
Indian Testing Board

PREFACE

This book is result of our quest for excellence in the field of test automation. This journey started when Aditya (or Adi as we all fondly call him) and I left our respective jobs and started company of our own, *QAAgility*. As the name suggested, our focus was Quality Assurance and achieving Agility in that. We were mainly aimed at providing testing service with an edge and our main distinguisher was the agility, and agility was largely driven by automation.

Scouting the Test Automation market there was no way that we would have missed on Selenium. In order to cater for the Selenium related requirements, we actively looked out for Selenium expects and also interviewed few them. Eventually we found that there was real dearth of Selenium professional not only in India but globally. This situation lead us to evaluate and explore the tool on our own to fulfill our client's requirements. We documented our learnings as we picked up the tool and used it to resolve various test automation related issues.

This documentation turned into a training course that we started to offer in public as well as corporate training platform. While this was happening, we unknowingly became the 'flag-bearers' for Selenium as preferred automation tool in the market. We were extremely convinced regarding the utility of the tool and wanted to propagate it to the best of our ability, somehow it was felt that we owed it to the tool. However, there were some road blocks.

Being an open-source tool has made Selenium popular however it is a double-edge sword as it can easily turn counter-productive. At times what happens that when you adopt a tool and you don't have to pay for it, you tend not to plan and strategize on the actual implementation of the tool. This would also include untrained or self-learned test automation engineers who might have the skewed picture of the tool and limited awareness of the features. This was also due to fact that the testers who wished to learn this tool were manual testers with limited programming language. When you are evaluating a tool which is free you tend to give up at the first issue that you face, it becomes a 'show-stopper'.

So there were many organizations and testers who started to evaluate Selenium but gave up too soon upon come across technical difficulties, and they could do that as there was no real investment made for the tool cost. We were witness to all this and our training course started to impart knowledge of the tool to the budding 'test automators' who were maily manual testers and then there were experts who were continuously compare it to other popular Test Automation tools, especially the paid ones. So we had to tread that road keeping balance between the technical details while training the participants.

Our training courses evolved such they could get testers start automation work quickly and made the learning curve less steep. The practical content of the training programs have been transformed into this book. We have tried to give to enough details and step-by-step instructions and tips to get started with the tool and fast track your learning.

As we are getting more and more involved with Selenium 2.0, we feel even more excited about the tool and keep us going with more motivation and zeal than ever.

Ashish Mishra

Aditya Garg

CONTENTS

INTRODUCTION

Introduction

History

Selenium was invented in 2004 by Jason R. Huggins and team. Initially it was not called 'Selenium'. But then, even they were not aware of the fact that they were inventing a tool. They were simply looking for a solution to the problem that they were facing in the application. They initially named the solution as JavaScript Functional Tester [JSFT] but then it slowly evolved it as an Open source browser based integration test framework built originally by Thoughtworks. It was 100% Javascript and HTML and was designed to make test writing easy. It had ability to run whole suites of tests or individual tests and also to step through individual tests. It was cross browser – IE 6/7, Firefox .8+, Opera, Safari 2.0+

Story about Selenium

Selenium was extracted from a web-based (Python + Plone!) time-and-expense (T&E) application at ThoughWorks. One of the mandates for the new T&E app was that it needed to be fast. The expense reports can get pretty long for people who travel a lot. No matter how many default rows were put in a blank expense form, people often needed to add more rows of expense items to their reports. So they added an "Add row" button to the expense report form. To make this fast and scalable, they decided to use a button that triggered JavaScript to dynamically add one blank row to the form. At the time (Spring 2004), however, JavaScript was considered buggy and evil by most web developers.

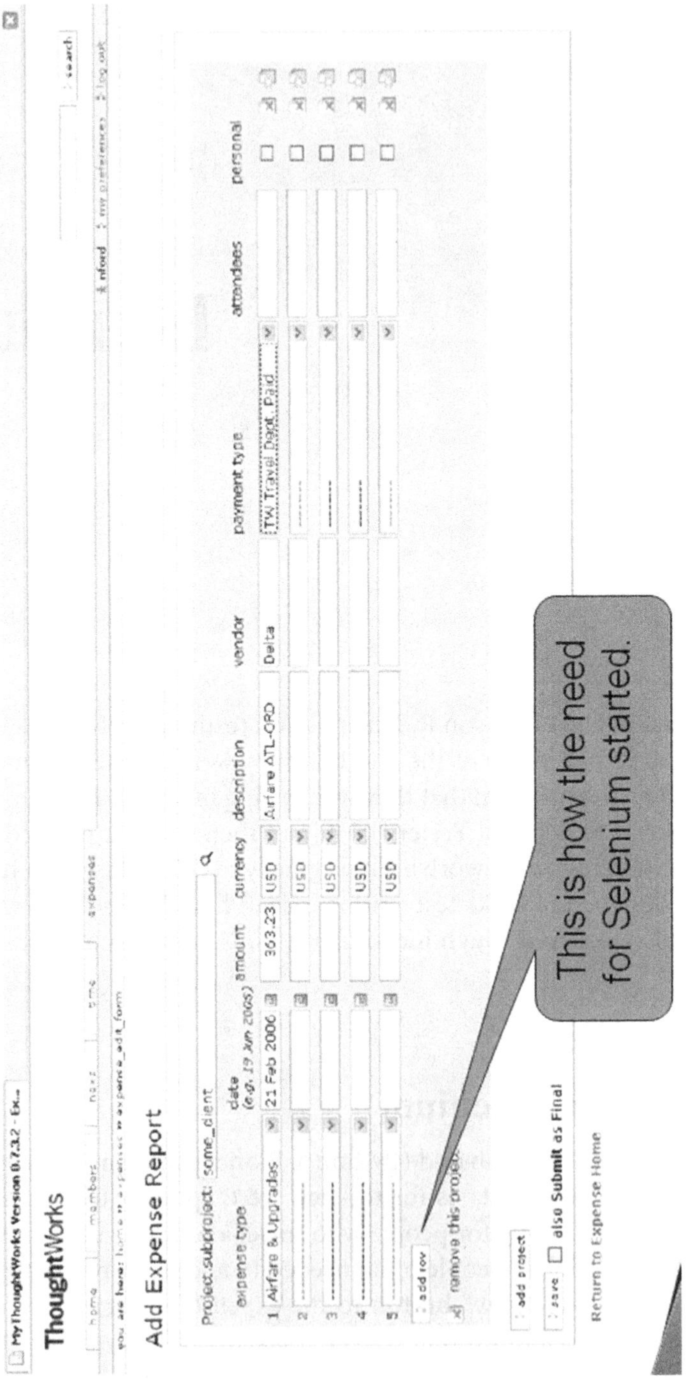
ThoughtWorks
Add Expense Report
Project:subproject: some_client
expense type
date (e.g. 19 Jun 2005)
amount
currency
description
vendor
payment type
attendees
personal
Airfare & Upgrades
21 Feb 2006
363.23
USD
Airfare ATL-ORD
Delta
TW Travel Dept. Paid
add row
remove this project
add project
save
also Submit as Final
Return to Expense Home
This is how the need
for Selenium started.

They had a really difficult time testing that little "Add row" button and it broke often. One week "Add row" would be working in Mozilla (Firefox was pre-1.0), but broken in Internet Explorer and vice versa.

They had a very tiny budget and commercial testing tools were - and still are - ridiculously over-priced on a per-seat basis. The T&E project was done the "Agile Way" - every developer does testing - so shelling out thousands of dollars per developer for a testing tool wasn't going to happen. Never mind the fact that there were no commercial tools that did what we needed anyway!

After many months of trial and error and various code workarounds, they came to the conclusion they needed a testing tool that would let them functional-test JavaScript-enhanced web user interfaces (aka "DHTML" or now "Ajax"). There were no commercial apps at the time that could do this. So they needed to write our own tool and Selenium was born.

But why the name 'Selenium'?! After all Selenium is a chemical element with the atomic number 34, represented by the chemical symbol Se. It is a nonmetal, chemically related to sulfur and tellurium, and rarely occurs in its elemental state in nature. Absolutely no link with software lest testing!!!

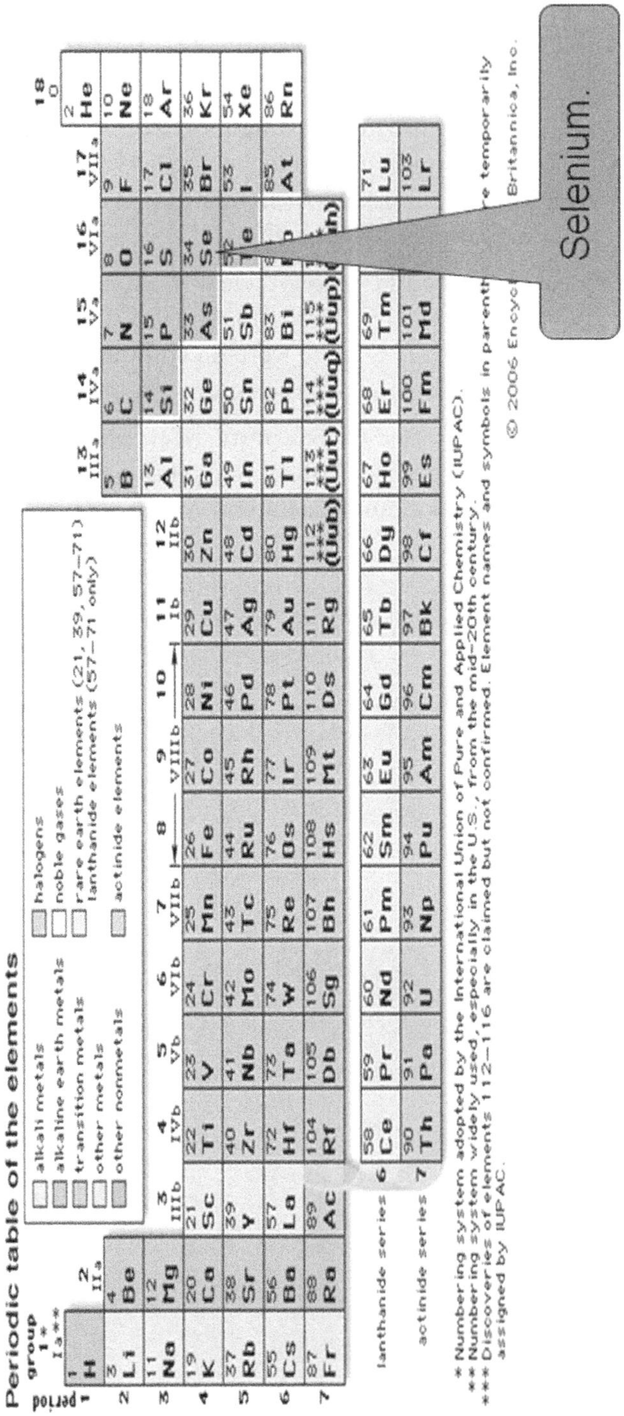
Periodic table of the elements
alkali metals
alkaline earth metals
transition metals
other metals
other nonmetals
halogens
noble gases
rare earth elements (21, 39, 57–71)
lanthanide elements (57–71 only)
actinide elements
lanthanide series
actinide series
Selenium.
* Numbering system adopted by the International Union of Pure and Applied Chemistry (IUPAC).
** Numbering system widely used, especially in the U.S., from the mid-20th century.
© 2006 Encyclopædia Britannica, Inc.

Selenium is used for treating "Mercury" Poisoning.

Hint: At that time tools like Quick Test Professional and Quality Center is developed by Mercury Interactive Corporation (Now HP owns it).

What is Selenium

Selenium is a portable software testing framework for web applications.

The tests can be written as HTML tables or coded in a number of popular programming languages and can be run directly in most modern web browsers.

Selenium can be deployed on Windows, Linux, and Macintosh.

Selenium is used for UAT (User Acceptance Test).

Selenium Components

- IDE
- RC
- Grid

Selenium IDE (SIDE) is a complete Integrated Development Environment (IDE) for Selenium tests (previously known as Selenium Recorder).

Firefox extension that allows recording and editing of tests

Allows easier development of tests

Selenium IDE Features:

➢ Record and playback

➢ Intelligent field selection will use IDs, names, or XPath as needed

➢ Auto complete for all common Selenium commands

➢ Walk through test cases and test suites.

➢ Debug and set breakpoints

➢ Save tests as HTML, Java, PHP and other such formats

➢ Support for Selenium user-extensions.js file

➢ Option to automatically assert the title of every page

Getting The Source-Code

Licensing

Selenium is open source software, released under the Apache 2.0 license and can be downloaded and used without charge. For more details visit http://www.gnu.org/licenses/gpl.html

Windows, Linux or Mac

Selenium is available for operating systems such as Windows, Linux and Mac.

EXERCISES

1. What are the Testing Tools you know?
2. Do you know any testing Tool which tests cross-browser compatibility?
3. Find any five testing tools. Provide brief description about the tool.
4. Find any 5 differences between the Functional Unit Test Tools you know and Selenium.
5. What is a Open Source Project?
6. What is a GPL (General Public License)?
7. What are the web development mark-up languages you know?
8. What are the scripting languages you know?

1

TEST AUTOMATION

What is Test Automation

Test Automation is much talked about topic in the world of software testing and quality. But before we get into Test Automation, let's figure out what is software testing? The classical definition says "Software testing is a process used to identify the correctness, completeness and quality of developed computer software." However in real world, testing can never establish the correctness of the software. It can only find defects—it cannot prove that there are none left to discover.

This process is carried out either manually , using automation tools, but mostly it is combination of both.

Manual Testing is defined as developing and executing tests that rely primarily on direct human interaction throughout the entire test case - especially in terms of evaluating correctness and ascertaining test status.

Automation Testing is defined as developing and executing tests that can run unattended, comparing the actual to expected results and logging status. The rest of the book will concentrate primarily on automation testing.

Simply put, "Automated Testing" is automating the manual testing process currently in use. Minimal setup includes:

Detailed Test Cases

Predictable "Expected Results"

Dedicated Test Environment

And most importantly dedicated and skilled resources.

The obvious benefits of test automation can be listed as below:

- ➢ Longer term reduction in the cost of testing
- ➢ Accelerate time to market
- ➢ Reduce cost of quality
- ➢ Continuous Integration and Environment readiness
- ➢ Consistency
- ➢ Better coverage
- ➢ Increased confidence in code
- ➢ Job satisfaction
- ➢ Testability

Automated testing is expensive in terms of cost. It does not replace the need for manual testing or enable you to down-size your testing department. Automated testing is an addition to your testing process.

However, test automation can be cost-effective by following some of the time-tested techniques. It is recommended that there is an automated test strategy defined for Automation projects. This automated test strategy may not be the same for all the projects, as it needs to take into account the environment and risks identified for that project, as with the strategy for manual testing. This needs to define the business goals and objectives for the use of Automated Testing. As well as being aligned with the business goals it also needs to fit within the testing process.

Once the strategy is put in place a set of corresponding measurements must be defined to track whether the automated testing is meeting the goals and objectives.

Having talked about automation, it needs to be considered that sometimes it makes sense to execute manual tests first before executing automated tests for a number of reasons. It may not be economic or appropriate at that time to automate. Not all tests are suitable to automate.

The following list is considered to be "good practice" for the successfully use of test automation to ensure a reasonable level of Return On Investment (ROI):

- ➢ The test process is clearly defined and facilitates the use of existing test artefacts
- ➢ Test automation requirements are clearly defined
- ➢ Test automation has a defined architectural approach and supporting design to facilitate:
    - A robust implementation that provides appropriate levels of reliability
    - Repeatable automated tests
    - Minimisation of software change impacts to the automated tests
    - Clearly understood and documented levels of interdependency
- ➢ Test automation standards are defined and followed
- ➢ Test automation effort must be planned, documented, monitored and measured

- Clear definition of roles and responsibilities for use of the developed framework and its ongoing support and maintenance.
- A champion has been clearly identified within the organisation to perform a cultural change management role to facilitate adoption and use of the framework within the organisation
- Test environment is controlled to ensure a high level of stability which enables repeatability

Most Commonly Used Test Automation Tools

Tool name	*Produced by*	*Latest version*
HP QuickTest Professional	HP	11.5
IBM Rational Functional Tester	IBM Rational	8.1.0.3
Parasoft SOAtest	Parasoft	9.0
Ranorex	Ranorex GmbH	3.0
Rational robot	IBM Rational	2003
Selenium	Open source	1.5.0
SilkTest	Micro Focus	2010
TestComplete	Smart Bear Software	8.2
TestPartner	Micro Focus	6.3
Visual Studio Test Professional	Microsoft	2010
WATIR	Open source	1.8.0rc1

Test Automation Environment

For a successful Test Automation, we need to pick up the test environment carefully. We will be using the following tools while we learn Test Automation using Selenium. This will effectively constitute our test automation environment.

Selenium IDE

Selenium IDE is the Firefox plug-in that does record-and-playback of interactions with the browser. Use this to either script simple scripts, or to speed up creation of Selenium RC scripts.

Minimum Recommended Version 1.0.10

Download from: http://seleniumhq.org/download/

Java

For execution of our test cases Java Runtime Environment (JRE) is sufficient. But since we will also be doing lot of development work thus we would need Java Development Kit (JDK).

Minimum Recommended Version JDK 5+ (Java 1.6.xx)

Download from: http://www.oracle.com/technetwork/java/javase/downloads/index.html

Eclipse

Eclipse is a multi-language software development environment comprising an integrated development environment (IDE) and an extensible plug-in system. It is written mostly in Java and can be used to develop applications in Java and, by means of various plug-ins, other programming languages including Ada, C, C++, COBOL, Perl, PHP, Python, Ruby (including Ruby on Rails framework), Scala, Clojure, and Scheme. The IDE is often called Eclipse ADT for Ada, Eclipse CDT for C/C++, Eclipse JDT for Java, and Eclipse PDT for PHP. We will use JDT.

Minimum Recommended Version : Galileo

Download from: http://www.eclipse.org/downloads/

Selenium-RC

Selenium Remote Control (RC) is a test tool that allows you to write automated web application UI tests in any programming language against any HTTP website using any mainstream JavaScript-enabled browser.

Minimum Recommended Version 1.0.3

Download from: http://selenium.googlecode.com/files/selenium-remote-control-1.0.3.zip

2

GETTING STARTED WITH SELENIUM IDE

Installing Firefox

Visit the Firefox download page like http://www.getfirefox.com in any browser (e.g. Microsoft Internet Explorer). The page will automatically recommend the best version(s) of Firefox for you.

For installing and running Selenium RC, we need to have Firefox version 3.6.x. To access the older versions of firefox go to the URL http://www.mozilla.org/en-US/firefox/all-older.html

Click on the green download link to download the Firefox installer, then Run the file. It is recommended that you exit all your other running programs.

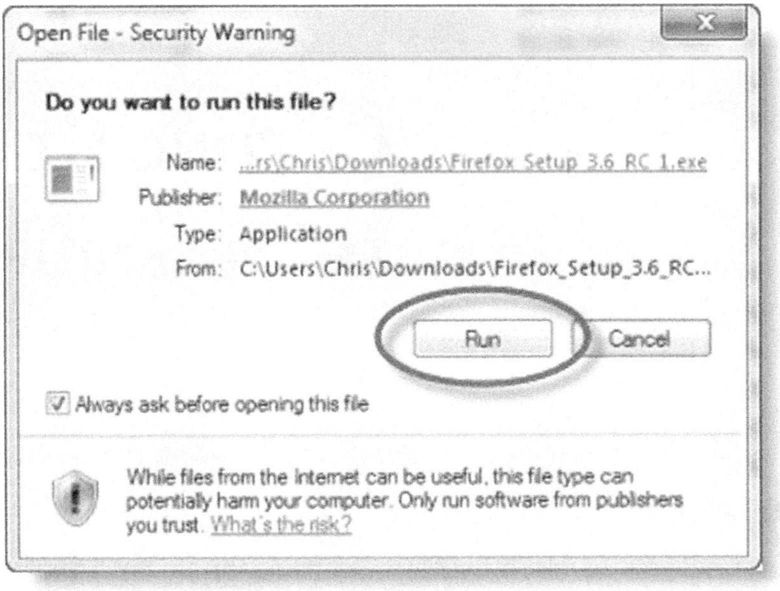

➢ **(Windows Vista / Windows 7**) You may see a User Account Control message. In this case, allow the setup to run by clicking Yes.

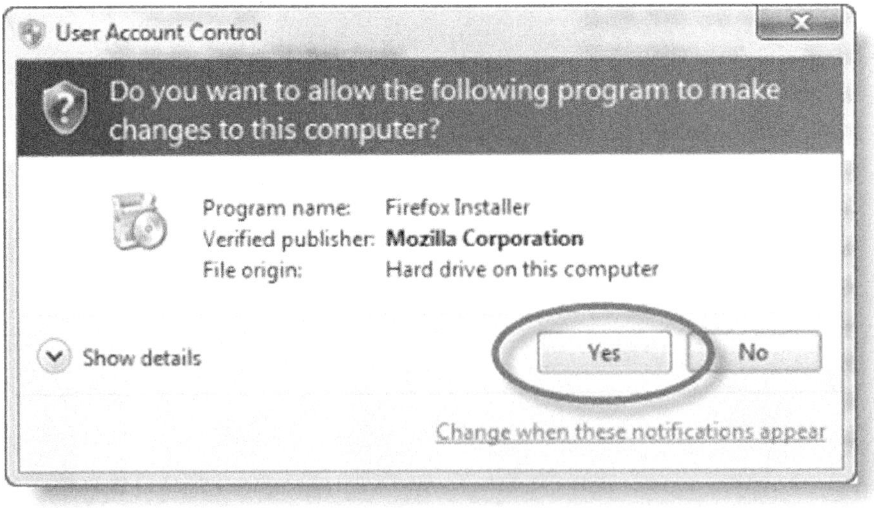

You will be greeted with a welcome screen. Click Next to continue. This will bring you to the Setup Type screen. A **Standard** setup is selected by default, which will install Firefox with a recommended configuration that will work for most users.

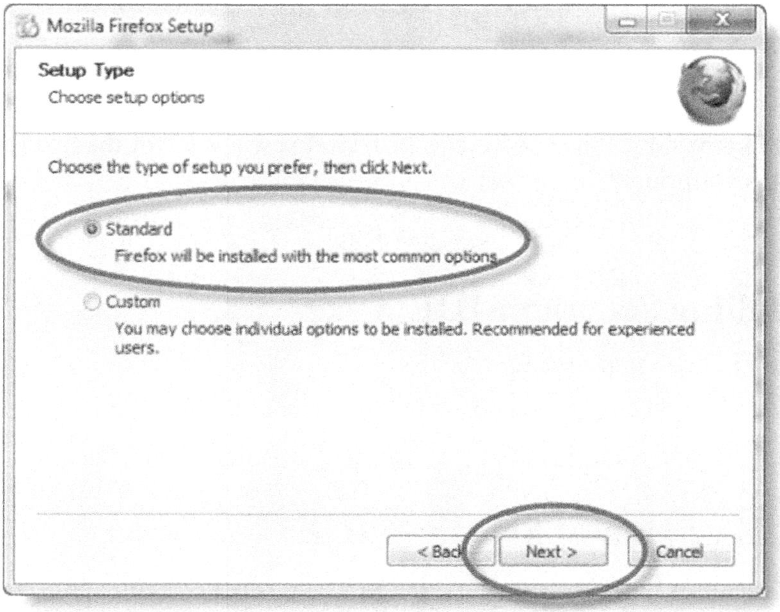

➢ Check **Use Firefox as my default browser** if you want to use Firefox when you open a link in your mail application, an Internet shortcut, or any HTML document. Click Next.

Once the installation is complete, close the setup wizard by clicking Finish.

If the "Launch Firefox now" checkbox is checked, Firefox will start for the first time immediately after you click Finish button.

Installing Selenium-IDE

Installing Selenium is a two step process:

First: If Firefox is not installed in your machine then Install Firefox (min version 3.6)

Second: If Selenium IDE is not installed on your machine then Install Selenium IDE Plug In

Is there an IE version of Selenium IDE?

No, at this time Selenium IDE works for Firefox only. You can write your test scripts via IDE and then use the Selenium Core TestRunner or Selenium RC to execute them on IE.

Installations Steps:

- ➢ Open the Firefox browser window (*1)
- ➢ In the navigation tool bar type the below URL:
  - – seleniumhq.org
- ➢ In the menu tabs, Click on Download (*1)

- ➢ Click on version number to download, click on the Firefox extensions link extension .xpi (*2)

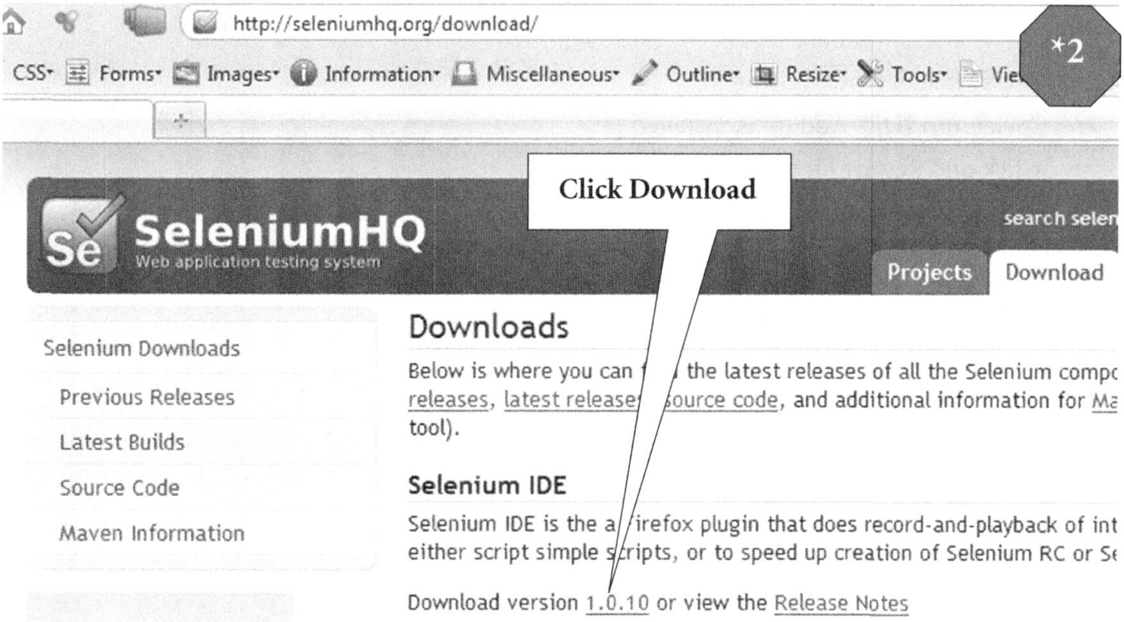

➢ If any installation warning message as below comes, click on Allow (*3)

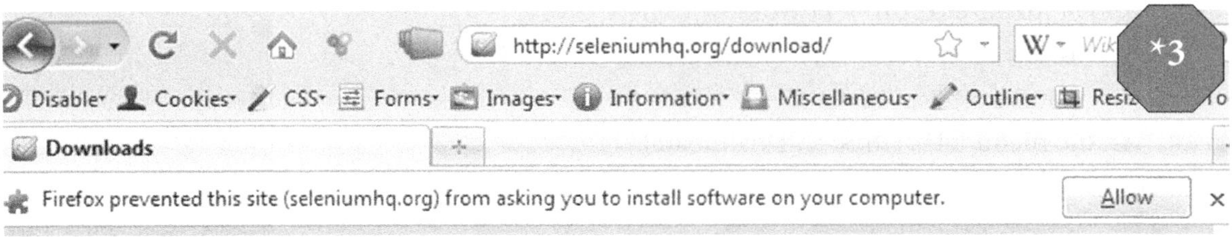

➢ When the Software Installation Window appears, select "Selenium IDE" (*4)

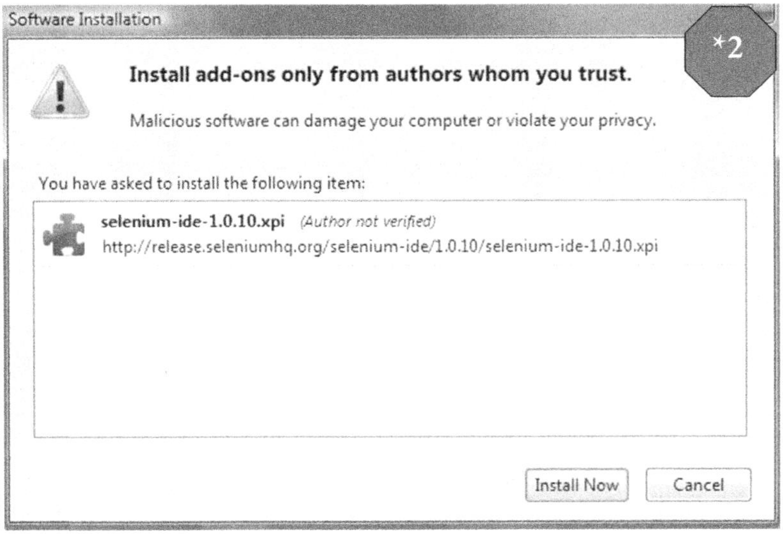

➢ Press "Install Now" button

➢ "Selenium IDE" Add on is installed (*5)

➢ Click on "Restart Firefox" button

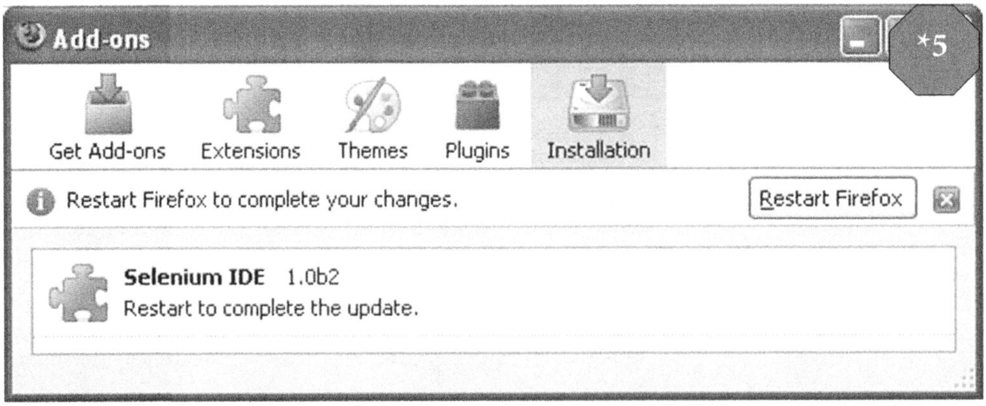

➢ Now, in the Firefox browser go to Tools and verify whether "Selenium IDE" is displayed (*6).

➢ If found, then the Selenium IDE installation is completed. (Congrats!)

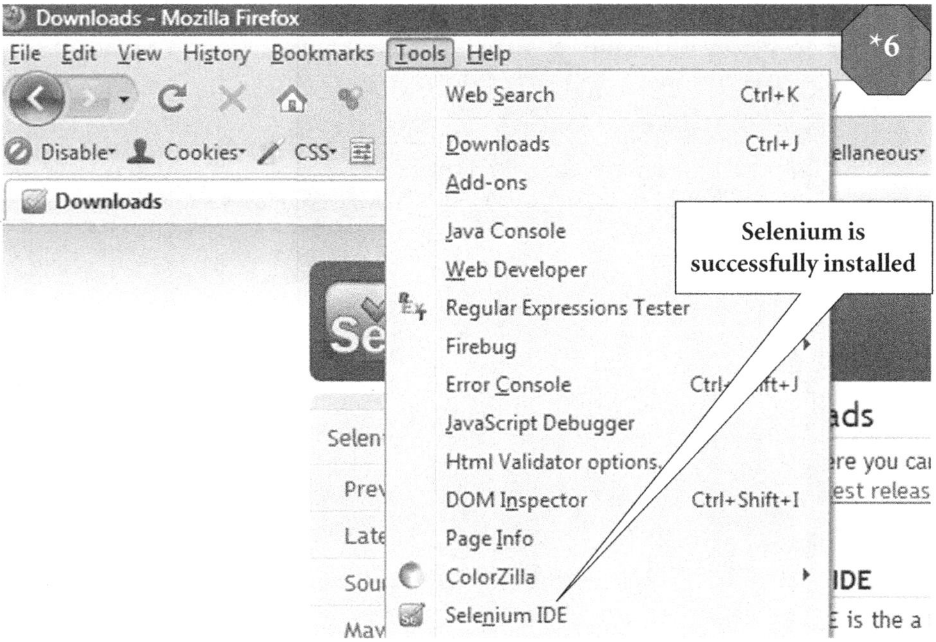

Recording a Script with the IDE

➢ For our initial simple automated test follow the below steps
- Open Firefox browser (*1)
- In the navigation bar enter www.ge.com
- Go to Tools → Selenium IDE (*2)

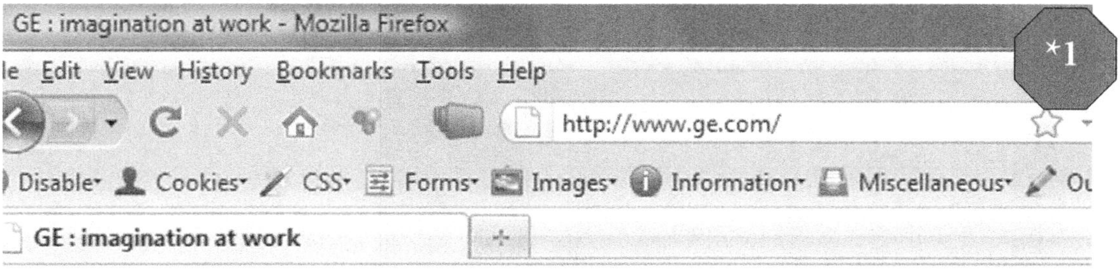

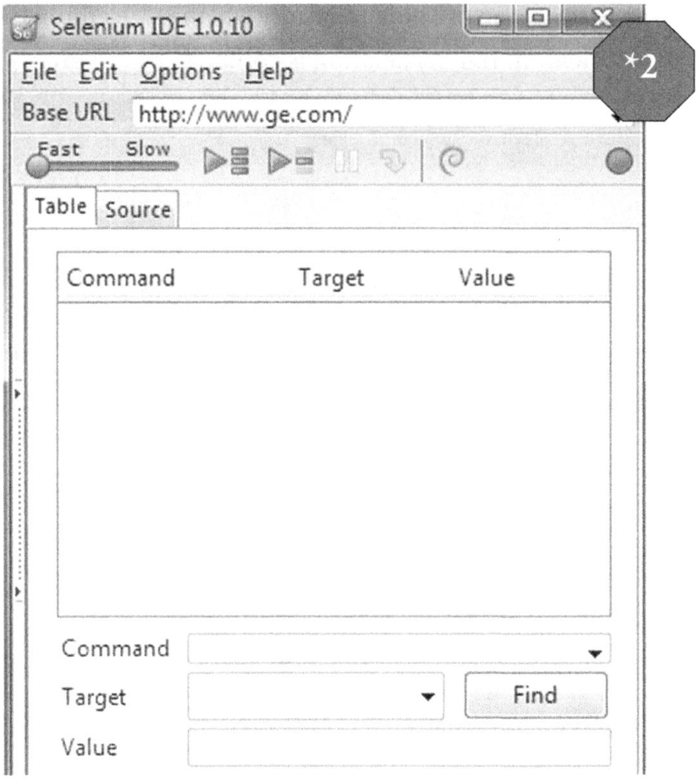

- Click the Red round button at the right side (*3)
- Now go to the other Browser window
  - In the Search text box enter "energy efficient" then click Search button (*4)

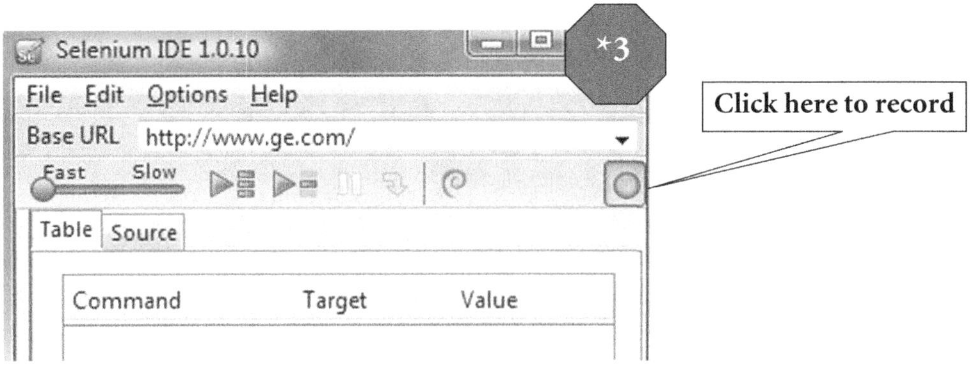

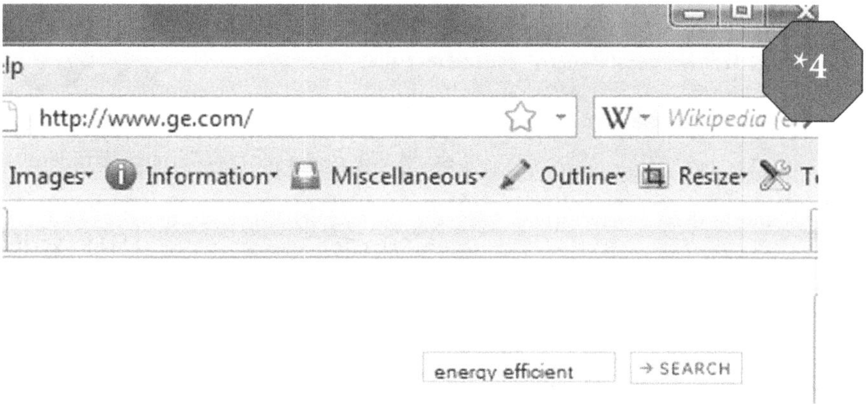

- ➢ Right click on the Firefox window (*5)
  - – Select assertTitle exact:GE Results
- ➢ Highlight “energy efficient” word (*6)
  - – Select VerifyTextPresent

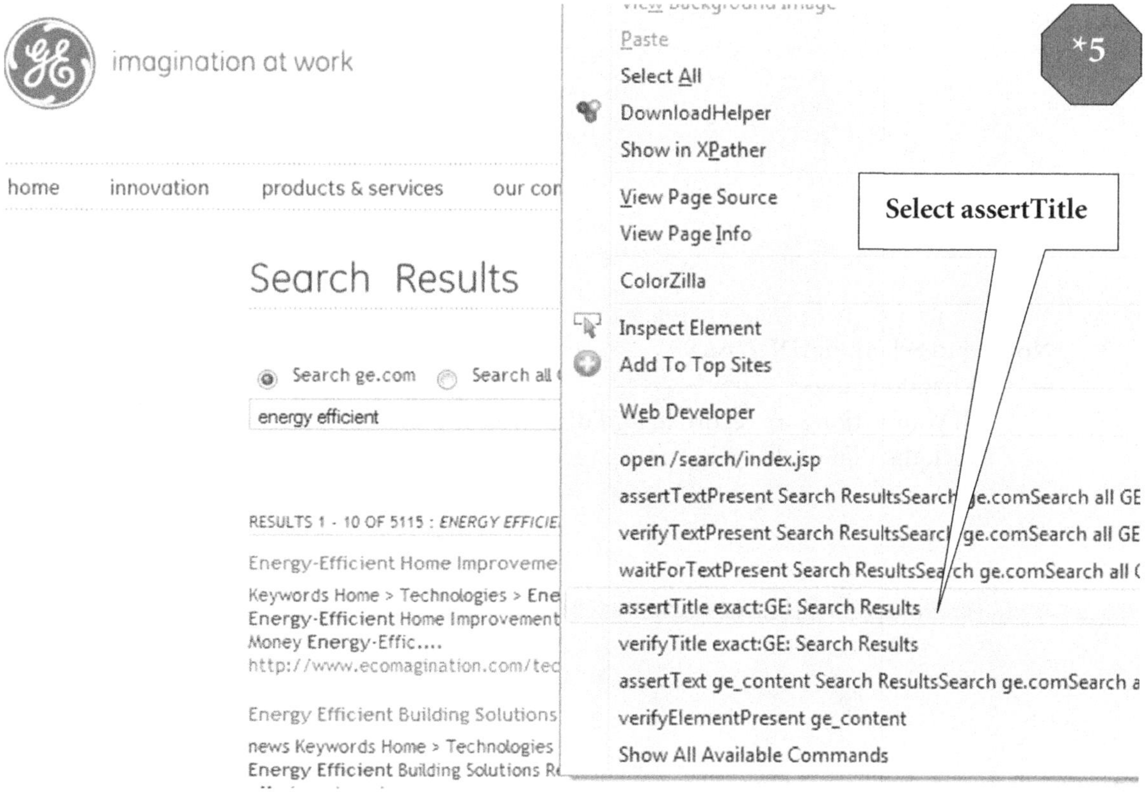

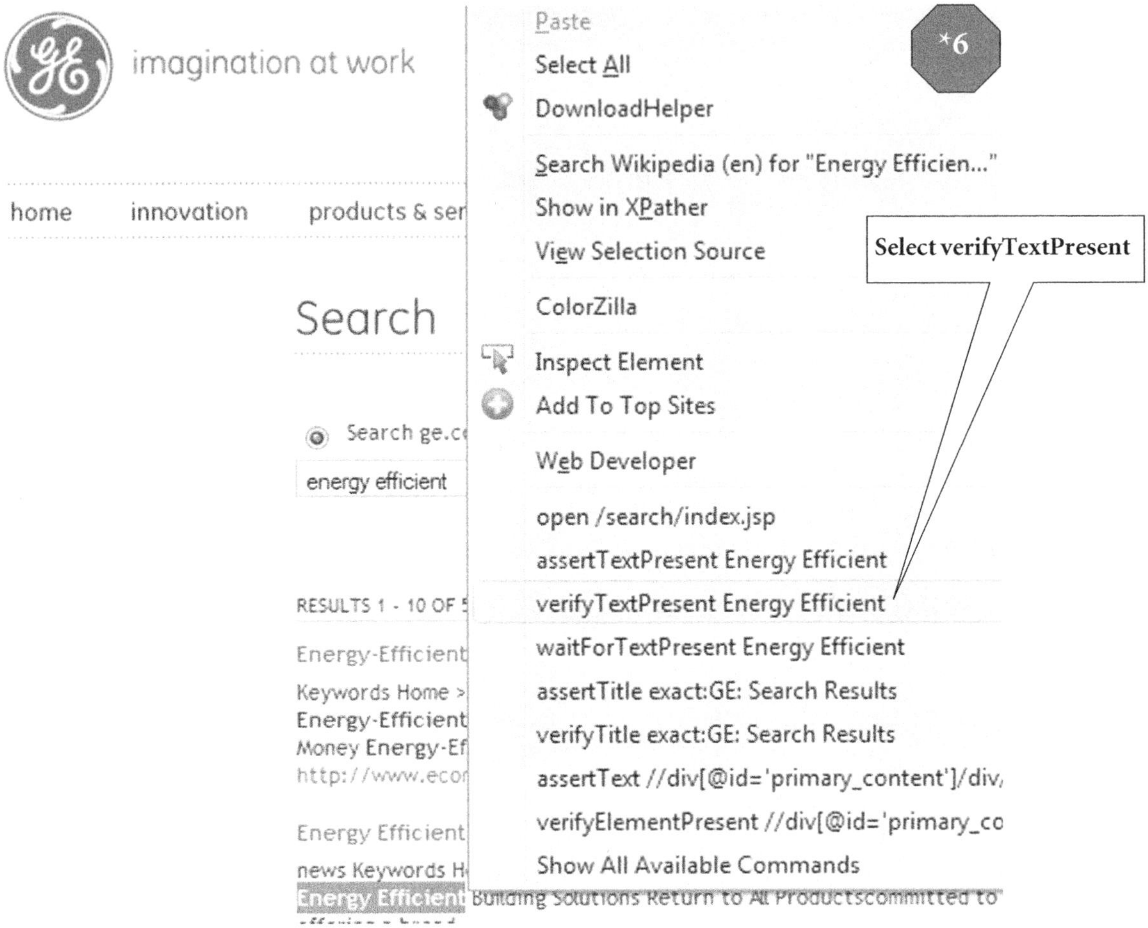

- Now go to Selenium IDE (*6A)
  - What do you see?
  - All your actions are recorded and displayed sequentially under Command Table Tab
  - Click the Red circle again to stop recoding the actions.

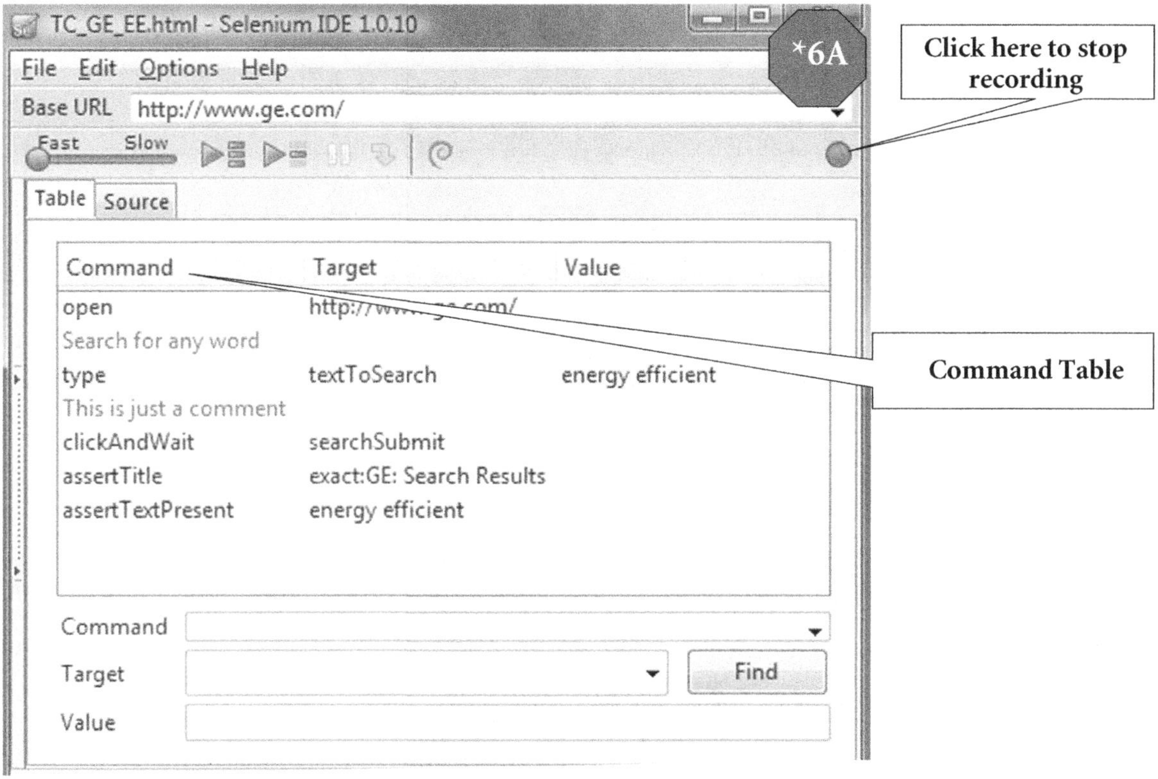

Save the Test Case

- Now Save the Test Case
  - File → Save Test Case (Short Cut, Ctrl+S) (*7)
  - Browse to "C:\BasicSelenium\Week1\Ex"
  - Enter name "TC_GE_EE.html" (*8)

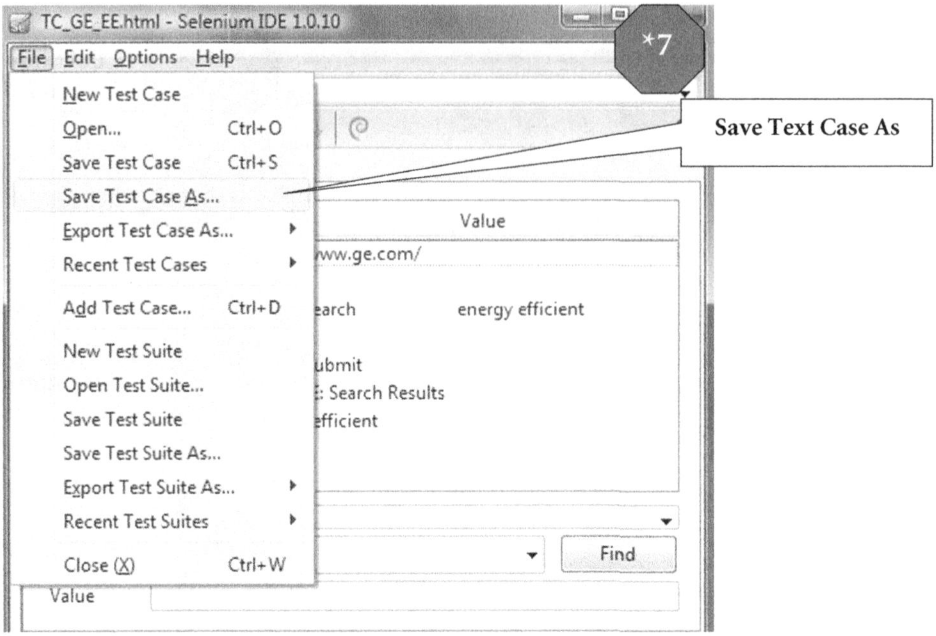
TC_GE_EE.html - Selenium IDE 1.0.10
File
Edit
Options
Help
New Test Case
Open... Ctrl+O
Save Test Case Ctrl+S
Save Test Case As...
Export Test Case As...
Recent Test Cases
Add Test Case... Ctrl+D
New Test Suite
Open Test Suite...
Save Test Suite
Save Test Suite As...
Export Test Suite As...
Recent Test Suites
Close (X) Ctrl+W
Value
Find
*7
Save Text Case As

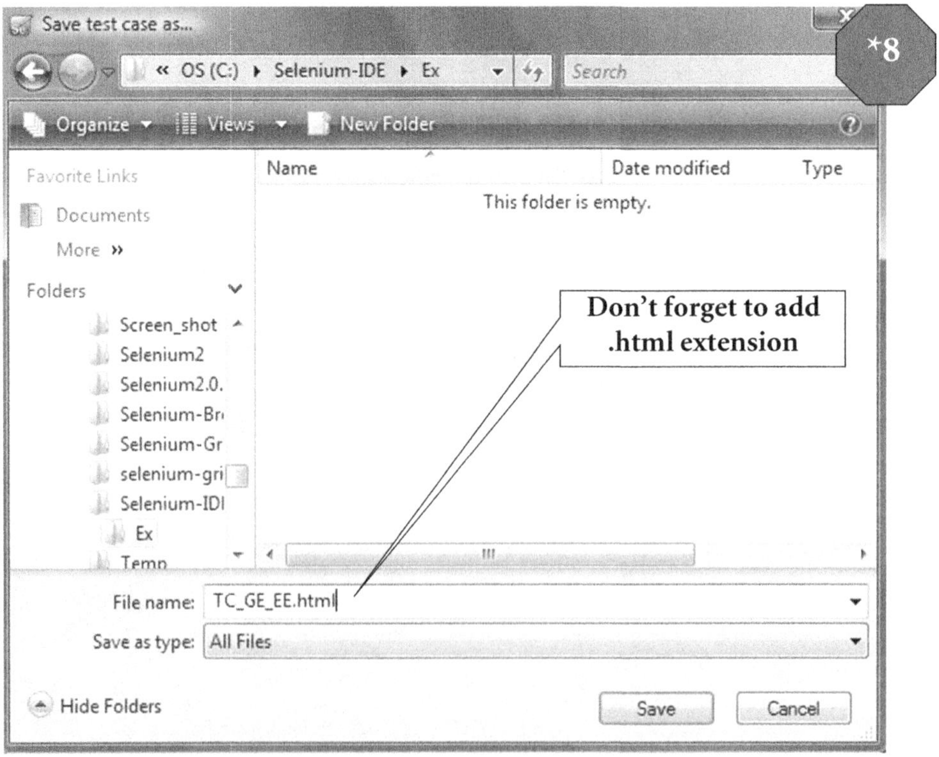
Save test case as...
« OS (C:) ▸ Selenium-IDE ▸ Ex
Search
Organize
Views
New Folder
Favorite Links
Documents
More »
Folders
Name
Date modified
Type
This folder is empty.
File name: TC_GE_EE.html
Save as type: All Files
Hide Folders
Save
Cancel
*8
Don't forget to add .html extension

- Congrats!!
- You have completed recording the first automatic test case using Selenium IDE
- Now we'll play back the recorded Test (*9)

Test Play-Back

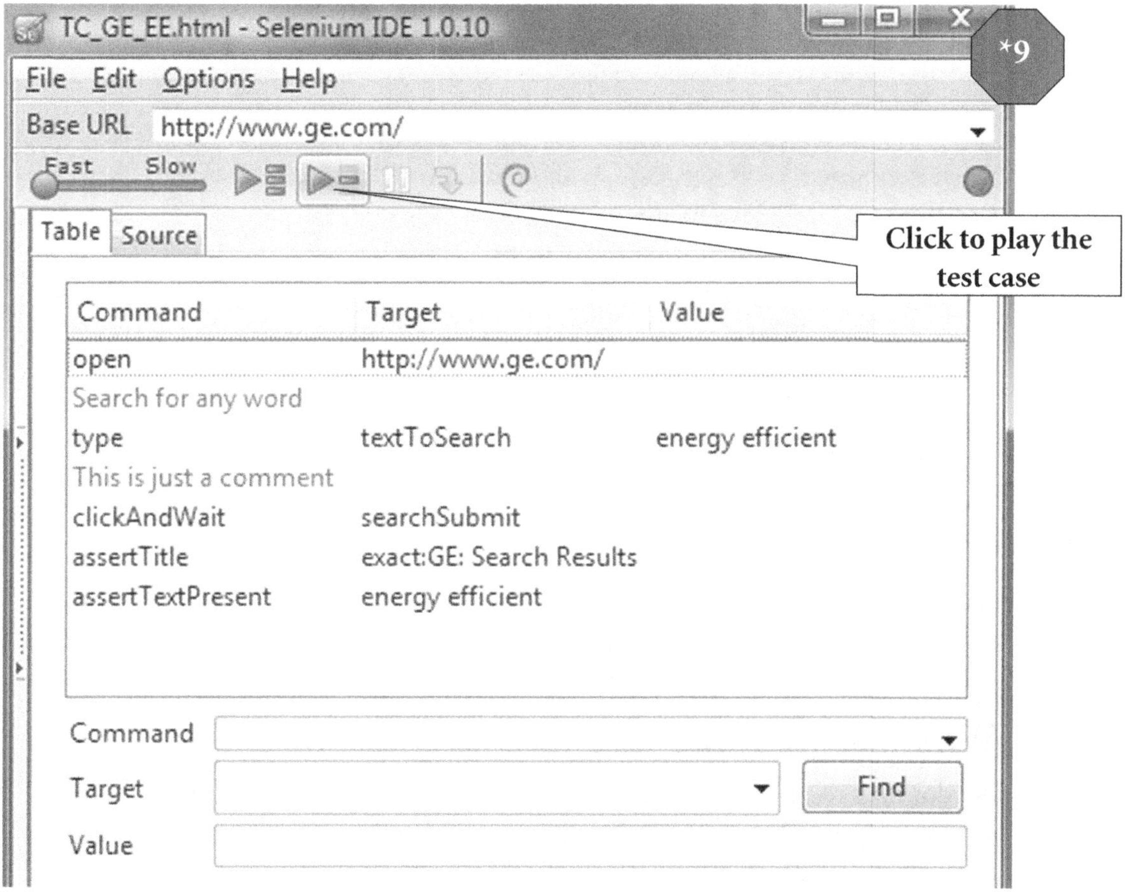

- The commands will be executed one by one and the recorded actions will now be played back in the browser window(*10)

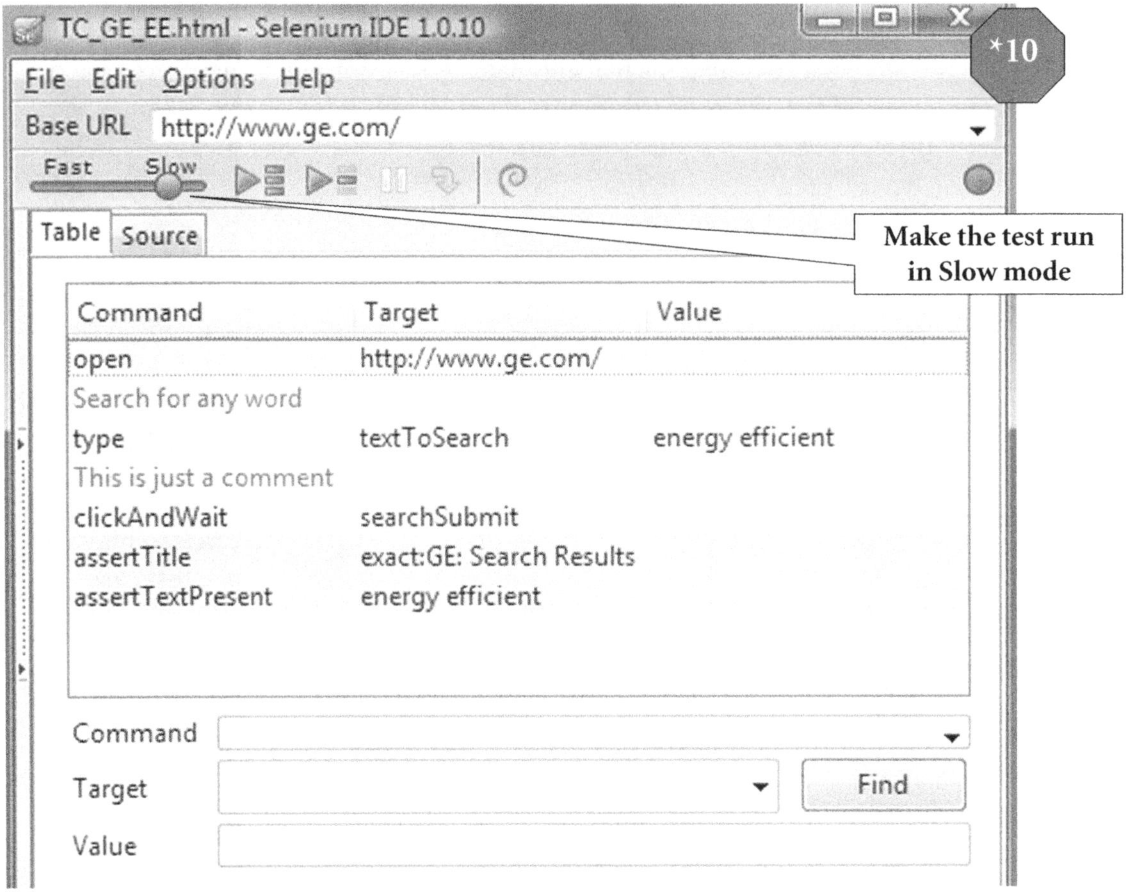

What did we test?

So what did we do? Let's recap

- Open a specific URL (http://www.ge.com)
- Search for a specific text ("energy efficient")
- Check whether the windows title matches "GE Search Results"
- Check whether the result set contains "energy efficient" text
- If you see all the command line rows turns at the end of the test Green color, then the test is passed. If a specific test failed it will be shown with Red color.

Must do Exercise

- Create a new Test: TC_YAHOO_EE.html on similar lines to TC_GE_EE.html
- Create a new Test: TC_GOOGLE_EE.html on similar line to above

Test Condition Failure

Let's make the test fail, how we will do that? We will change the expected title of the page to "GE: New Search Results" and run the test case again.

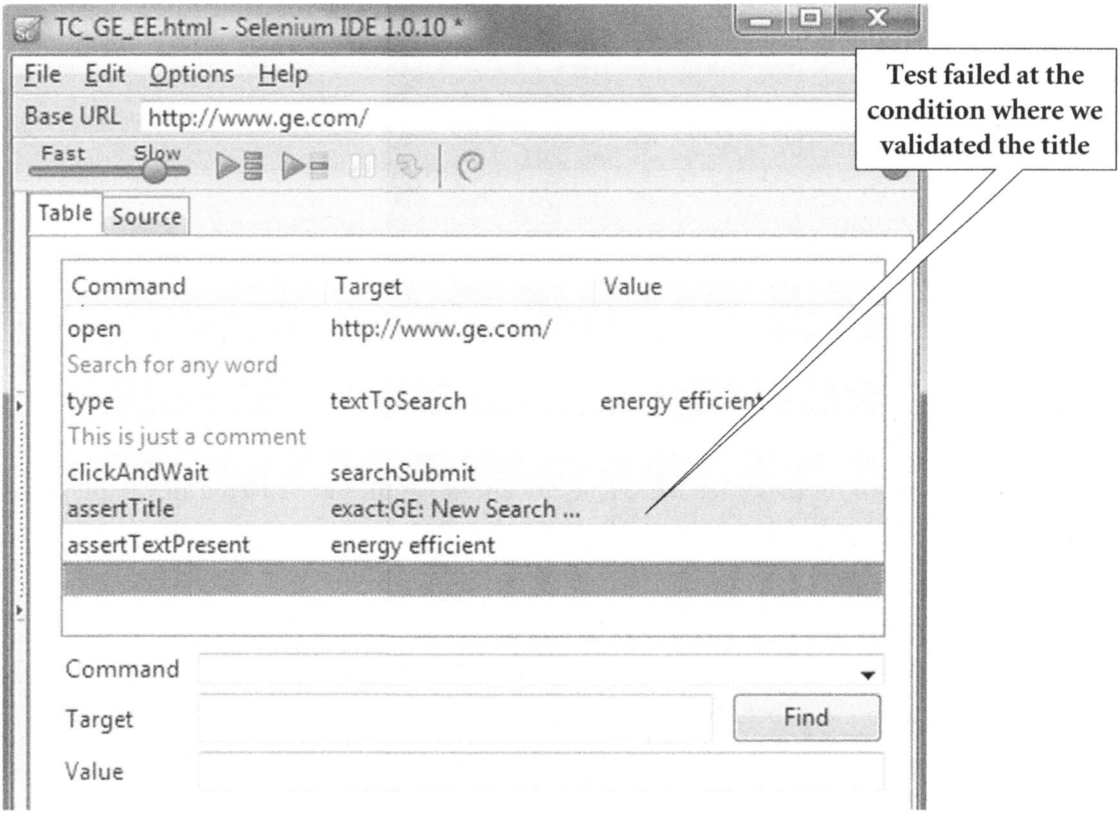

Why did this test condition fail?

The test case was recorded to validate the Title of the page exactly as "GE: New Search Results" however the title was found to be "GE: Search Results" thus the error was found and was highlighted as Red color to that step.

Things to Note

- ➢ Don't close the parent Firefox browser
- ➢ To notice the play back of test case, keep it in slow mode
- ➢ Keep the Firefox browser window small size and Selenium IDE next to it. (*11)
- ➢ You can notice the steps done in both the windows simultaneously.

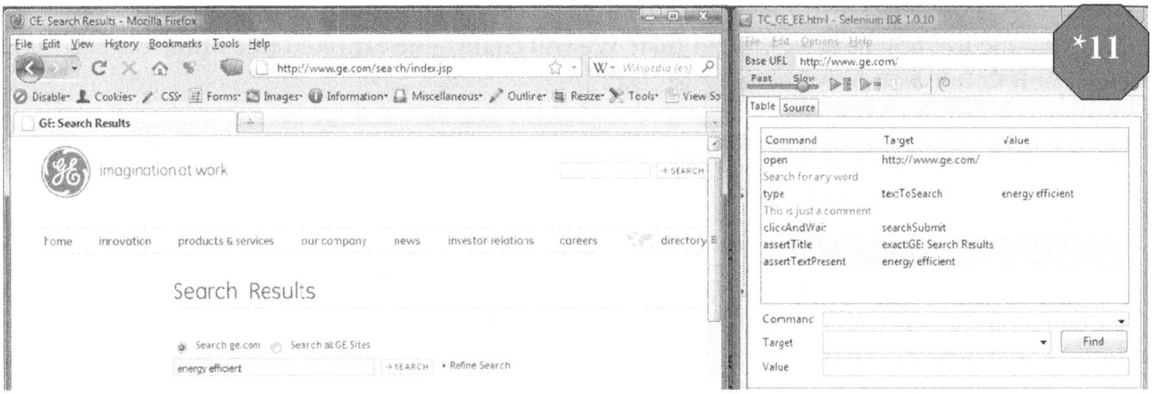

Further Reading

The detailed description of the other Basic and Advanced features are covered in Chapter 6 and Chapter 7.

EXERCISES

1. Why do you choose Selenium over QTP for automation?
2. What are the limitation of Selenium?
3. Find the advantages of following testing Tools:
   - Watir/WET (For Ruby)
   - LiquidTest (Web App Agile Functional Testing)
   - StoryTestIQ (STIQ, Selenium + FitNesse)

- Bromine ("QC" for Selenium)
- CubicTest (Eclipse Plug-in)
- Frankenstein (Java SWING Testing Framework)

4. Find the advantages of following testing frameworks:
   - JUnit,TestNG (Java)
   - NUnit (.Net)
   - Unittest (Python)
   - RSpec, Test::Unit (Ruby)
5. Test Specification –
   - Open a specific URL (www.amazon.com)
   - Select "Books" under Search Select List
   - Search for a specific text ("selenium IDE") in #1 page
   - Sort by "Price: Low to high"
   - Check whether the windows title matches "Amazon.com: selenium IDE: Books"
   - Check whether the result set contains "Selenium IDE" text
   - Click the link #2
   - Check whether the result set contains "Selenium IDE" text
6. Test Specification –
   - Open a specific URL (http://www.barnesandnoble.com)
   - Search for a specific text ("Javascript") in #1 page
   - Sort by "Price – Low to High"
   - How do you check "Online Price: $$$" is in sorted order?

3

INSTALL JAVA

Checking Java

- Go to Start → Run → cmd
  - Java –version (*1)
- If you see an older version (< 1.5) it is better to uninstall it.

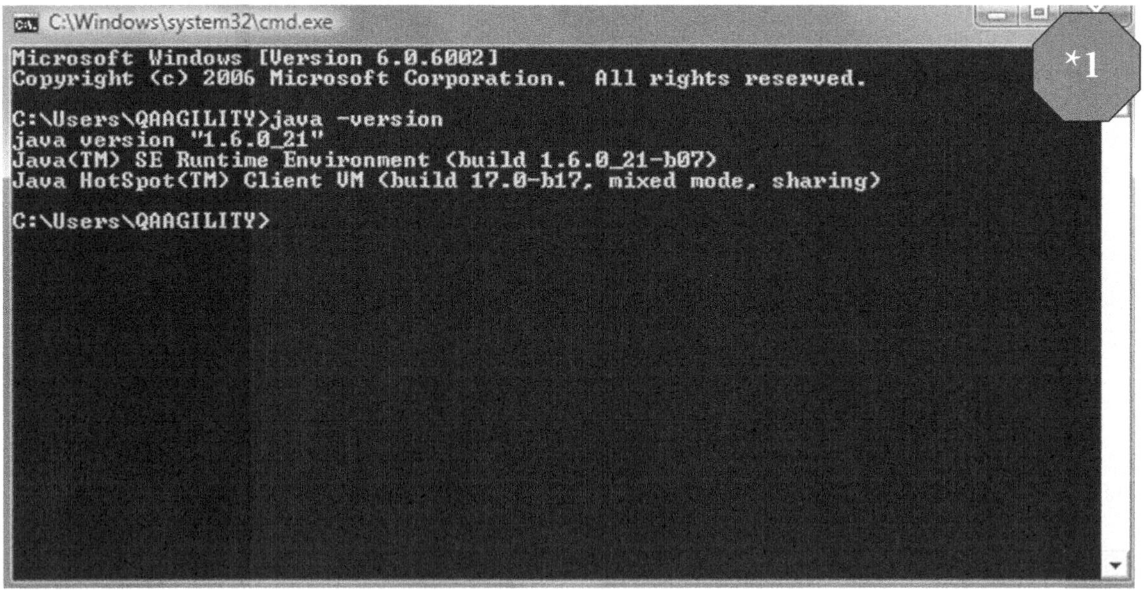

Remove Older versions of Java

Why should I remove older versions of Java from my system?

The latest version of Java is always the recommended version as it contains updates and improvements to previous versions. You can confirm that you have the latest version by visiting the Java Verification page.

Over time, you may have installed multiple versions of Java to run available Java content. In the past, each Java update was installed in separate directories on your system. However, Java updates are now installed in a single directory.

Should I Remove Older Versions of Java?

We highly recommend users remove all older versions of Java from your system.

Keeping old and unsupported versions of Java on your system presents a serious security risk.

Removing older versions of Java from your system ensures that Java applications will run with the most up-to-date security and performance improvements on your system.

Do I need older versions of java?

The latest available version is always compatible with the older versions. However, some Java applications (or applets) can indicate that they are dependent on a particular version, and may not run if you do not have that version installed. If an application or web page you access requires an older version of Java, you should report this to the provider/developer and request that they update the application to be compatible with all Java versions.

How can I remove older versions of java?

You can safely remove older versions of Java from your system by following the instructions given in the pages below.

Remove older versions of Java in the same way as you would remove any other software from your Windows computer.

Windows 7 and Vista - Uninstall Programs

1. Click **Start**
2. Select **Control Panel**
3. Select **Programs**
4. Click **Programs and Features**

5. Select the program you want to uninstall by clicking on it, and then click the **Uninstall** button.

You may need administrator privileges to remove programs.

Windows XP - Uninstall Programs

1. Click **Start**
2. Select **Control Panel**
3. Click the **Add/Remove Programs** control panel icon
4. The Add/Remove control panel displays a list of software on your system, including any Java software products that are on your computer. Select any that you want to uninstall by clicking on it, and then click the **Remove** button.

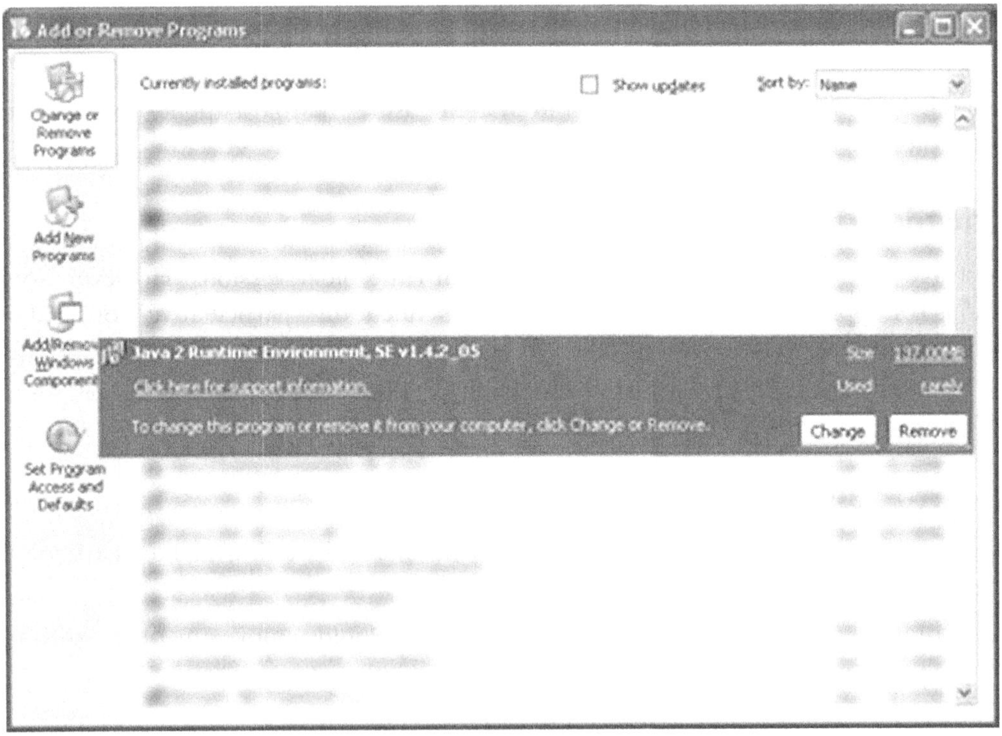

Installing JDK

Go to http://www.oracle.com/technetwork/java/javase/downloads/index.html

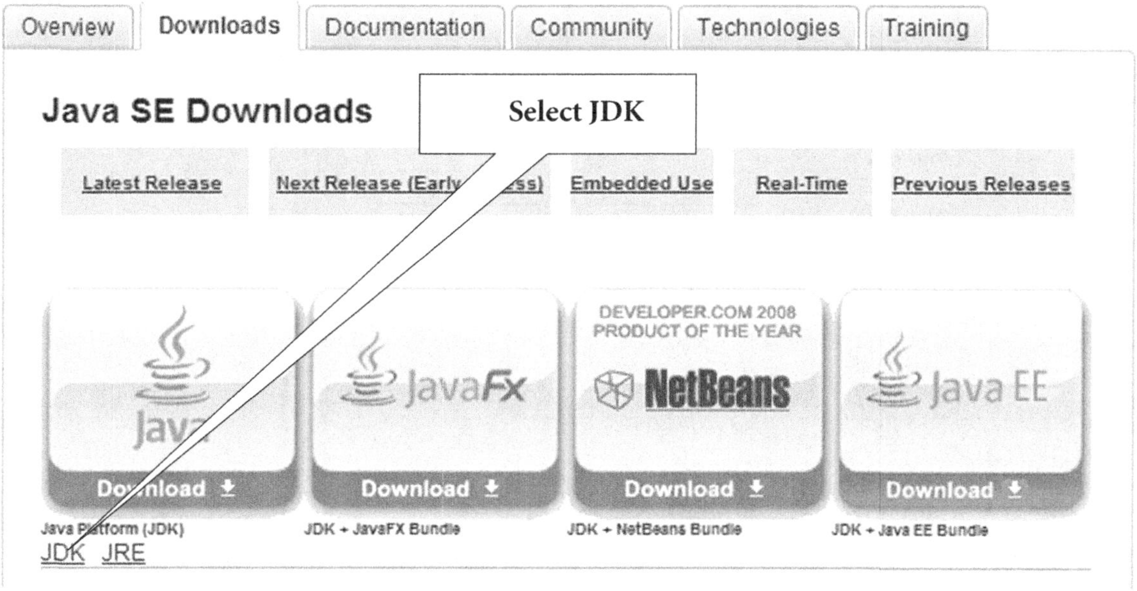

Note: Difference between JDK and JRE

JDK or the Java Development Kit is a set of a Java compiler, a Java interpreter, developer tools, Java API libraries, documentation which can be used by Java developers to develop Java-based applications.

JRE or the Java Runtime Environment is a minimum set that includes a Java interpreter, Java API libraries, Java browser plug-in, which make up the minimum environment to execute Java-based applications.

You need JDK, if at all you want to write your own programs, and to compile them. For running java programs, JRE is sufficient.

JDK includes a JRE as subset.

Select Platform and Language and click Continue.

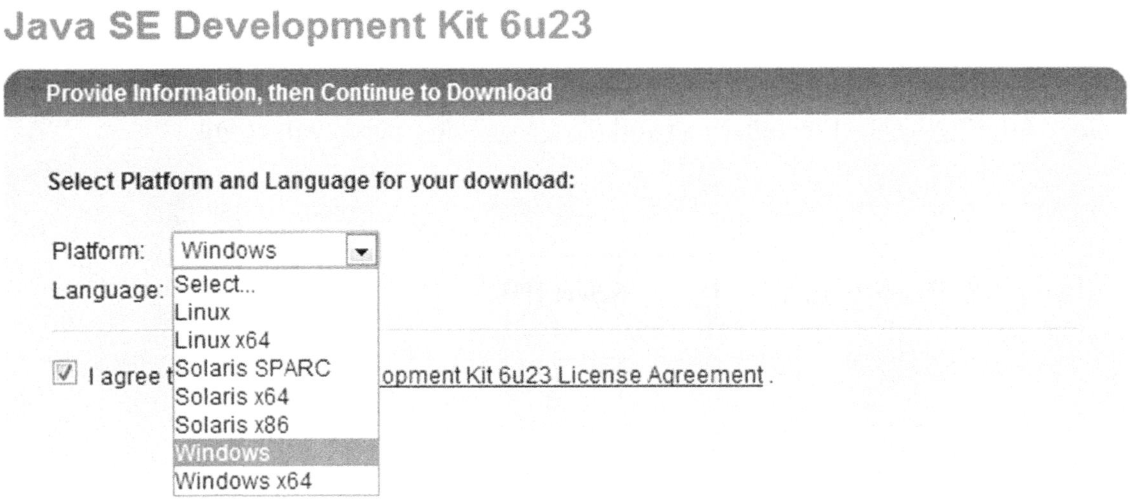

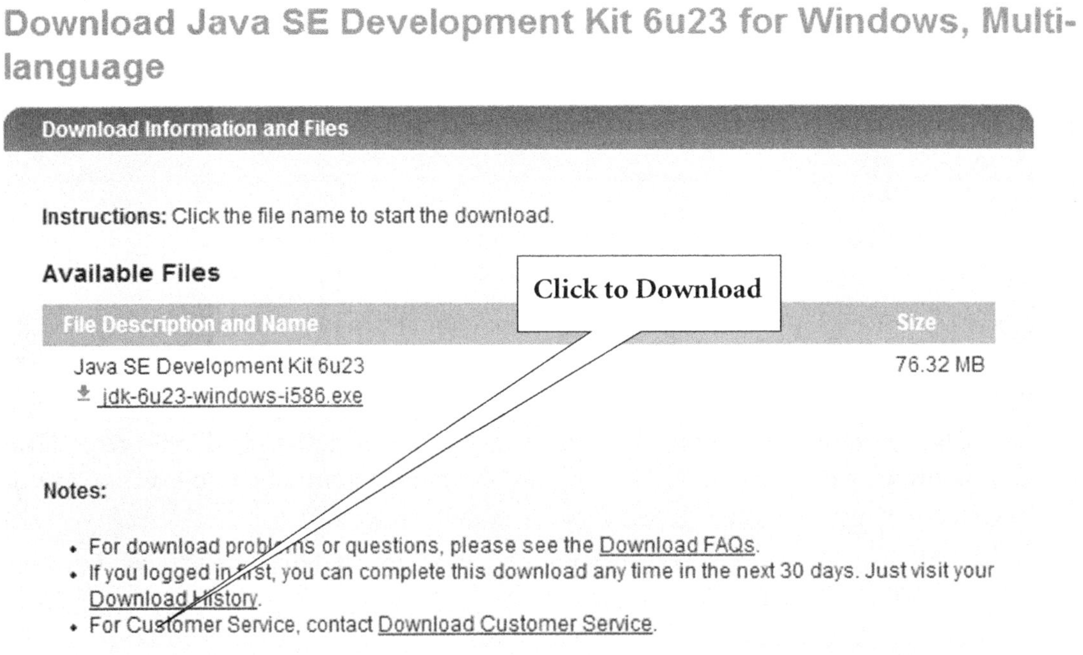

Save the JDK installable and run it. Accept the Security warnings and terms and continue with installation.

Verify the version again.

Go to Start → Run → cmd

- Java –version

➢ If you see newer version (>= 1.5) displayed you have successfully installed JDE.

4

Useful Tools for writing Test Cases — Firefox Add-Ons

- Firefox Add-ons allows extending the functionality of the Firefox browser.
- Large selection of add-ons available.
- Read the reviews and choose what you need the most.
- I have selected many add-ons which will enhance your learning of Selenium IDE testing.
- These Add-ons make your life easier by doing the expected jobs within your browser, instead of looking for an answer outside.

Dom Inspector

- Document Object Model (DOM) Inspector is a tool that can be used to inspect and edit the live DOM of any web document or XUL (XML User Interface Language) application.
- The DOM hierarchy can be navigated using a two-paned window that allows for a variety of different views on the document and all nodes within.
- This add-on depends on binary changes to Firefox, and will not work with Firefox 2.
- Inspects the structure and properties of a window and its contents.
- URL to Add:
  - https://addons.mozilla.org/en-US/firefox/addon/6622
  - Click Add to Firefox
  - Press Install Now button
  - Press Restart Firefox Now button

Firebug

- Firebug integrates with Firefox to put a wealth of development tools at your fingertips while you browse. You can edit, debug, and monitor CSS, HTML, and JavaScript live in any web page.
- Firebug 1.2 requires Firefox 3. Firefox 2 users should install the older 1.05 version of Firebug.
- URL to Add:
  - https://addons.mozilla.org/en-US/firefox/addon/1843
  - Click Add to Firefox
  - Select Firebug and Press Install Now button
  - Press Restart Firefox Now button

Venkman Javascript Debugger

- Venkman is the code name for Mozilla's JavaScript Debugger.
- Venkman aims to provide a powerful JavaScript debugging environment for Mozilla based browsers.
- URL to Add:
  - https://addons.mozilla.org/en-US/firefox/addon/216
  - Click Add to Firefox
  - Select JavaScript and Press Install Now button
- Press Restart Firefox Now button

Web Developer

- Adds a menu and a toolbar with various web developer tools.
- URL to Add:
  - https://addons.mozilla.org/en-US/firefox/addon/60
  - Click Add to Firefox
  - Select Web Developer and Press Install Now button
  - Press Restart Firefox Now button

Regular Expression Tester

- Allows you to test regular expressions. The tool includes options like case sensitive, global and multi-line search, color highlighting of found expressions and of special characters, a replacement function incl. back references, auto-closing of brackets, testing while writing and saving and managing of expressions..
- URL to Add:
  - https://addons.mozilla.org/en-US/firefox/addon/2077
  - Click Add to Firefox
  - Select Regular Expression Tester and Press Install Now button
  - Press Restart Firefox Now button

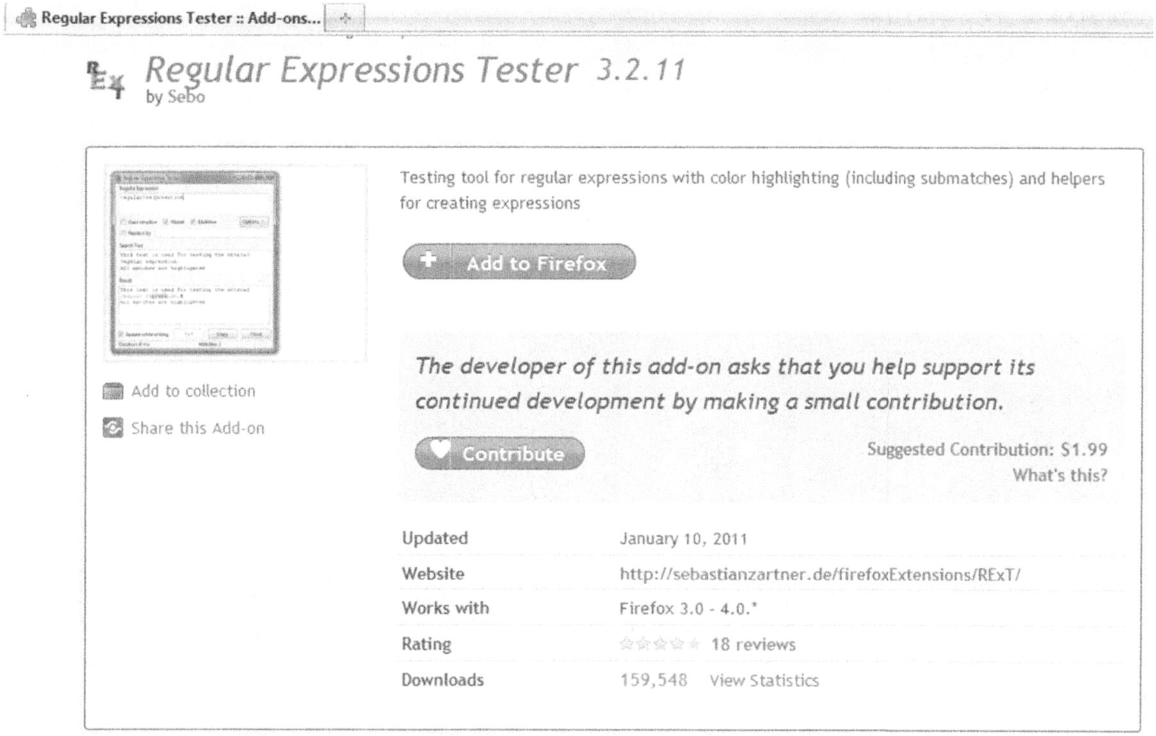

HTML Validator

- HTML Validator adds HTML validation inside Firefox and Mozilla. The number of errors of a HTML page is seen on the form of an icon in the status bar when browsing. W3C Validator for HTML 4.01 and XHTML.
- URL to Add:
  - https://addons.mozilla.org/en-US/firefox/addon/249
  - Click Add to Firefox
  - Select Html Validator and Press Install Now button
  - Press Restart Firefox Now button
  - Select SGML Parser (w3.org uses the same)
  - Go through the user guide for more information

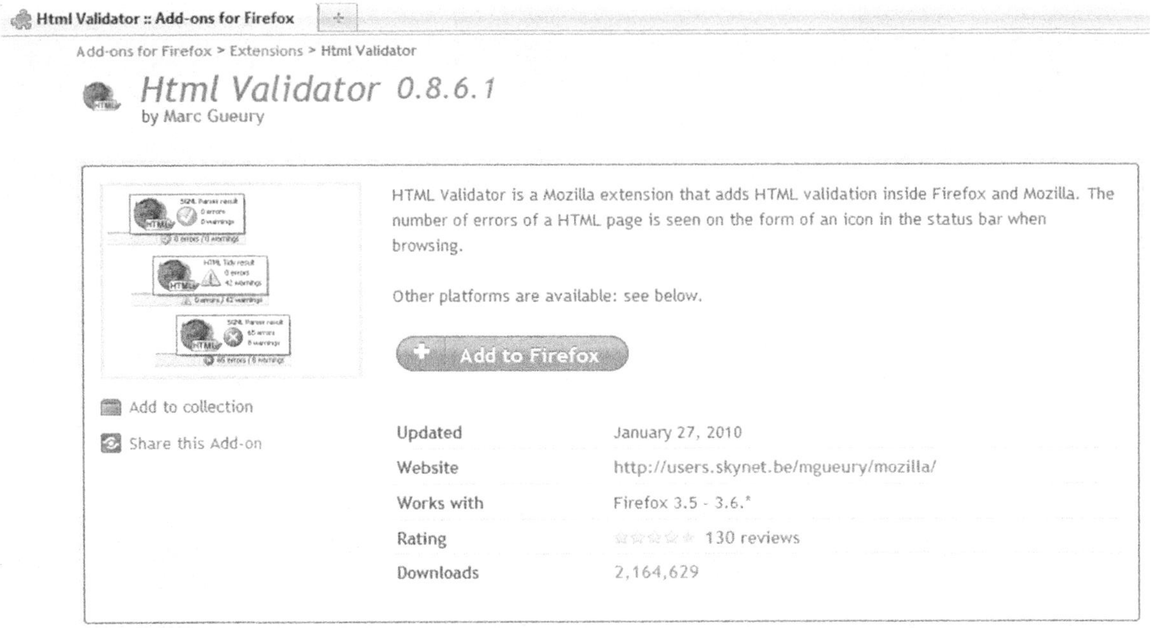

Xpather

- XPath generator, editor, inspector and simple extraction tool. Since FF3, it requires DOM inspector plug-in .
- URL to Add:
    - https://addons.mozilla.org/en-US/firefox/addon/1192
    - Click Add to Firefox
    - Select XPather and Press Install Now button
    - Press Restart Firefox Now button

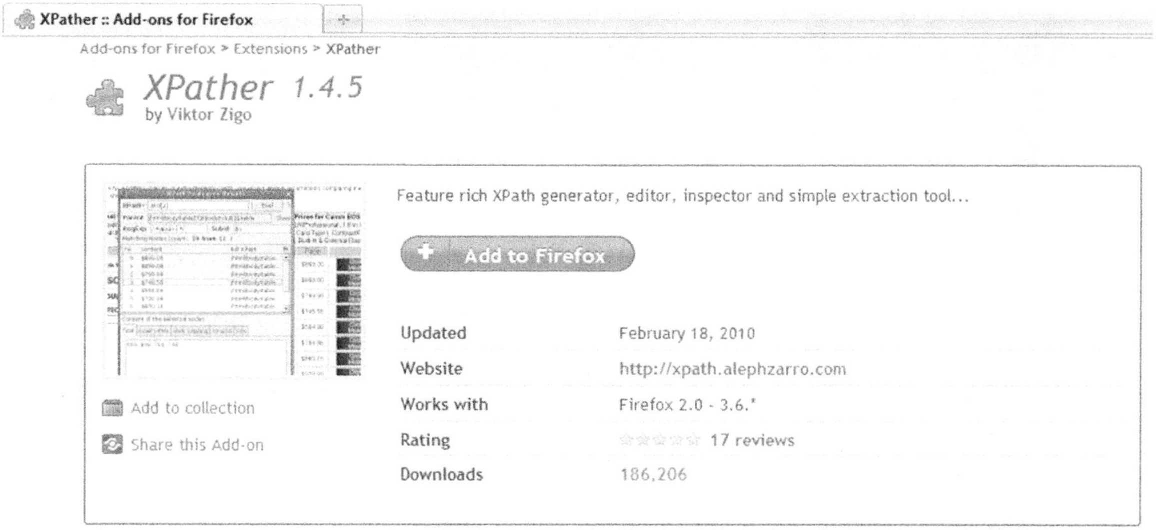
XPather :: Add-ons for Firefox
Add-ons for Firefox > Extensions > XPather
XPather 1.4.5
by Viktor Zigo
Feature rich XPath generator, editor, inspector and simple extraction tool...
Add to Firefox
Updated
February 18, 2010
Website
http://xpath.alephzarro.com
Works with
Firefox 2.0 - 3.6.*
Rating
17 reviews
Downloads
186,206
Add to collection
Share this Add-on

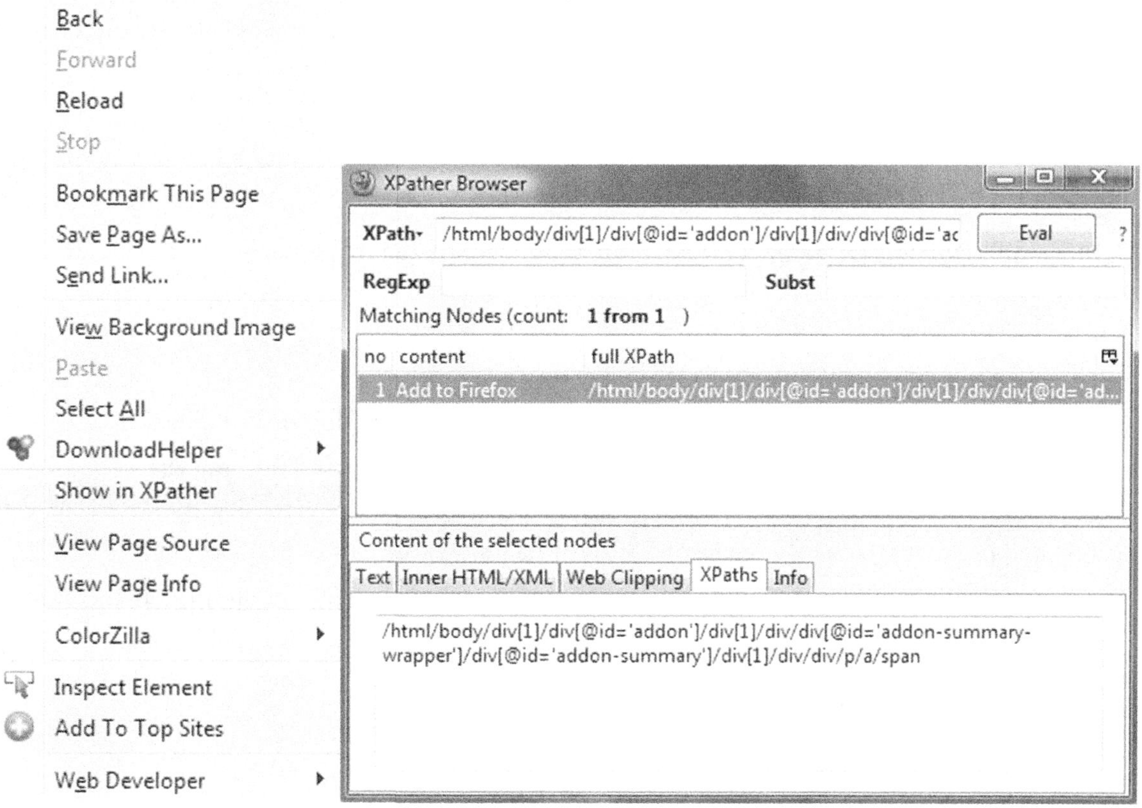
Back
Forward
Reload
Stop
Bookmark This Page
Save Page As...
Send Link...
View Background Image
Paste
Select All
DownloadHelper
Show in XPather
View Page Source
View Page Info
ColorZilla
Inspect Element
Add To Top Sites
Web Developer
XPather Browser
XPath /html/body/div[1]/div[@id='addon']/div[1]/div/div[@id='ac
Eval
RegExp
Subst
Matching Nodes (count: 1 from 1)
no content full XPath
1 Add to Firefox /html/body/div[1]/div[@id='addon']/div[1]/div/div[@id='ad...
Content of the selected nodes
Text
Inner HTML/XML
Web Clipping
XPaths
Info
/html/body/div[1]/div[@id='addon']/div[1]/div/div[@id='addon-summary-wrapper']/div[@id='addon-summary']/div[1]/div/div/p/a/span

5

Basic HTML Theory

You cannot escape HTML, it is almost synonymous with website development and structure. No matter what is the technology or programming language used to create the website, the output is always in HTML. In this chapter we will look at the nuances of HTML that will be required to use Selenium.

What is HTML?

HTML is abbreviation for **H**yper**T**ext **M**arkup **L**anguage. As the name has it, it's a programming language.

Let's do a breakup:

- Hypertext is simply a piece of text that works as a link.
- Markup Language is a way of writing layout information within documents.

Basically an HTML document is a plain text file that contains text and nothing else.

When a browser opens an HTML file, the browser will look for HTML codes, known as tags, in the text and use them to change the layout, insert images, or create links to other pages.

Since HTML documents are just text files they can be written in even the simplest text editor.

A more popular choice is to use a special HTML editor - maybe even one that puts focus on the visual result rather than the codes - a so-called WYSIWYG editor ("What You See Is What You Get").

HTML TAGS

HTML Tags are basically instructions to the browser to display the information in a certain manner. All the HTML tags are enclosed in < and >. For a computer alphabet 'A' is simply an 'A' and it doesn't care for whether it is bold, italics, big or small. We need to use certain tag to tell the browser that the alphabet will be displayed as bold. For example the line "This text is **bold"** needs to be written as below using the HTML Tag:

This text is <b>bold</b>.

Notice that the <b> is the starting tag and </b> is the closing tag. There always has to be an associated closing tag.

HTML PAGE STructure

All HTML pages consist of head and body.

- The head contains the text and tags that do not show directly on the page.
- The body has text and tags that are shown directly on the page.

There needs to be <HTML> tag tell the browser where to start and end the page. Please look below for example for a basic HTML web page:

```
<html>
<head>
<!— This section contains comments regarding the page. —>
</head>
<body>
<!— This section contains what you want to show on the page. —>
</body>
</html>
```

The Head Section

The head section of the webpage includes all the stuff that does not show directly on the resulting page.

The <title> and </title> tags encapsulate the title of the page. The title is what shows in the top of your browser window when the page is loaded.

Quite often the head section contains javascript which is a programming language for more complex HTML pages.

Finally, more and more pages contain codes for cascading style sheets (CSS). CSS is a rather new technique for optimising the layout of major websites.

We will be using JavaScript and CSS while we create tests of Selenium IDE.

The BODY Section

The body of the document contains all that can be seen when the user loads the page.

There are different aspects of HTML that are used in Body section, including:

- Text
  - Formatting
  - Resizing
  - Layout
  - Listing
- Links
  - To local pages
  - To pages at other sites
  - To bookmarks
- Images
  - Inserting images (GIF and jpg)
  - Adding a link to an image
- Backgrounds
  - Colors
  - Images
  - Fixed Image
- Tables
- Frames
- Forms
- Metatags
- Hexadecimal Colors

HTML Tables

Tables are used on websites for two major purposes:

- The obvious purpose of arranging information in a table

- The less obvious - but more widely used - purpose of creating a page layout with the use of hidden tables.

However we are looking at the HTML tables from the view of Selenium IDE test cases/suites. As we have seen already the Selenium Test Cases and Test Suites are stored as HTML tables.

Now let's look at the HTML table structure and related tags.

Tables are defined with the <table> tag.

To insert a table on your page you simply add these tags where you want the table to occur:

```
<table>
</table>
```

The above table would be of no use since it has no rows and no columns.

ROWS:

To add rows to your table use the <tr> and </tr> tags.

Example:

```
<table>
<tr></tr>
<tr></tr>
</table>
```

COLUMNS:

You can divide rows into columns with <td> and </td> tags:

Example:

```
<table>
<tr> <td>This is row one, column one.</td> <td>This is row one, column two.</td> </tr>
<tr> <td>This is row two, column one.</td> <td>This is row two, column two.</td> </tr>
</table>
```

Result:

This is row one, column one.	This is row one, column two.
This is row two, column one.	This is row two, column two.

This page has shown the core basics of tables. In addition to these, there are different options for customizing your tables.

This should make you comfortable in the HTML concepts that are required for Selenium IDE Test Cases/Suites. Now let's move on to see how can we review, create and modify the HTML code of the Selenium IDE Test Cases/Suite.

EXERCISES

1. Create a simple page introducing yourself, how old you are, what you do, what you like and dislike.
2. Modify the introduction to include a bullet list of what you do and put list the 5 things you like most and dislike as numbered lists.
3. Create another page about your favourite hobby, and link it to (and from) your main page.
4. Center something, and put a quote on one of your pages
5. Put an existing image on a web page.
6. Create a table, use a heading and at least one use of rowspan/colspan
7. Create a table with Calendar for the current month.
8. Color a page and some text within the page.
9. Add links to your favorite websites.

6

CREATE SELENIUM TEST SUITE

Concept of Test Case and Test Suite

Selenium understands two types of files

- ➢ Test Case
- ➢ Test Suite

Every test must be contained within a test suite.

Both test cases and test suites are defined by using simple tables in HTML.

Test Suites are needed to group the Test Cases in a particular sequence depending upon the Test Requirements so that they can run in the order defined the Test Suite.

Format of Selenium Test

Selenium HTML Table commands are called Selenese commands.

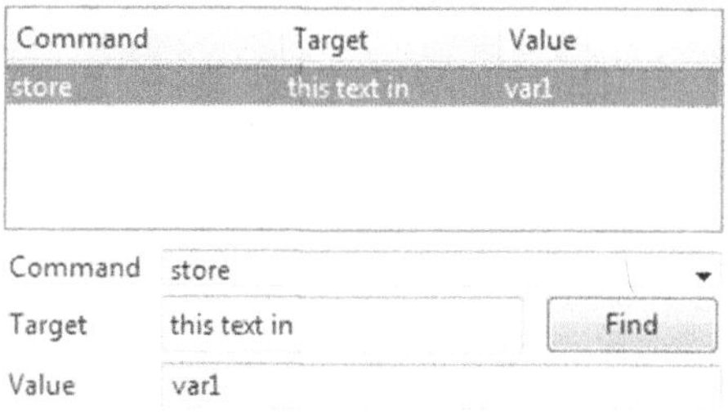

Selenese provides simplicity and does not require actual coding to be done. You need to aware of the functionality of these Selenese commands and use them as per your Testing requirements.

Selenese defined in HTML Table with 3 columns

- ➢ First Column: Selenium command
- ➢ Second Column: Required first parameter

➢ Third Column: Optional second parameter

Note: To avoid confusion, please try NOT to remember the Selenese commands by "Target" and "Value", instead use first parameter and second parameter since the first parameter doesn't always stores the target and second parameter doesn't always stores the value. As depicted in the figure above, the store command is storing "this text in" value in the target variable "var1" which is exactly opposite to the labels the labels for the fields!

Format of Selenium Test Suite

The format of Selenium Test Suite is similar to a Test Case, it is also an HTML table. However the difference being that it points to the Selenium Test Cases and lists them in one column.

Download the TS_EE.jar file from http://www.qaagility.com/downloads/SeleniumBook/ Unzip/ Decompress the .jar file in a folder.

Just double Click on the HTML file and open the "TS_EE.html" in any browser.

Click the individual test cases link and you will see that it will open the HTML code of the Test Cases stored in the test suite.

TC_Yahoo_EE		
open	http://m.www.yahoo.com/	
type	p	energy efficient
clickAndWait	search-submit	
waitForTextPresent	Energy Efficient	
verifyTitle	energy efficient - Yahoo! Search Results	

GE Test Case 1		
open	http://www.ge.com/	
type	textToSearch	energy efficient
clickAndWait	searchSubmit	
assertTitle	exact:GE: Search Results	
assertTextPresent	energy efficient	

TC_Google_EE		
open	http://www.google.com/	
type	q	energy efficient
clickAndWait	btnG	
waitForTextPresent	energy efficiency	
assertTitle	energy efficient - Google Search	

Selenium Test Case writing in HTML

You can update or even write the Selenium Test directly in HTML and load in the IDE and run it.

However, please note that Selenium is very sensitive to the format of the table.

All selenium command rows must have three columns else they will not be recognised as commands.

Try it yourself: If you edit the test script in HTML editor and add the forth column to the command then the content of the forth column is taken as extension to the content of the third column itself.

I don't see many reasons why would anyone write the test cases from scratch in HTML instead of recording them in IDE, however there might be a need to manually update them as per the requirement.

Similar to Test Cases the Test Suites can also be created directly using HTML editor as they are nothing but one-column HTML table. Let's have a deeper look at ways to create Test Suites.

Test Suites can be created in two ways:

- Editing the Basic Test Suite
- Using Add Test Case Method

Editing the Basic Test Suite

This is manual way of editing Test Suite.

If you have only one test case (TC_GE_EE.html) in your test suite named TS_EE.html and you want to add another Test Case TC_Google_EE.html to the Test Suite. As the first step open it Wordpad (or other HTML Editor of your choice).

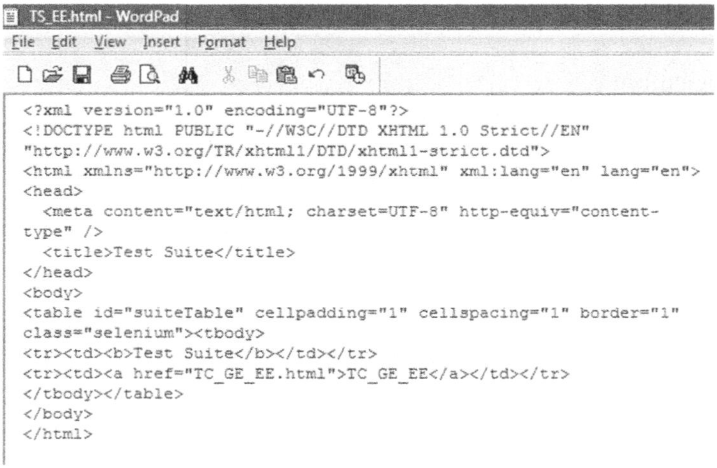


```
<?xml version="1.0" encoding="UTF-8"?>
<!DOCTYPE html PUBLIC "-//W3C//DTD XHTML 1.0 Strict//EN"
"http://www.w3.org/TR/xhtml1/DTD/xhtml1-strict.dtd">
<html xmlns="http://www.w3.org/1999/xhtml" xml:lang="en" lang="en">
<head>
  <meta content="text/html; charset=UTF-8" http-equiv="content-
type" />
  <title>Test Suite</title>
</head>
<body>
<table id="suiteTable" cellpadding="1" cellspacing="1" border="1"
class="selenium"><tbody>
<tr><td><b>Test Suite</b></td></tr>
<tr><td><a href="TC_GE_EE.html">TC_GE_EE</a></td></tr>
</tbody></table>
</body>
</html>
```

Add a line of code before the end of </tbody> tag

<tr><td><a href="TC_Google_EE.html">TC_Google_EE</a></td></tr>

File → Save then Exit.

Now you can double click and see the entire test suite in your browser.

Don't forget to keep all the test cases in the same directory

```
<tr><td><b>Test Suite</b></td></tr>
<tr><td><a href="TC_GE_EE.html">TC_GE_EE</a></td></tr>
<tr><td><a href="TC_Google_EE.html">TC_Google_EE</a></td></tr>
</tbody></table>
</body>
</html>
```

Try it yourself: Keep the test case that needs to be added in the Test Suite in a different folder and update the Test Suite HTML to run that test. Hint – You will need to use the relative path which mentioning the Test Case file name in the HTML code.

If you like this approach then you can edit the Test Suite in Wordpad when you want to:

- Change the name of the test cases
- Add, Remove, and Rename test cases
- Arrange order of test cases.

There is another way to do this which is simpler and does not involve any HTML editing.

Using Add Test Case Method

This time we'll use Selenium IDE to create the Test Suite for us.

Open Firefox

Open Tools → Selenium IDE

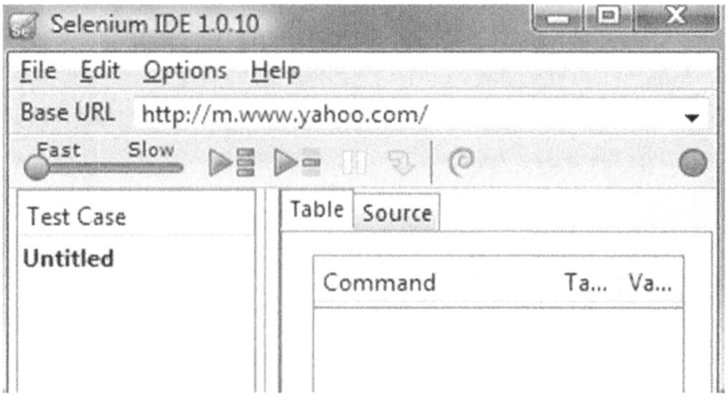

By default there will be one test case "Untitled", even though we don't want it in our Test Suite, we will need to keep it there for now since if we try to delete it, we will get a message "There must be at least 1 test case in a test suite".

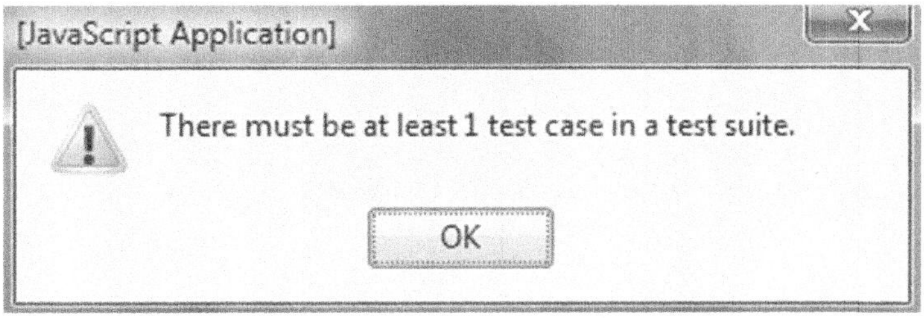

We will now select the first test case that we want to be part of our Test Suite TC_GE_EE.html.

File → Open → TC_GE_EE.html (*1)

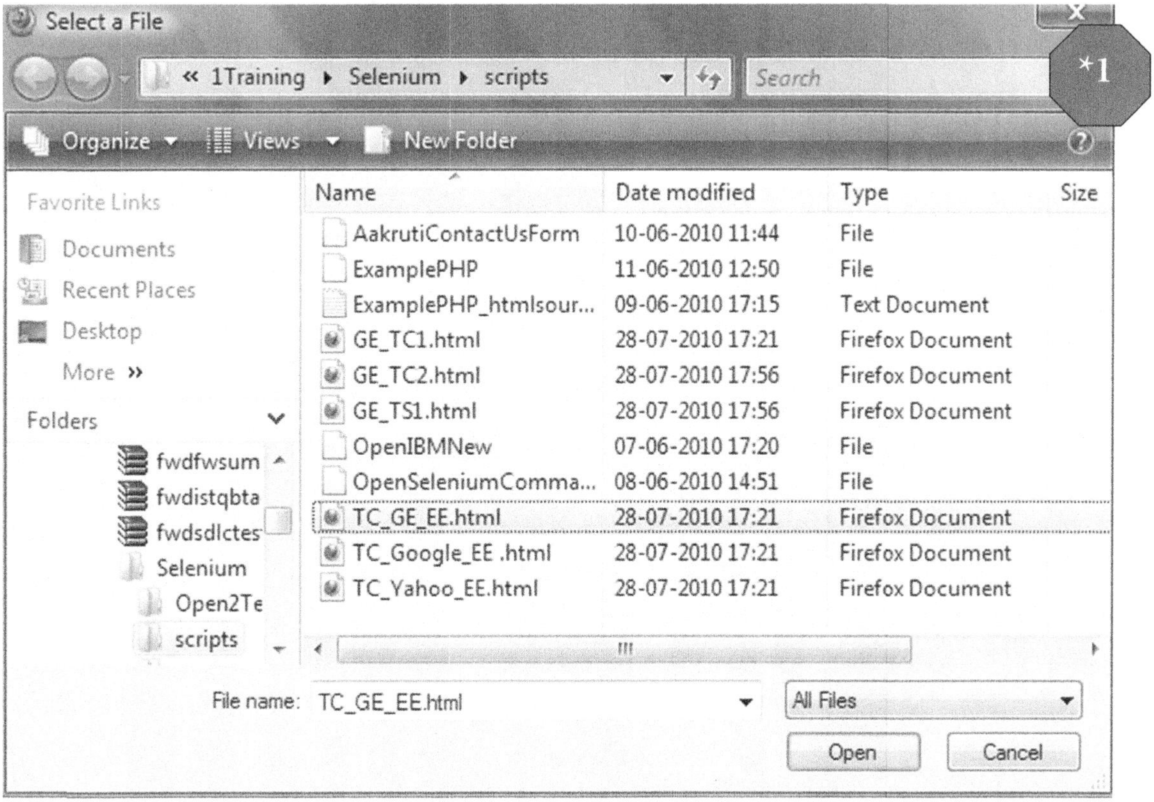

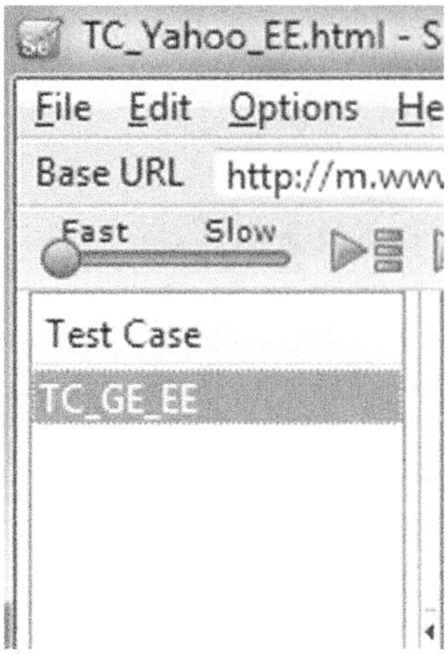

File → Add Test Case → TC_Google_EE.html (*2)

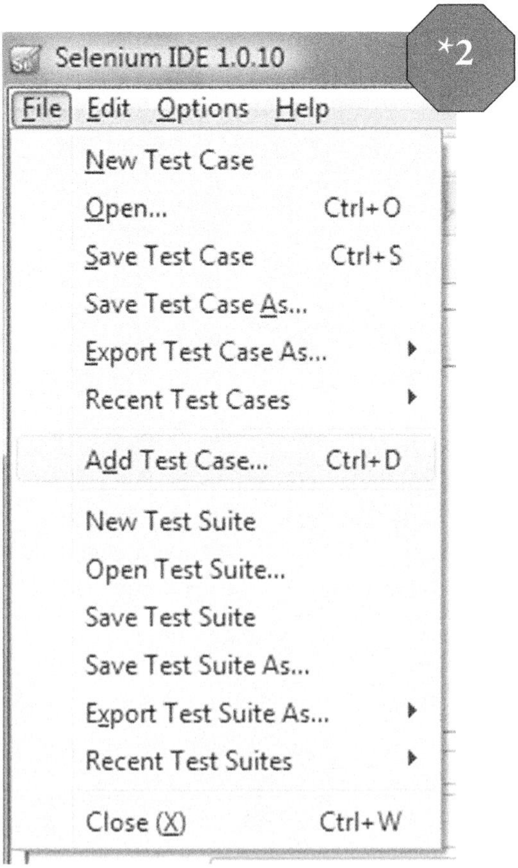

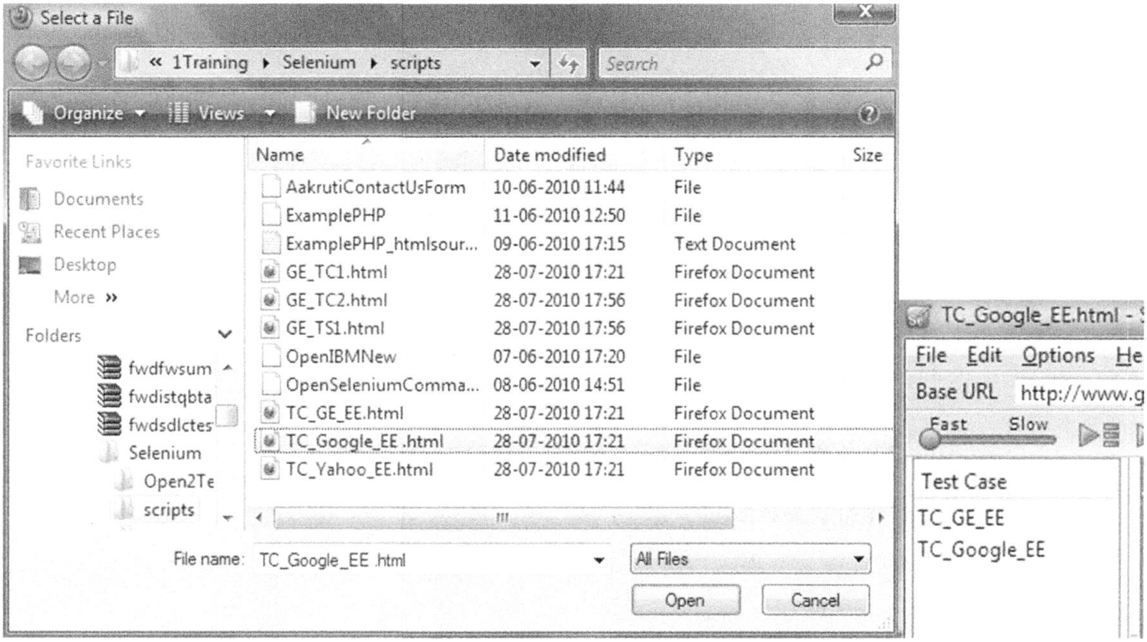

Press Ctrl+D (menu short-cut for Adding Test Case), Select TC_Yahoo_EE.html (*3)

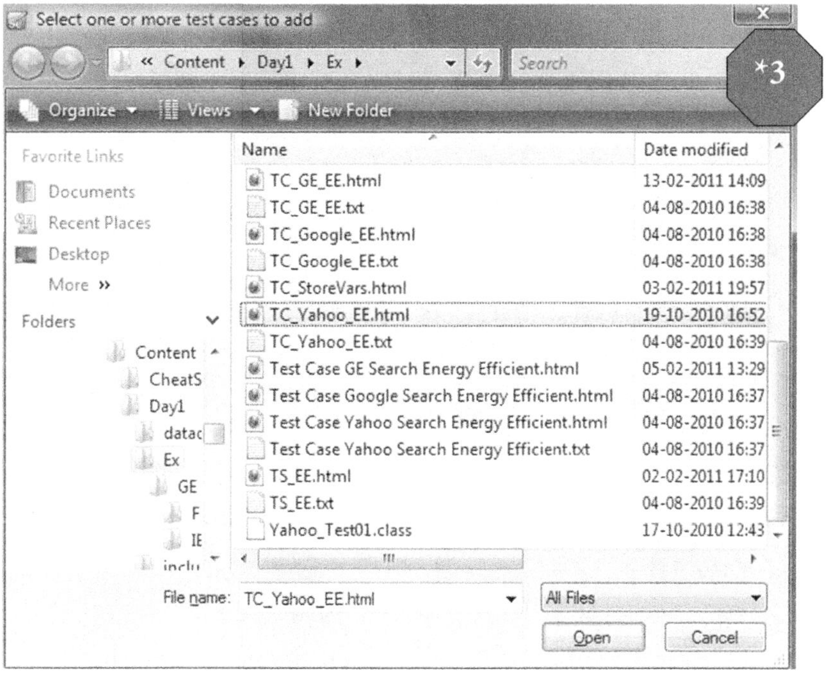

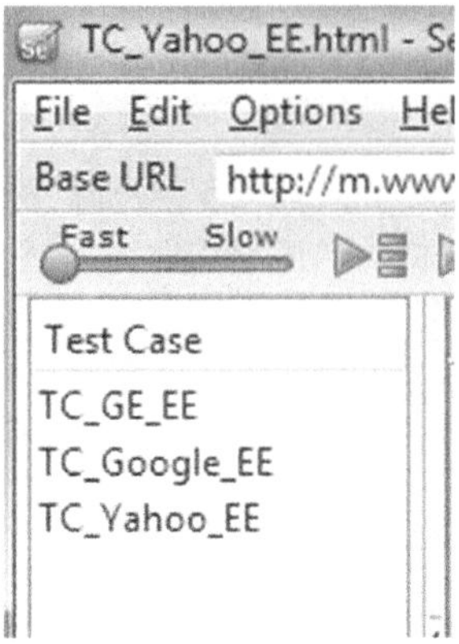

Now Enlarge the Test Case Section

You will see all your test cases listed

File → Save Test Suite As "TS_EE.html" (*4)

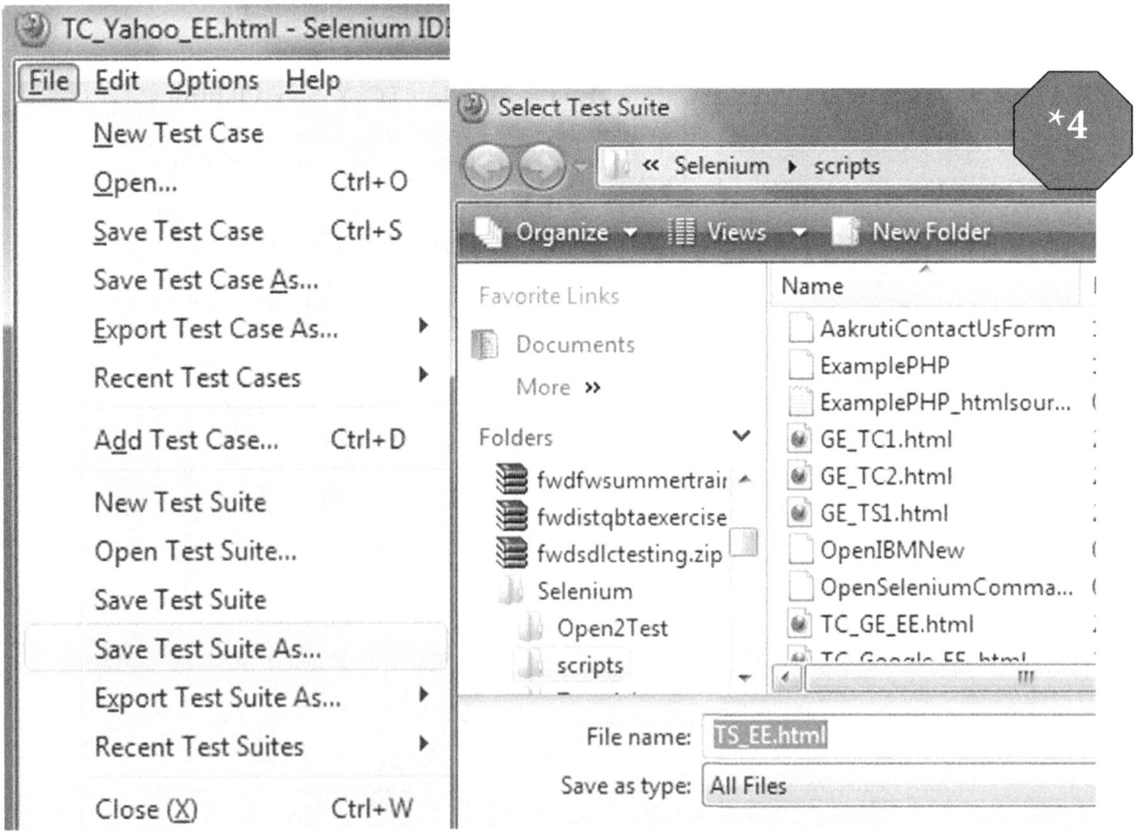

Now Click on the "Play Entire Test Suite" icon (*5).

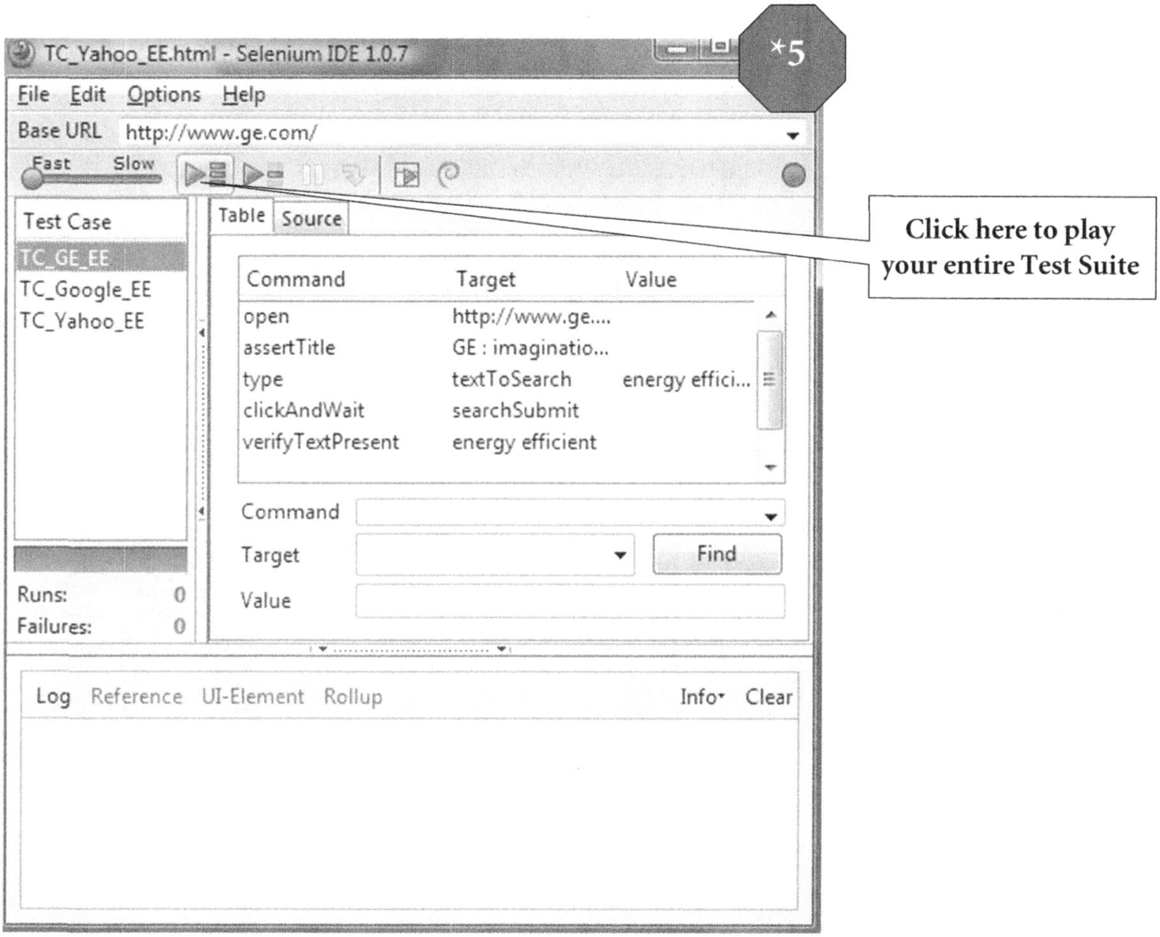

Edit Test Suite

If you need to edit the Test Suite then open the Test Suite

File → Open Test Suite…

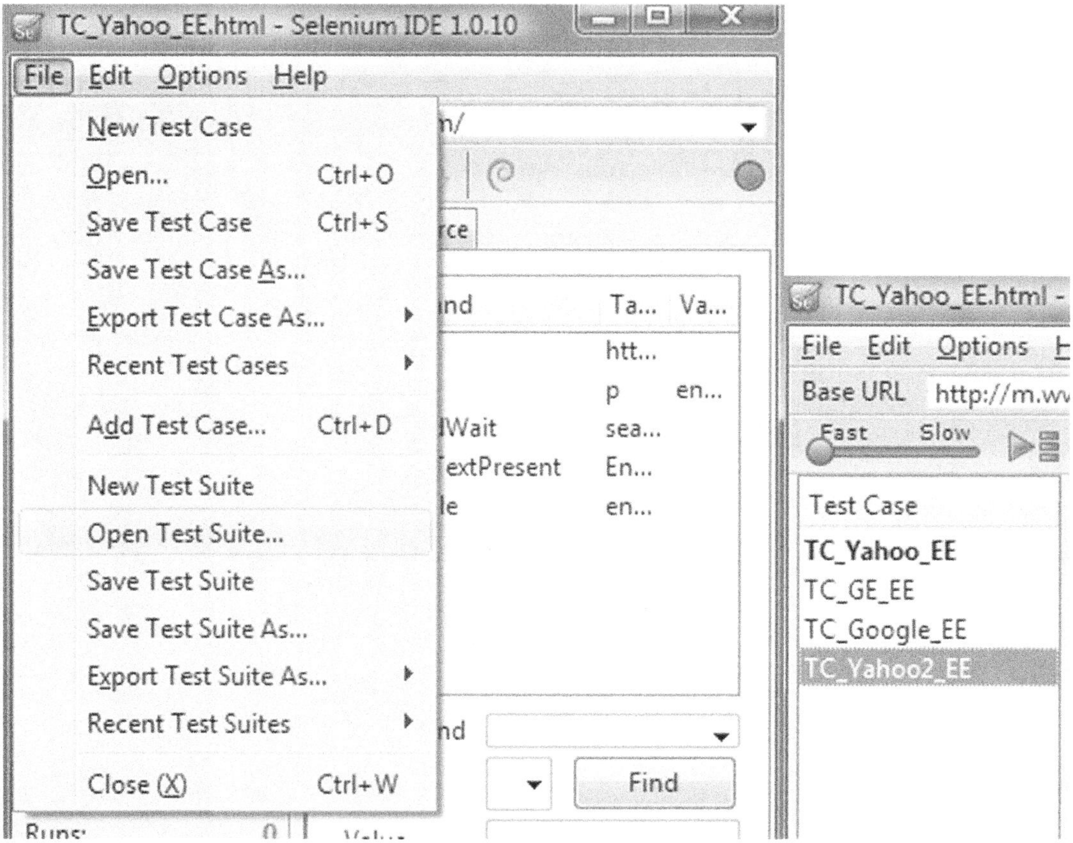

Right Click on the Test Cases list panel and choose the appropriate action. For e.g. if you chose "Delete" then the selected Test Case would be deleted.

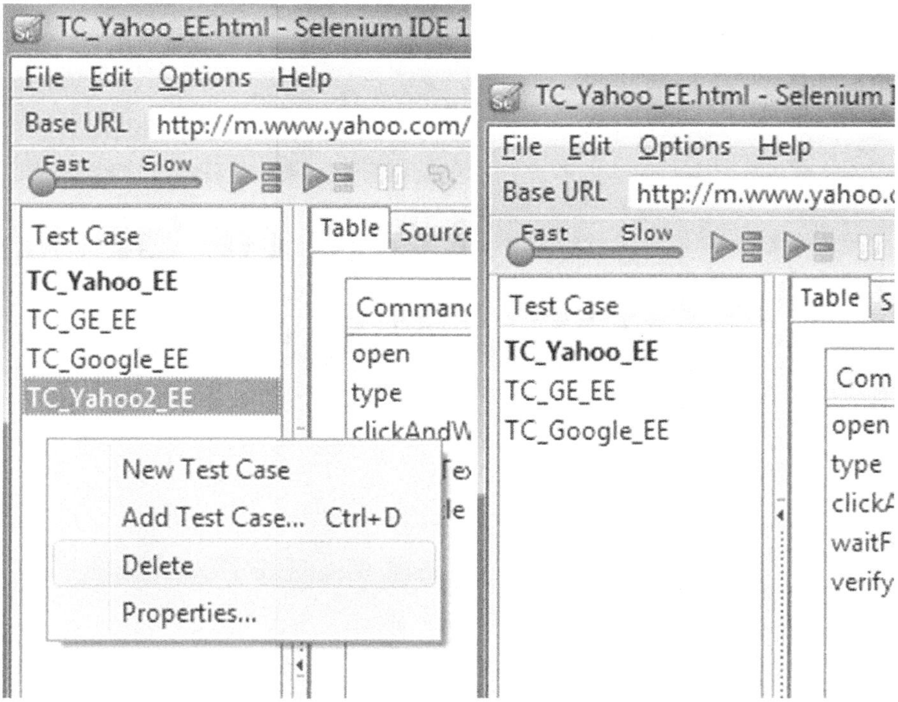

The other options would result in the associated actions.

It is as simple as that.

EXERCISES

1. Create a test suite with three Test cases that you have recorded in IDE. Run the individual test case independently and then run them as a Suite.
2. Change the sequence of execution of the Test cases from IDE. How will you do this without using the IDE interface?
3. If there was a failure of an Assert command in one of my test case then will execution of my test suite halt?
4. Can the test cases of the test suite be places in different folders? What are the implications of this?

7

Tour of Selenium IDE—Simple Features

Selenium IDE contains the following menus:

- File, Edit, Options, Help

Test Running IDE Provides

- Test Case List View
- Record/Review Test Case View
- Table/Source Test Case View
- Log/Reference/UI-Element/Rollup View

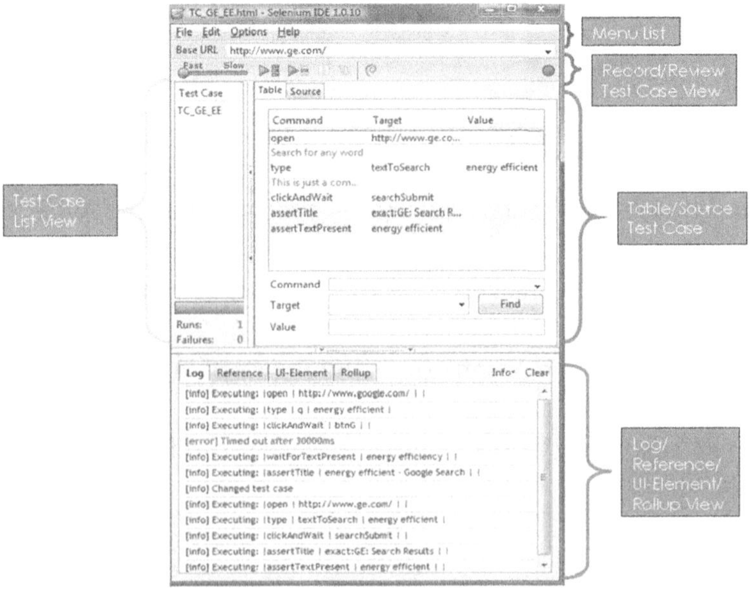

Selenium IDE Menu Options

File Menu

It allows you to create, open, save, export and to view recent test cases.

Allows you to create, open, save and to view recent test suites.

Close menu item will allow you to save/discard last changes before closing the current test case/ suite.

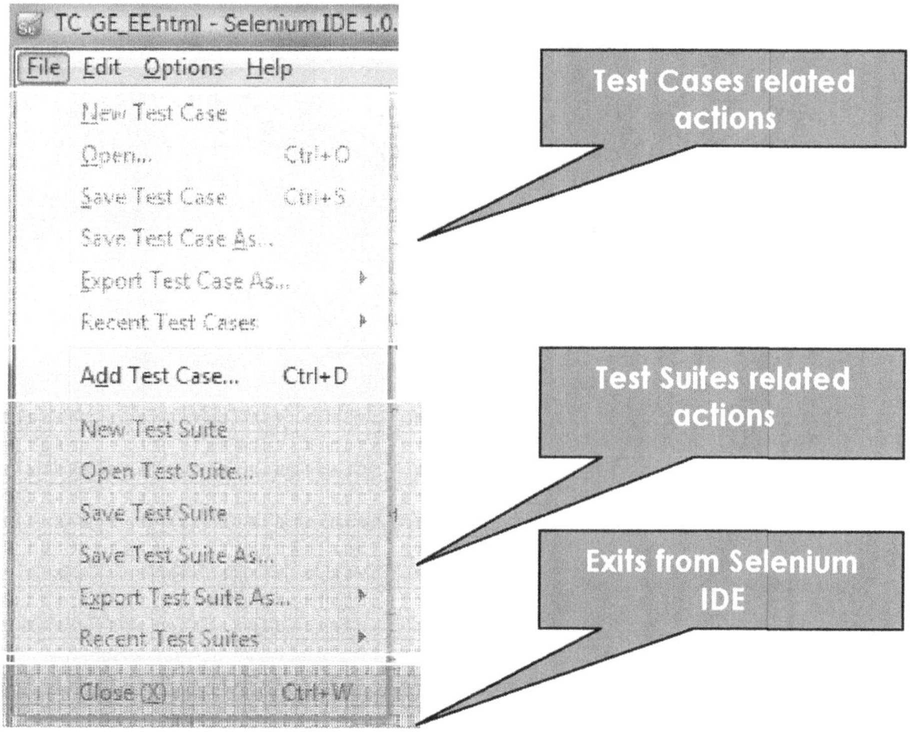

Please note that Selenium IDE does not provide any way to Close a particular Test Case

Export Test Case As...

In Selenium IDE exporting Test Cases Available for the following languages:

- HTML
- Java
- JUnit

- TestNG
- Groovy
- C#
- Perl
- PHP
- Python
- Ruby

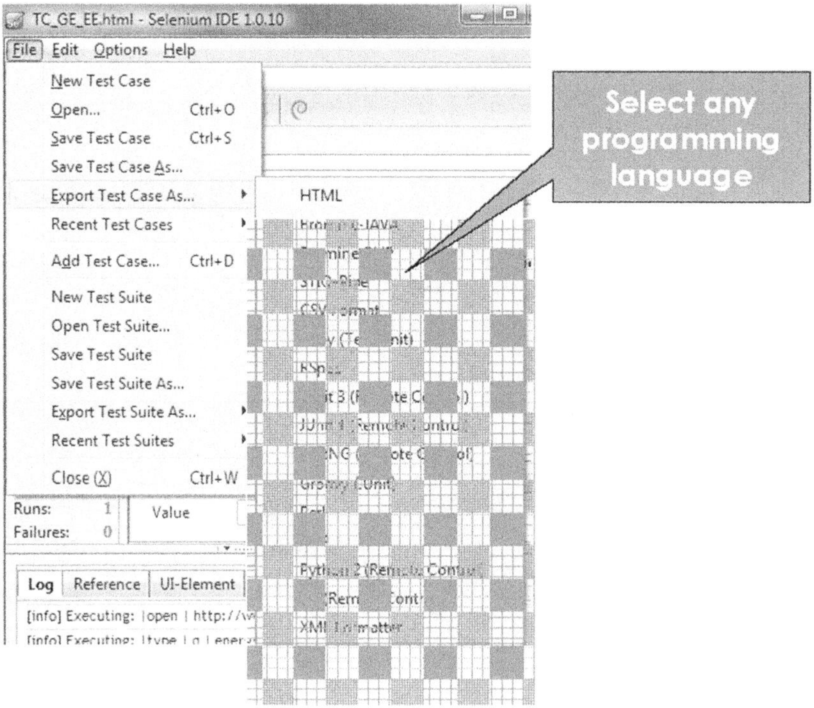

Edit Menu

Edit Menu allows you to redo or undo the actions you have performed

Allows you to Select All or Partial Test cases then cut, copy, paste and delete them.

Also, when the clipboard format (will be discussed later in Advanced Features chapter) is selected on a specific language. Holds the copy in that specific language format.

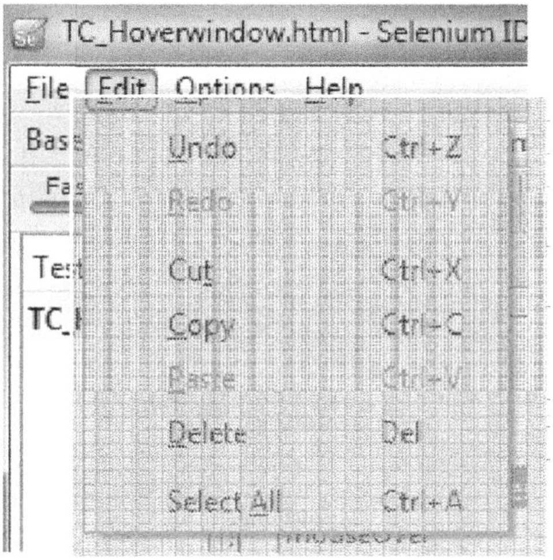

Options Menu

Allows you set default values under **General** Options (*1)

Allows you to add new Formats for test cases (*2)

Select a specific format to use in the Selenium IDE (*3)

Select a clipboard format to copy from Selenium IDE (*4)

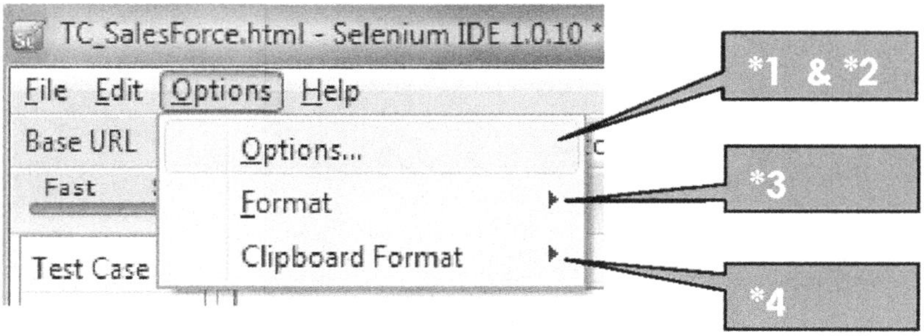

These options we will look in details in the sections below.

Options Menu – General Tab

➢ Allows you to set default values for
  - Encoding format of test files (UTF-8, UTF-16)
  - Timeout value (15000, 45000)

- ➢ Allows you add extensions
  - Selenium Core (user-extensions.js)
  - Selenium IDE extensions
- ➢ Settings to
  - Remember Base URL, Record assertTitle automatically, Record absolute URL, Activate Developer Tools, Start recording immediately on open

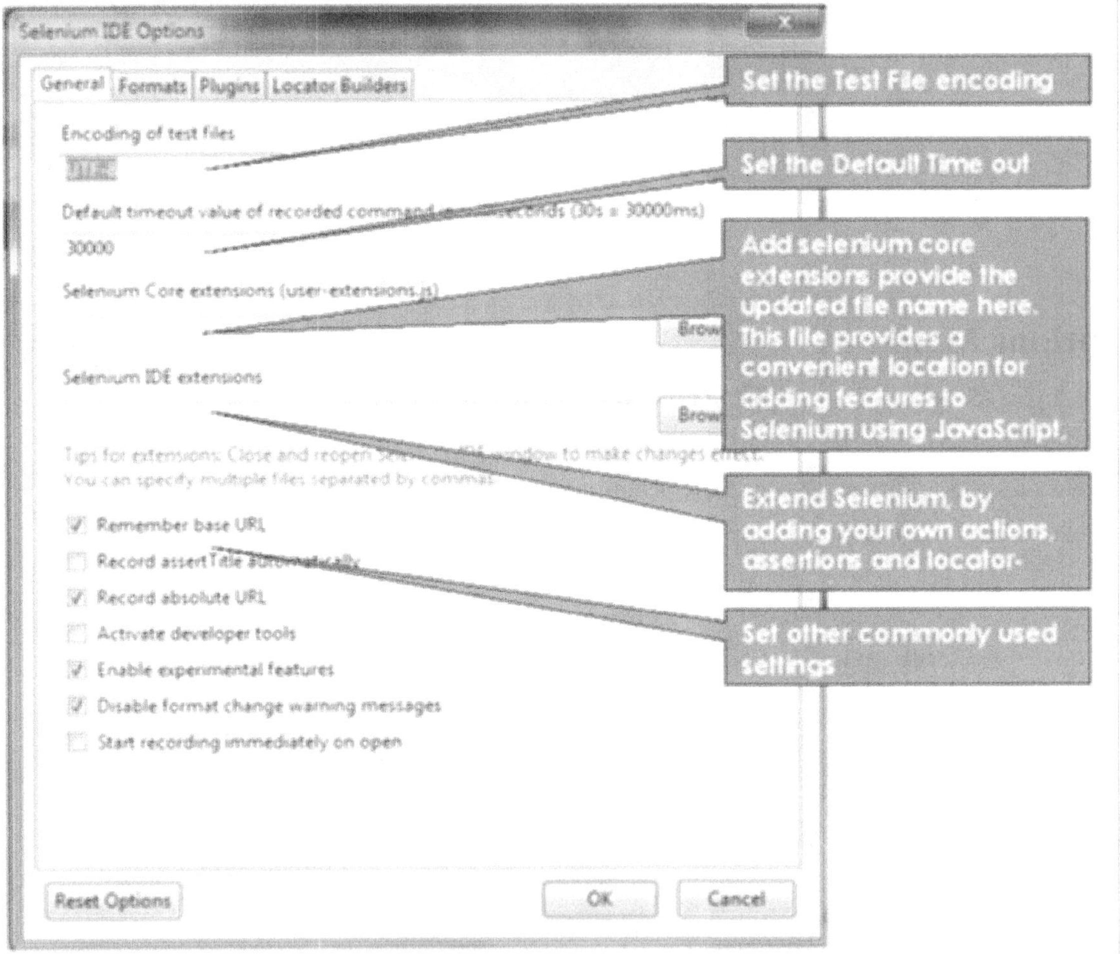

The options are described as below:

➢ Remember base URL – This option records the starting URL of the application under test. For e.g in this test the Base URL is recorded as http://www.ge.com

- Record assertTitle automatically – For every new page opened while recording an "assertTitle" command is added automatically.
- Record absolute URL – This will record the URLs fully and not relative to the base URL.

For e.g. relative URL will be recorded as below:

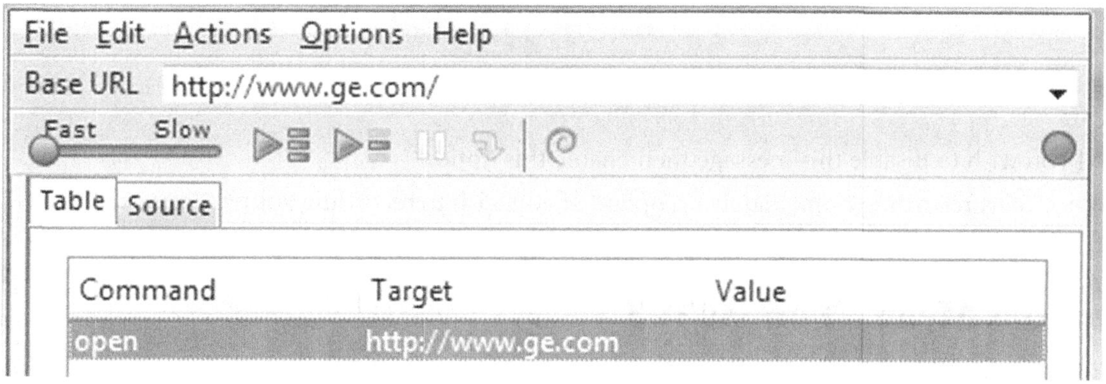

Absolute URL will be as below:

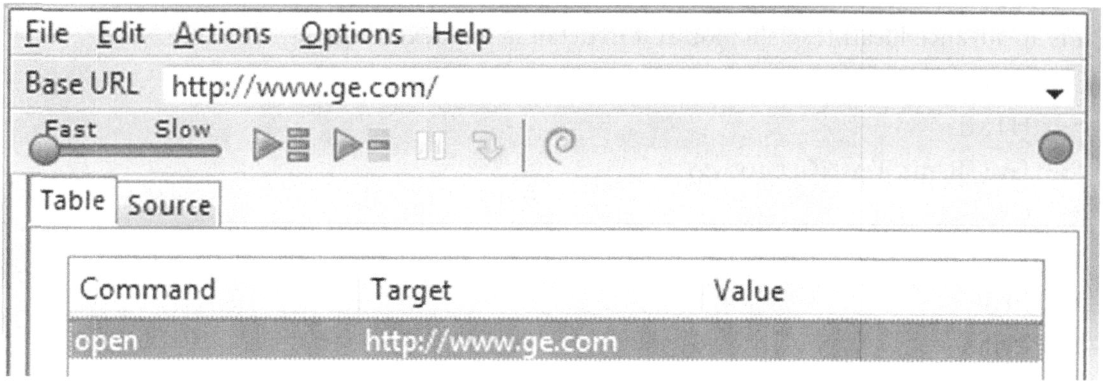

- Activate developers tools – You will need to restart the IDE every time you make changes to the Core or IDE extension user-extension.js file, however with this option enabled you need not do that and changes to the js file will take effect immediately.

- Enable experimental features – The formats available to convert the IDE code to Java or PHP code using option Options-Format has been termed as experimental. If you need this options then enable this else the menu Options – Format will be grayed out.
- Disable format change warning messages – Whenever you will switch the IDE code to another format using Options – Format, you will get following warning message:

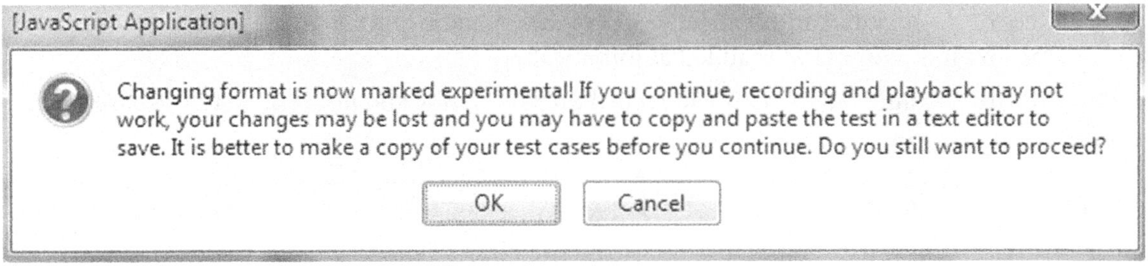

If you wish to disable this message then enable this option.

- Start recording immediately on open – If you wish to recording your actions as soon as IDE is opened then enable this option.

Options Menu – Format Tab

Allows you to **add** a new language format for test cases.

Allows you to **view** the existing language format for test cases.

You can **modify** at the source code of each existing language formats.

It is an advanced feature, we'll look at it in detail in the next chapter.

Currently available language formats are:

- HTML
- Java (JUnit, TestNG, Groovy)
- C#
- Perl
- PHP
- Python
- Ruby

Other than the HTML, rest are handled by Selenium RC (Remote Control).

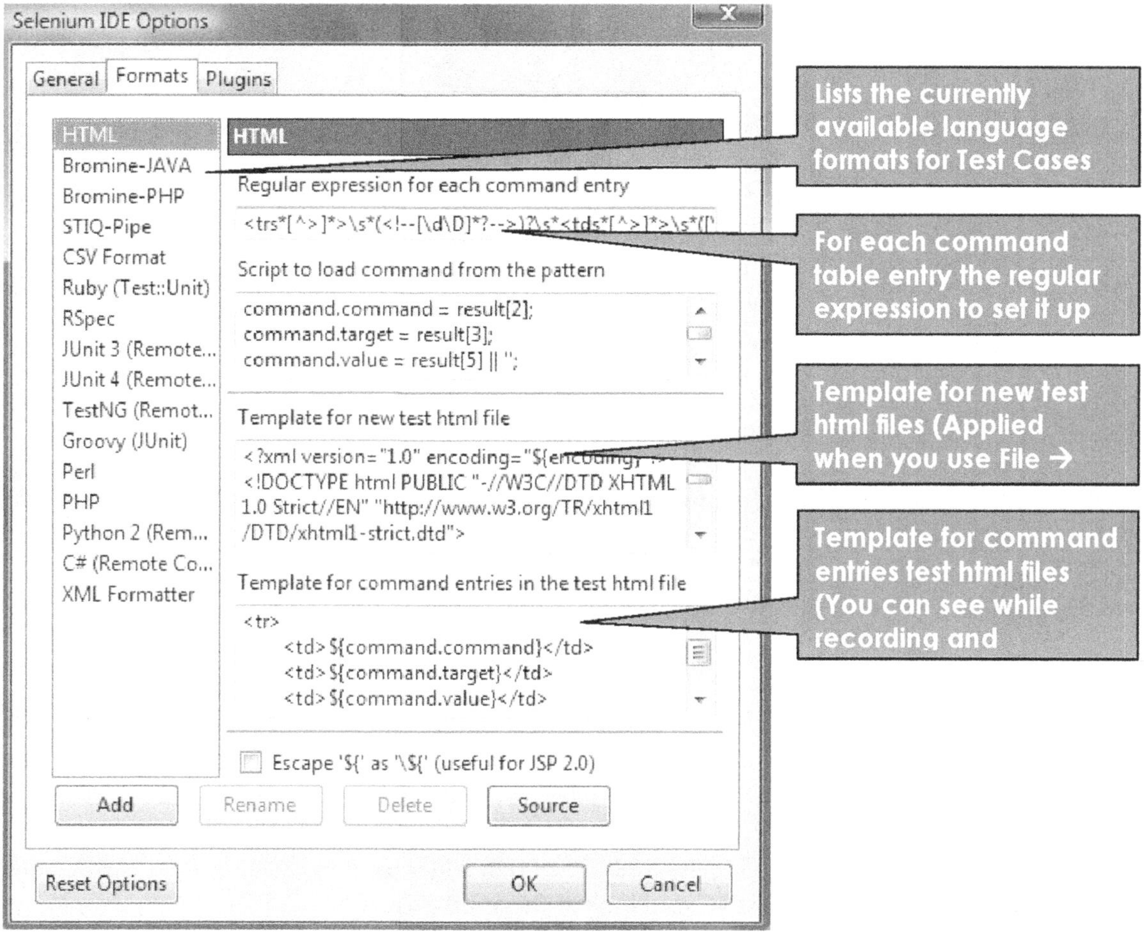

Options Menu – Format Menu Items

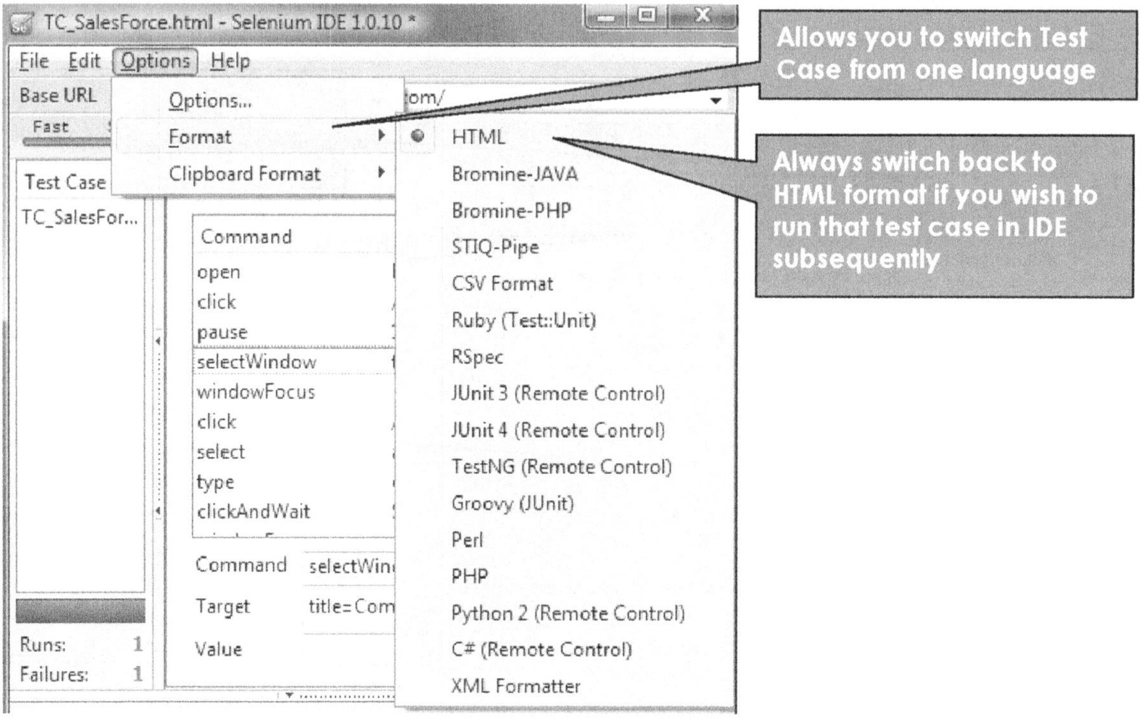

Exercise:

Open the recorded Test case TC_Google_EE.html in IDE and look at the Source Tab. Now change the Format of the Test Case to TestNG and look at the Source Tab.

Options Menu – Clipboard Format

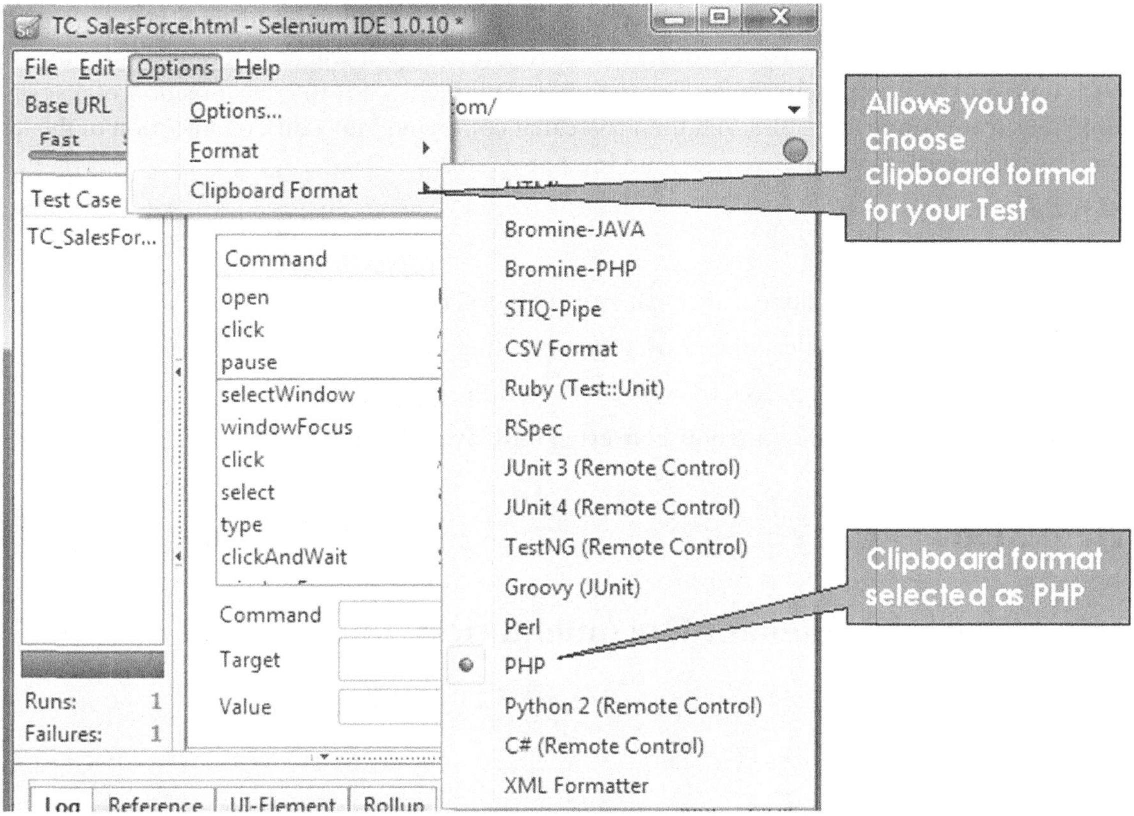

Exercise

Open the recorded Test case TC_Google_EE.html in IDE and look at the Source Tab. Now switch the Clipboard format to PHP and look at the Sorce Tab, notice that it remains the same. Now go back to the Table tab and select all the rows in the table (Control+A), Copy the content and paste in to Notepad. You will have the commands that you copied from the Table are pasted in PHP language code.

You can also select few rows from the Table as paste them to get the target language (PHP in this case) code for those Selenese commands.

Clipboard format helps us to quickly copy the code in our selected language and also for the selected rows, while not disturbing the original IDE HTML code.

What is clipboard?

Clipboard is a temporary storage area for information that you have copied or moved from one place and plan to use somewhere else. You can select text or graphics and then use the Cut or Copy commands to move your selection to the Clipboard, where it will be stored until you use the Paste command to insert it elsewhere. For example, you might want to copy a section of test case commands from command tables, and then paste that command into a different portion of the test case. The Clipboard is available in most Windows programs.

Try this out:

Open TC_Google.EE.html

Change the Options → Clipboard format → HTML to Java

In the Command Table Select one or multiple rows then right click and copy

Now Open your notepad, press Ctrl+v or Edit → Paste

You can see your commands are now converted into Java format

Help Menu

Help Menu – UI Element Documentation

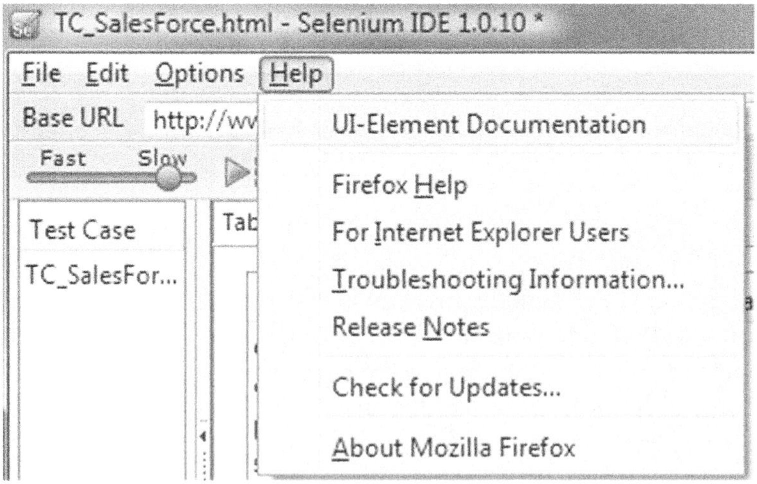

Help UI-Element Documentation is the only menu item related to Selenium

Rest of the Help menu items are as it is available as it is in Firefox browser

UI Element Documentation is a reference material, we'll see the contents when we deep dive on that subject.

Selenium IDE – GUI

Test Running IDE GUI (Graphical User Interface) Provides

- ➢ Test Case List View
- ➢ Record/Review Test Case View
- ➢ Table/Source Test Case View
- ➢ Log/Reference/UI-Element/Rollup View

Test Case List View

Test Case List View

- ➢ Test Case List View displays the test cases available within a test suite
- ➢ Allows you to monitor the progress of the test cases while you are running the test suite
- ➢ Displays the results of the test execution

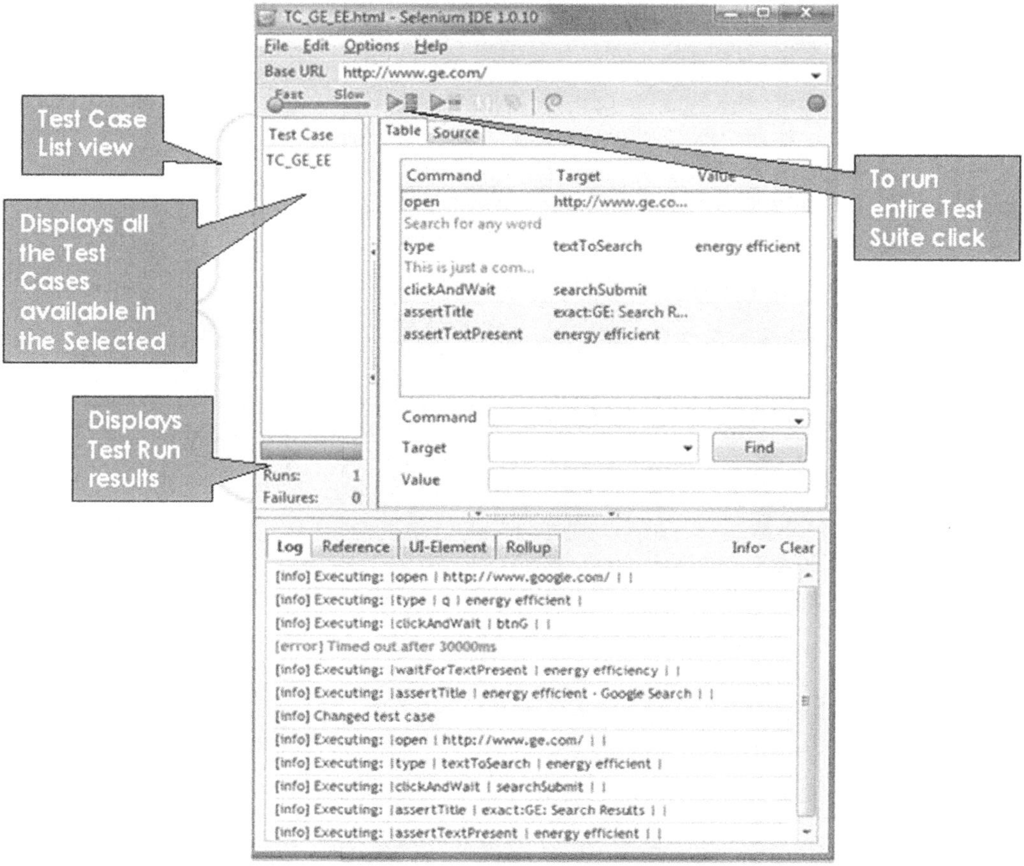

Record/Review Test Case View

Record/Review Test Case View

- Shows/sets the base URL of current test case
- Always better to verify the base URL shown is the one you are running the test case
- Allows you to set the speed of the test case execution
- Allows you to play current test case or the entire test suite
- Pass/Resume the test case
- Step through the test case
- Record a test case (Default mode when Selenium IDE is opened)
- Stop the current recording
- To play the test case with Test Runner
- To apply rollup rules

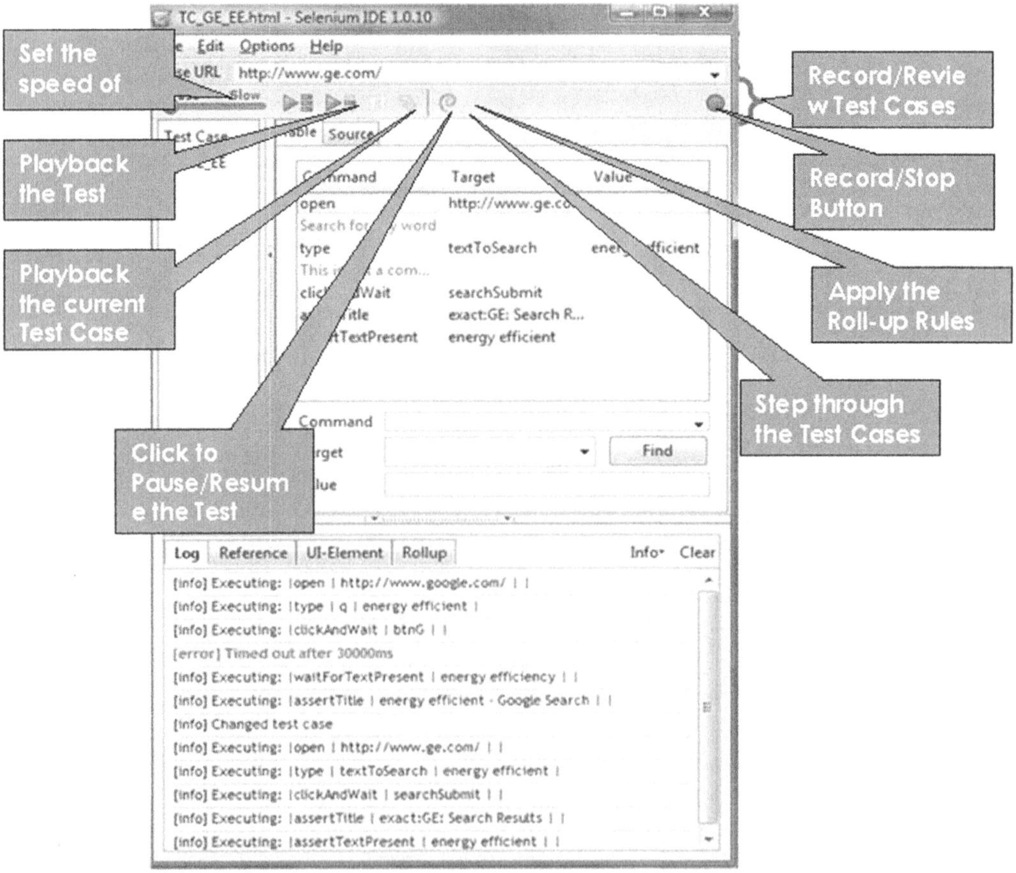

Table/Source Test Case View

Table/Source Test Case View

- ➢ Displays the current test case
- ➢ Allows you edit a specific test step
- ➢ Based on the language format selected, the "Source" displays the test case on that language format
- ➢ Test Case Table view displays the command, target and values for each step
- ➢ Displays the status of the test case execution Green indicates the step is passed. Red indicates the step is failed.
- ➢ Right Click allows you to
  - insert new commands
  - set breakpoints
  - execute a specific step
  - cut, copy, del a specific step or all the test cases

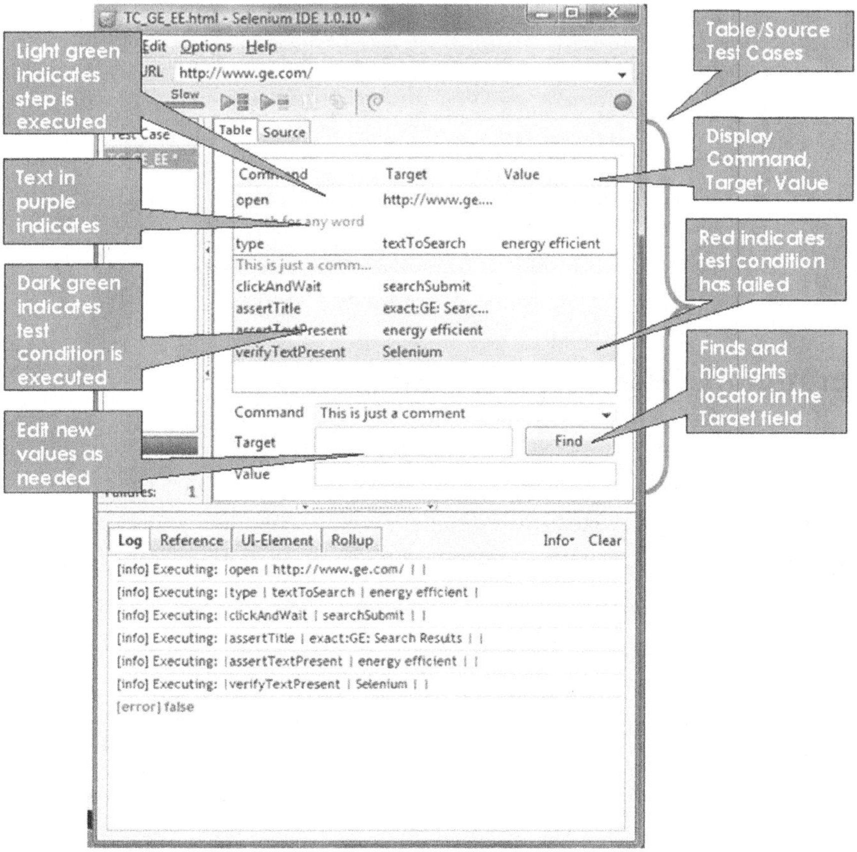

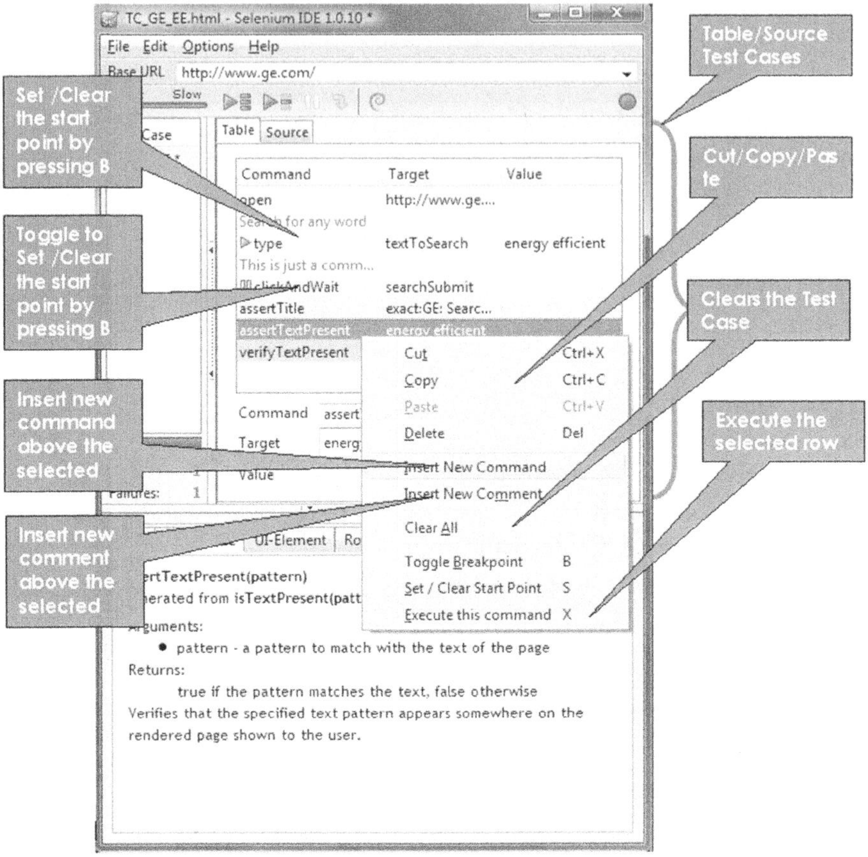

Log/Reference/UI-Element/Rollup View

Log View

- Provides current test case execution details
- Contains each step processed result
- Failed step will have a red text
- Log is filtered into 4 different categories
  - Debug – Debugging information
  - Info – Execution information
  - Error – Error Information (for failed test steps)
  - Warn – Any warnings

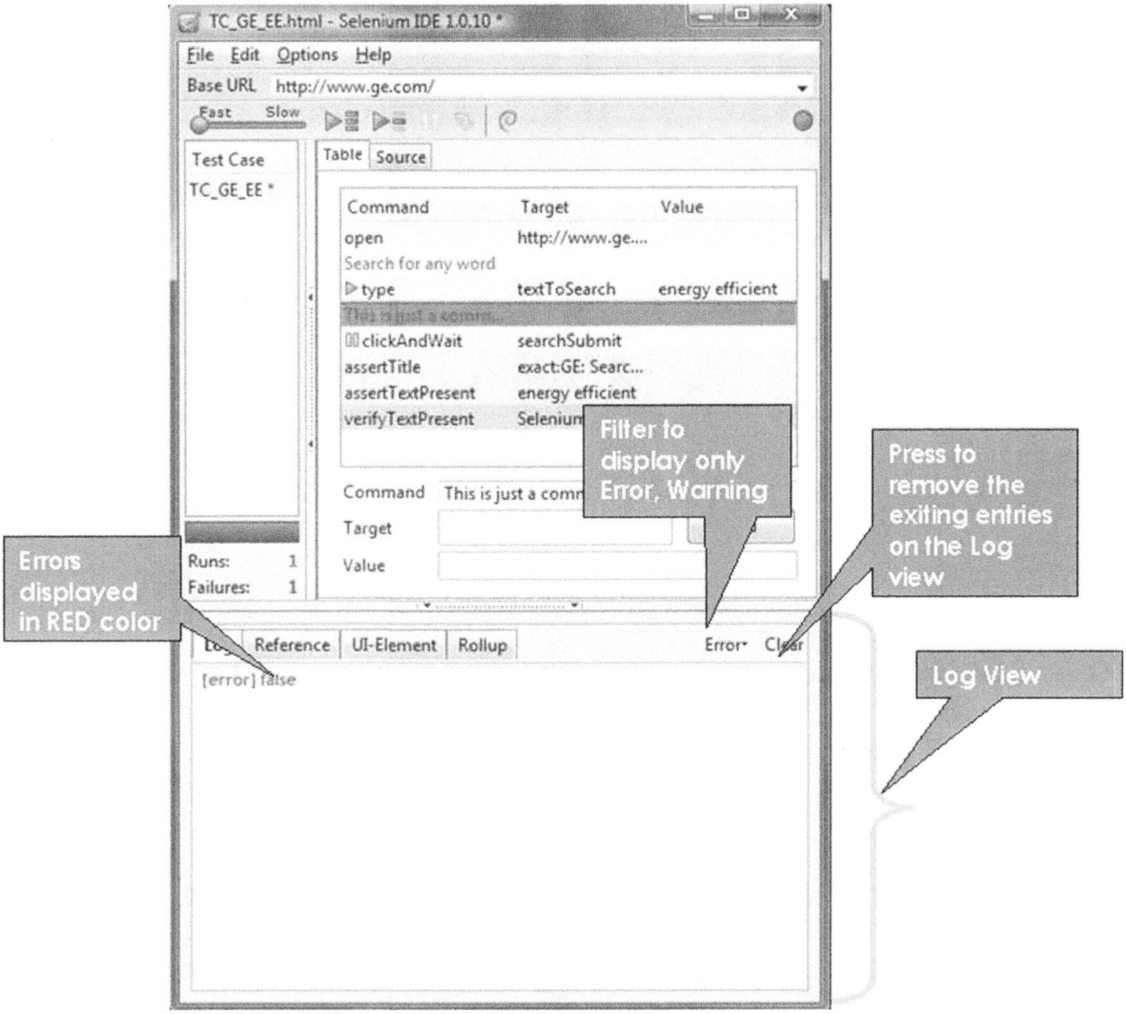

Reference View

- ➢ Provide current test steps command's reference details.
- ➢ Argument Details
- ➢ Generated from which command
- ➢ Details about the command

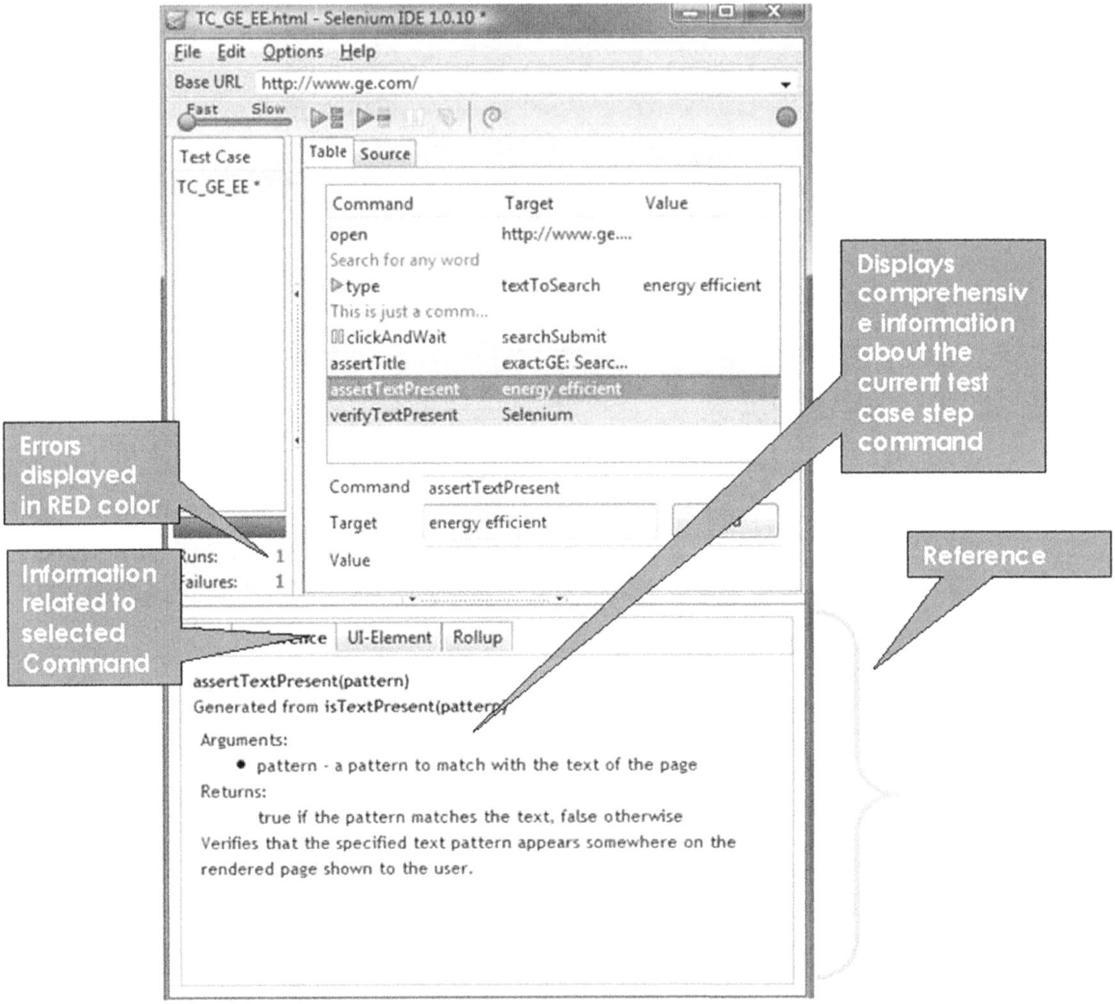
TC_GE_EE.html - Selenium IDE 1.0.10 *
File Edit Options Help
Base URL http://www.ge.com/
Fast Slow
Test Case
TC_GE_EE *
Table Source
Command Target Value
open http://www.ge....
Search for any word
type textToSearch energy efficient
This is just a comm...
clickAndWait searchSubmit
assertTitle exact:GE: Searc...
assertTextPresent energy efficient
verifyTextPresent Selenium
Command assertTextPresent
Target energy efficient
Value
Runs: 1
Failures: 1
UI-Element Rollup
assertTextPresent(pattern)
Generated from isTextPresent(pattern)
Arguments:
pattern - a pattern to match with the text of the page
Returns:
true if the pattern matches the text, false otherwise
Verifies that the specified text pattern appears somewhere on the rendered page shown to the user.
Displays comprehensive information about the current test case step command
Errors displayed in RED color
Information related to selected Command
Reference

EXERCISES

- Open a specific URL (http://www.barnesandnoble.com/)
- Search for a specific text ("Java") in #1 page
- By default only 10 items are listed.
- How do you verify only 10 items are present?
- Change the Items Per Page to 100.
- Verify whether it contains 100 per page.

8

Tour of Selenium IDE — Advanced Features

Options Menu

Adding New Format

Go to Tools → Selenium IDE → Options → Format Tab

Press the add button

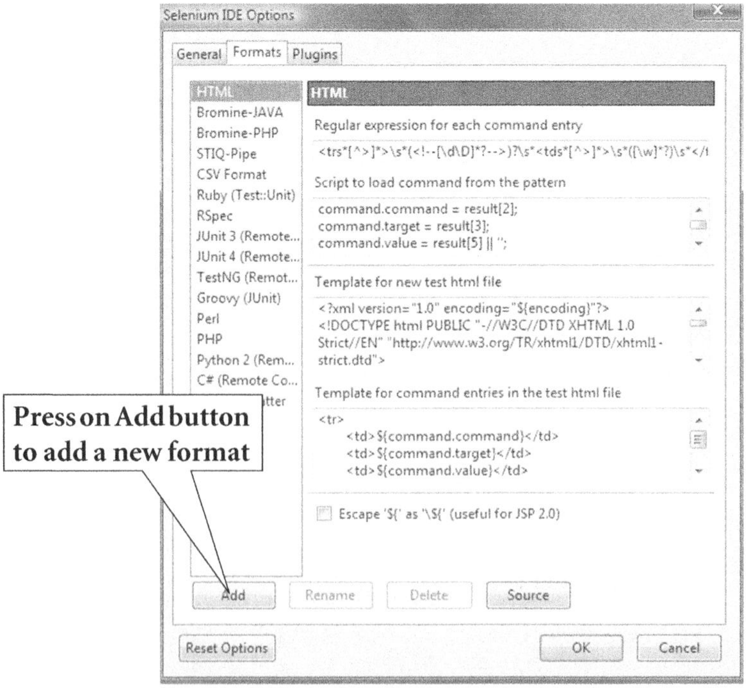

Provide the name of format as "CSV Format"

Download the "seleniumIDE_CSV.js" from http://www.qaagility.com/downloads/SeleniumBook/

Open "seleniumIDE_CSV.js" file in notepad, (From the folder where you have stored, right click on the file name and select Edit Option).

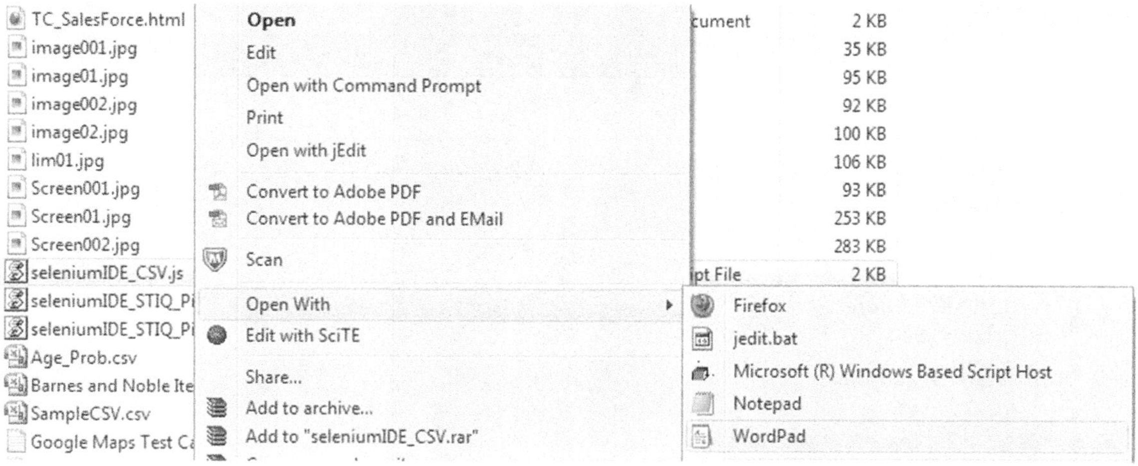

Press Ctrl+A to select all the Text from the notepad, and Press Ctrl+C to copy the contents

Paste the JavaScript contents in Selenium IDE Format Source window

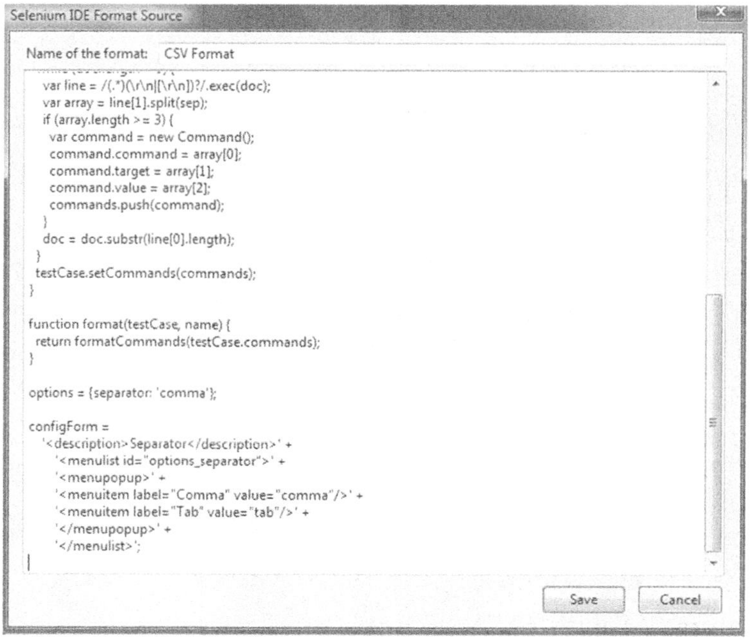

Press the "Save" button

Under the Separator Option, select "Comma" and Press "Ok" button

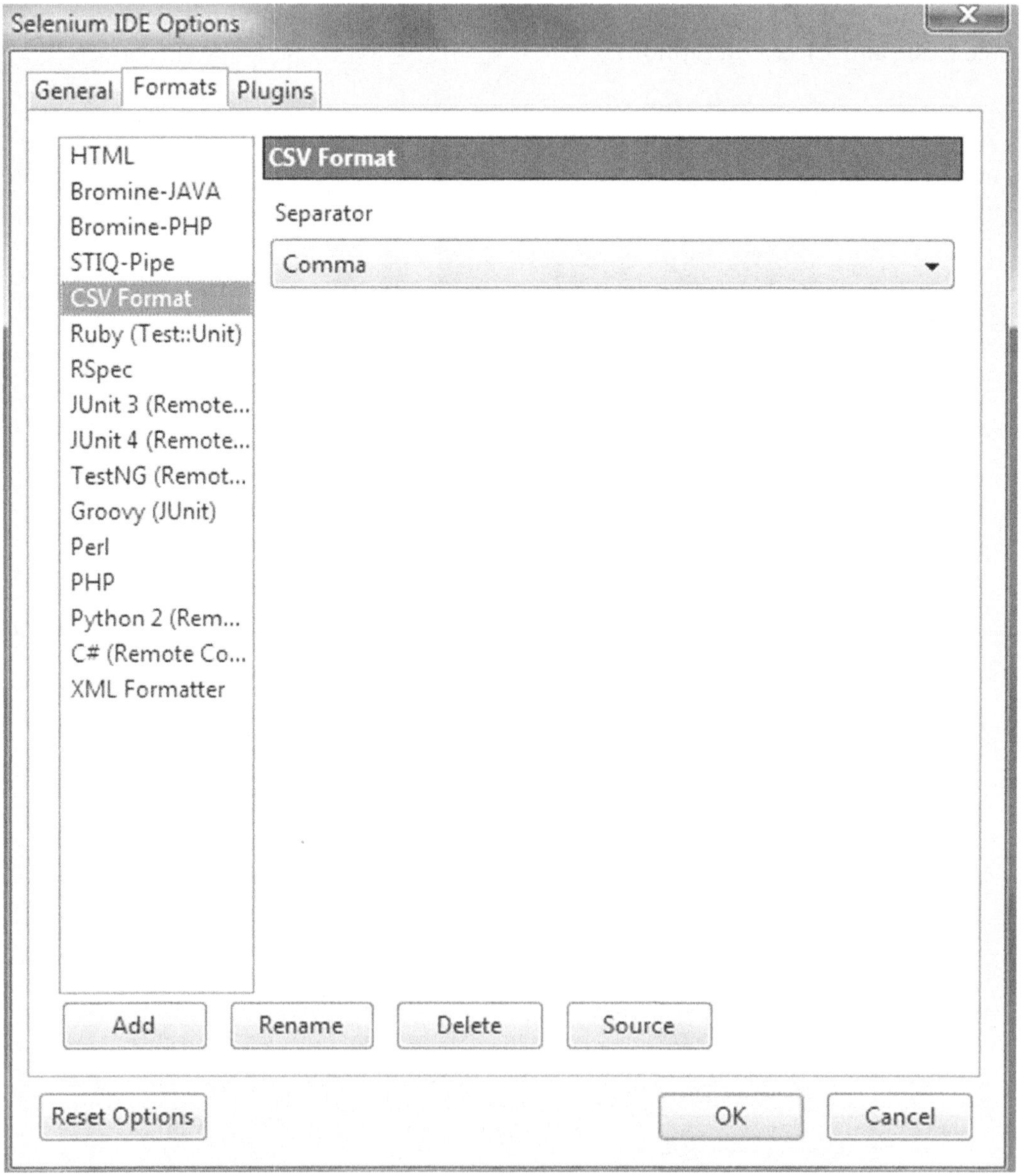

The other option is Tab delimited format and can be selected from the dropdown list.

Now we have created two new formats:

1. Comma Separated Values (CSV)

2. Tab Delimited Values (TDV)

We'll get into action to test the new formats

Open any of the existing test cases you have stored by going to

File → Open → TC_GE_EE.html

Select the Source Tab, what do you see, it is in html format

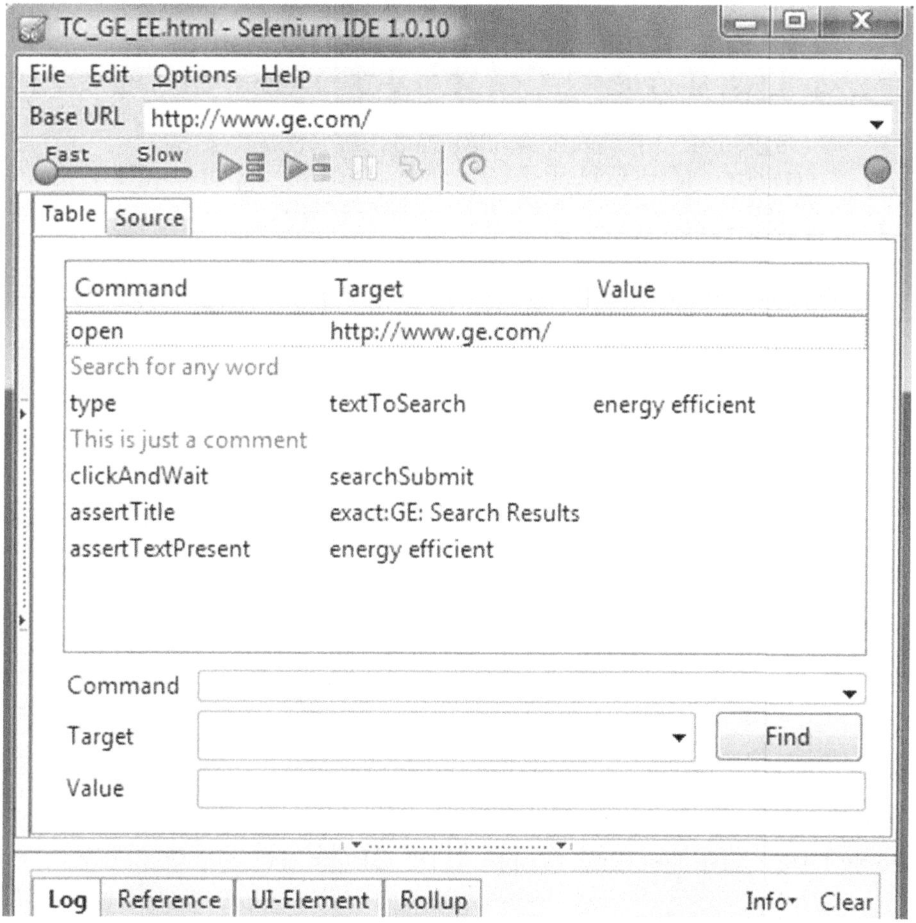

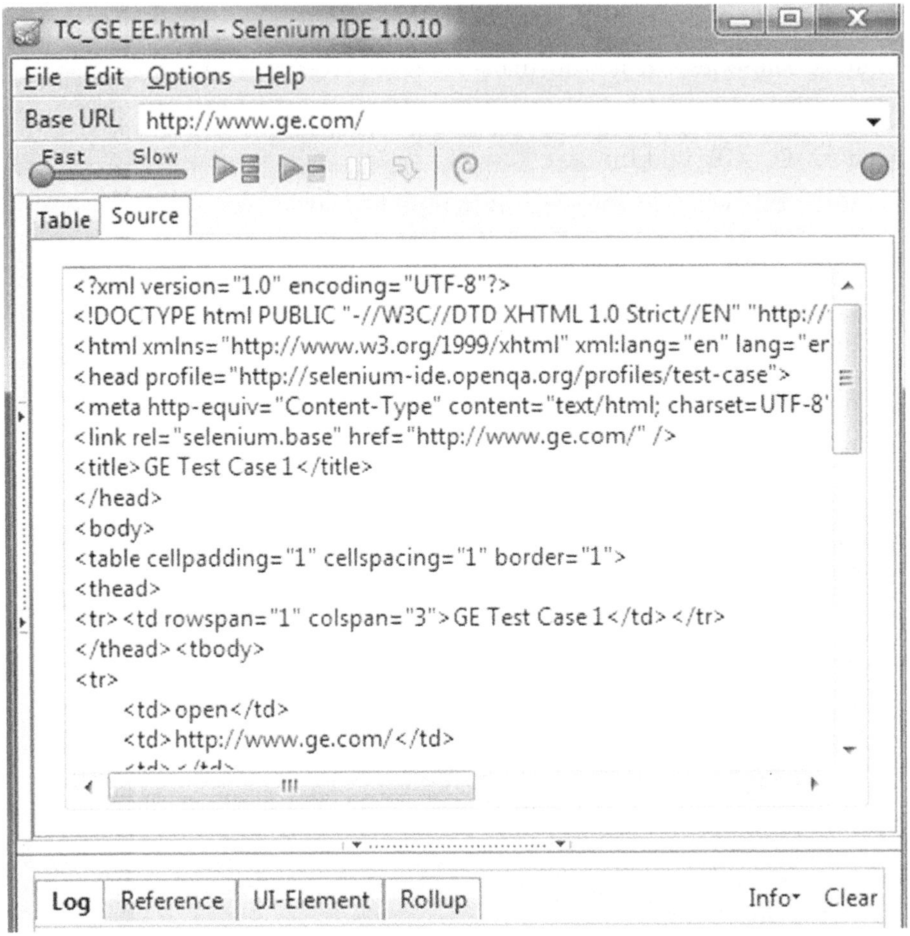

Go to Format ? Select CSV Format from the available options

Now look at the source Tab, it is converted into Comma Separated Value format.

Save by going File → Save Test Case As option, TC_GE_EE.csv

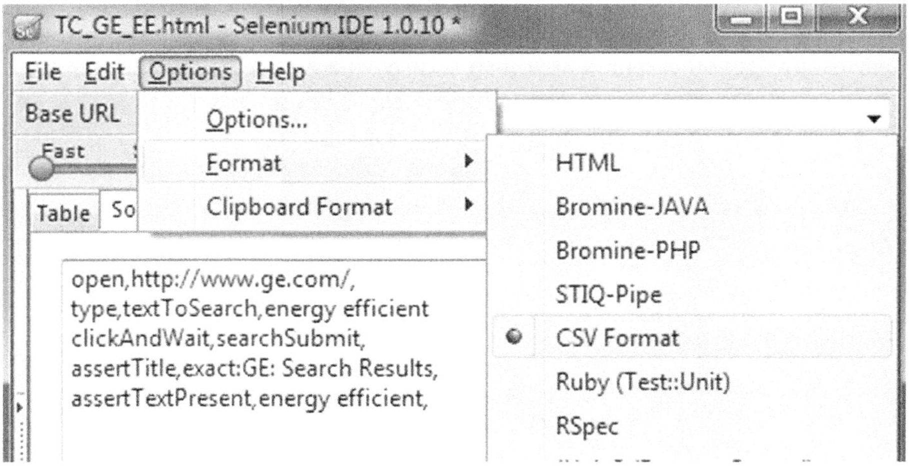
TC_GE_EE.html - Selenium IDE 1.0.10 *
File Edit Options Help
Base URL
Fast
Table
Options...
Format
Clipboard Format
HTML
Bromine-JAVA
Bromine-PHP
STIQ-Pipe
CSV Format
Ruby (Test::Unit)
RSpec
open,http://www.ge.com/,
type,textToSearch,energy efficient
clickAndWait,searchSubmit,
assertTitle,exact:GE: Search Results,
assertTextPresent,energy efficient,

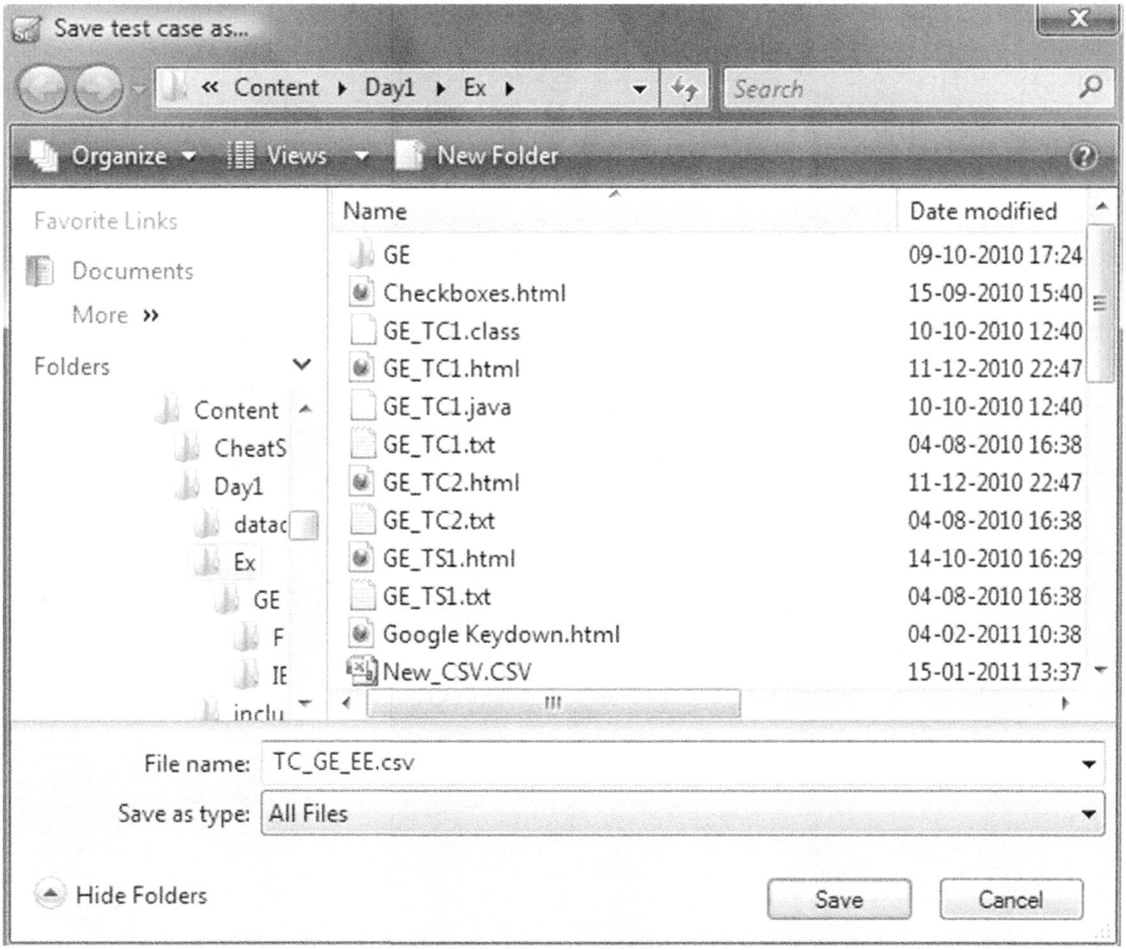
Save test case as...
« Content ▸ Day1 ▸ Ex ▸
Search
Organize
Views
New Folder
Favorite Links
Documents
More »
Folders
Content
CheatS
Day1
datac
Ex
GE
F
IE
Name
Date modified
GE 09-10-2010 17:24
Checkboxes.html 15-09-2010 15:40
GE_TC1.class 10-10-2010 12:40
GE_TC1.html 11-12-2010 22:47
GE_TC1.java 10-10-2010 12:40
GE_TC1.txt 04-08-2010 16:38
GE_TC2.html 11-12-2010 22:47
GE_TC2.txt 04-08-2010 16:38
GE_TS1.html 14-10-2010 16:29
GE_TS1.txt 04-08-2010 16:38
Google Keydown.html 04-02-2011 10:38
New_CSV.CSV 15-01-2011 13:37
File name: TC_GE_EE.csv
Save as type: All Files
Hide Folders
Save
Cancel

Open the TC_GE_EE.csv in Excel Application

With little formatting, you can look at your test cases in a nice formatted way in Excel Sheet.

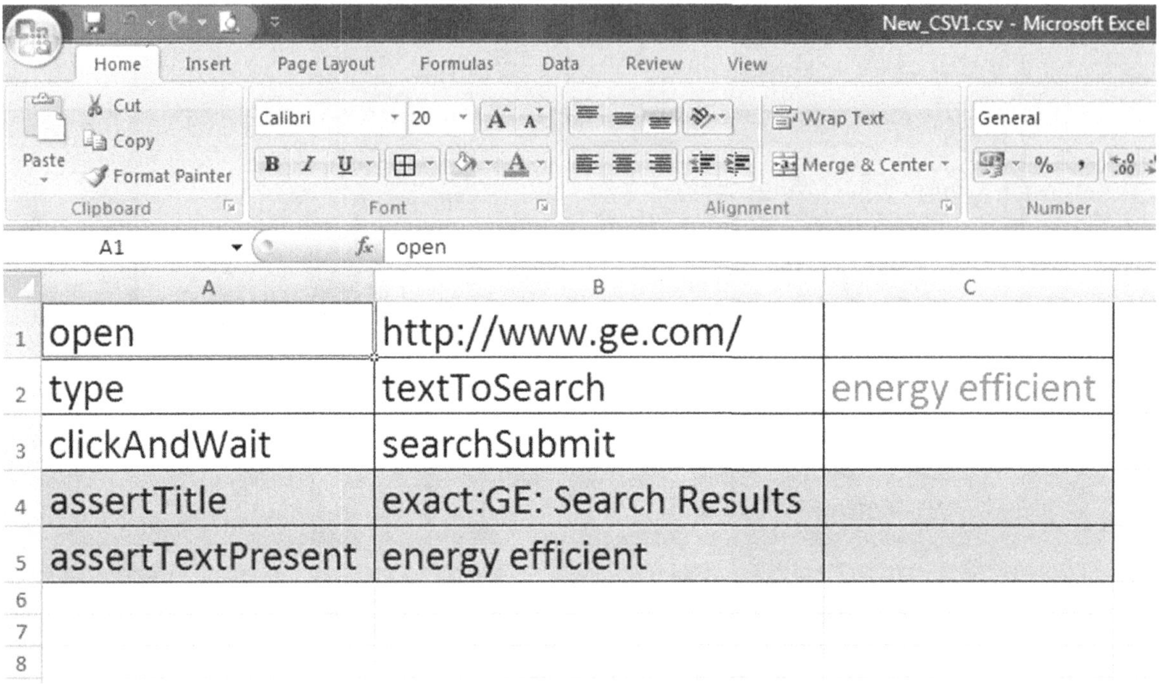

You can send your test cases to the Business Users easily through excel sheet.

If you are interested we can look at the JavaScript code which does this conversion.

Javascript Code for CSV Format

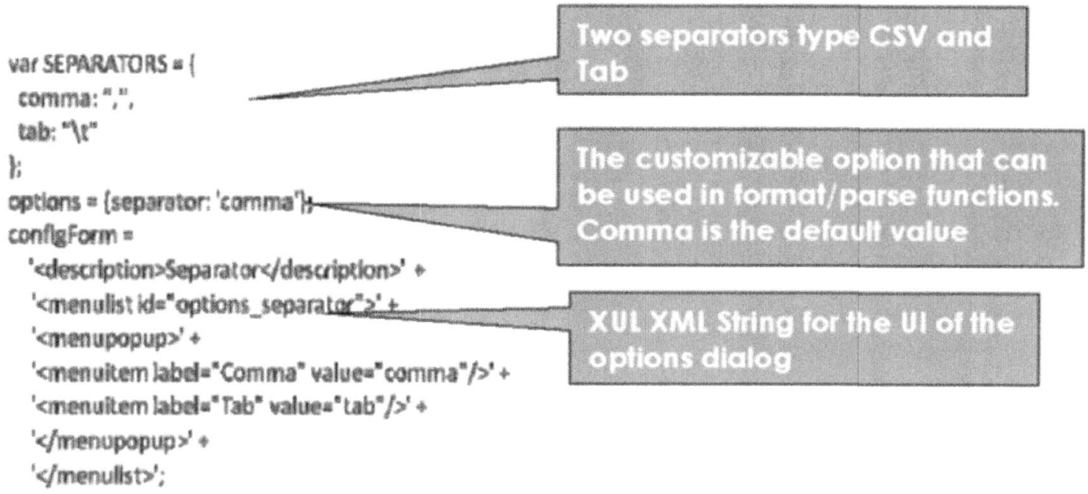

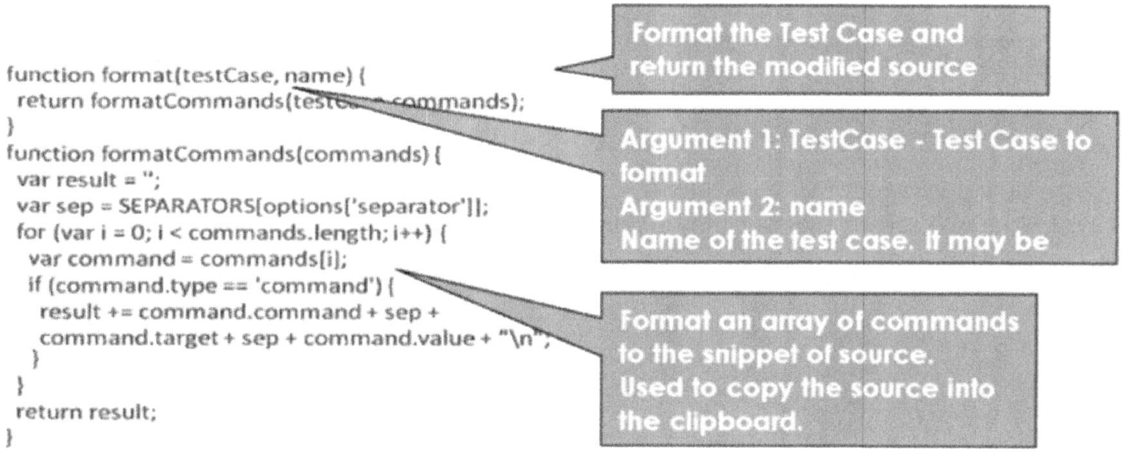

```
function parse(testCase, source) {
  var doc = source;  var commands = [];
  var sep = SEPARATORS[options['separator']];
  while (doc.length > 0) {
    var line = /(.*)(\r\n|[\r\n])?/.exec(doc);
    var array = line[1].split(sep);
    if (array.length >= 3) {
      var command = new Command();
      command.command = array[0];
      command.target = array[1];
      command.value = array[2];
      commands.push(command);
    }
    doc = doc.substr(line[0].length);  }
  testCase.setCommands(commands);}
```

Parse source file and update TestCase. Throw an exception if any error occurs

Argument 1: TestCase - Test Case to update
Argument 2: source - Source to parse

Source Line is parsed and in the IDE it is passed as Command, Target and Value

EXERCISES

1. How do you convert your HTML Selenese test cases to XML compliant format? (Hint: Your XML test cases should be read and processed by any XML parser)

9

Applying CSS to Selenium Test Cases

What is CSS

- What is CSS?
- CSS stands for Cascading Style Sheets
- Styles define how to display HTML elements
- Styles are normally stored in Style Sheets
- External Style Sheets can save you a lot of work
- External Style Sheets are stored in CSS files
- How to use it?
- I have created a simple CSS file which will change the look and feel of any Selenium HTML test cases.
- After downloading "Selenium.css" in your machine, you need to add the following HTML code in your existing test case.

```
<head>
<link rel="stylesheet" type="text/css" href="selenium.css" />
</head>
```

selenium.css

```
table {
   border: 4px solid black;
   background: Maroon;
   font-family: Verdana, Arial, sans-serif;
   font-size: 12px;
   font-weight: bold;
   text-align: center;
}
td {
   border: none;
   padding: 4px;
   margin: 0;}
```

```
thead {
   background: Darkgray;
   font-family: Verdana, Arial, sans-serif;
   font-size: 18px;
   font-weight: bold;
   text-align: center;
   color: #00ff00
}
tbody {
   background: Lightgrey;
   font-family: Verdana, Arial, sans-serif;
   font-size: 10px;
   font-weight: bold;
   text-align: left;
   color: Blue;
   }
```

Applying CSS to your Test Cases

1. Download Selenium.css from http://www.qaagility.com/downloads/SeleniumBook/
2. Download the Test Case - Demo - Add - Admin - Company Info - Company Structure.html from Exercises Section
3. Open the file in WordPad (Right Click on the file, Select Open With à WordPad)
4. Between the </title> and </head> tags insert the following HTML code
5. <link rel="stylesheet" type="text/css" href="selenium.css" />
6. File → Save As → CSS Applied - Test Case - Demo - Add - Admin - Company Info - Company Structure.html
7. File → Exit
8. Click and Open the "CSS Applied - Test Case - Demo - Add - Admin - Company Info - Company Structure.html" file in firefox browser.

See the CSS applied HTML Test Case below:

GE Test Case 1		
open	http://www.ge.com/	
type	textToSearch	energy efficient
clickAndWait	searchSubmit	
assertTitle	exact:GE: Search Results	
assertTextPresent	energy efficient	

EXERCISES

Create a CSS to apply for Selenium Suites

- TIP 1: You can use the same selenium.css as a base and start to create a new one
- TIP 2: When you open a test suite which should totally defer from the look and feel of test cases.
- TIP 3: You can easily distinguish test suites from test cases by applying unique CSS to each.
- TIP 4: Decide on the CSS formats before start writing the test cases and simply add them to the header of test scripts you record.

10

Selenium Concepts

Selenium Commands

A command is what tells Selenium what to do.

Selenium commands are broken down into 3 types:

- **Actions** – Command the browser to do something
- **Accessors** – Store/retrieve data from selenium variables
- **Asserts** – Verify that the browser is in a certain state

Actions

Actions are commands that generally manipulate the state of the application.

They do things like “click this link” and “select that option”.

If an Action fails, or has an error, the execution of the current test is stopped.

Many Actions can be called with the “AndWait” suffix, e.g. “clickAndWait”.

Action suffix tells Selenium that the action will cause the browser to make a call to the server, and that Selenium should wait for a new page to load.

Accessors

Accessors examine the state of the application and store the results in variables, e.g. “storeTitle”.

They are also used to automatically generate Assertions.

Asserts

Assertions are like Accessors, but they verify that the state of the application conforms to what is expected.

- Examples include "make sure the page title is X" and "verify that this checkbox is checked".

All Selenium Assertions can be used in 3 modes: "assert", "verify", and "waitFor".

- Example includes, "assertText","verifyText" and "waitForText".

When an "assert" fails, the test is aborted. When a "verify" fails, the test will continue execution, logging the failure.

This allows a single "assert" to ensure that the application is on the correct page, followed by a bunch of "verify" assertions to test form field values, labels, etc.

"waitFor" commands wait for some condition to become true (which can be useful for testing Ajax applications).

Selenium Parameters

Two types of Selenium Parameters

- **Locators** – Used to find elements in html trees
- **Pattern Matchers** – Used to verify values

Lots of locator types. Some examples are:

- Id based,
- X-Path based, DOM Based
- CSS selector based

Pattern matchers are typically exact matches or regular expressions

Selenium Element Locators

Element Locators tell Selenium which HTML element a command refers to.

Many commands require an Element Locator as the "target" attribute.

- Examples of Element Locator's include "elementId" and "document.forms[0].element".
- The format of a locator is: locatorType=argument.

To locate elements use identifier, id, name, DOM, CSS, XPath, and link. Without an explicit locator prefix, Selenium uses the following default strategies:

- DOM, for locators starting with "document."
- XPath, for locators starting with "//"
- identifier, otherwise

Selenium Element Filter

Element filters can be used with a locator to refine a list of candidate elements.

They are currently used only in the 'name' element-locator. Filters look much like locators, i.e.

- filterType=argument

Supported element-filters are:

- Based on their values match elements. It is useful for refining a list of similarly-named toggle-buttons.
  - value=patternValue
- Selects a single element based on its position in the list (starting from zero).
  - index=indexValue

Selenium String Match Patterns

Various Pattern syntaxes are available for matching string values:

- glob:patternValue: "Glob" is a limited regular expression syntax. Similar to DOS command-line wildcards. In a glob pattern, "*" represents any sequence of characters, and "?" represents any single character. Glob patterns match against the entire string.
- regexp:regexpValue: Match a string using a regular-expression. The full power of JavaScript regular-expression is available.
- exact:stringValue: Match a string value exactly, without using any wildcards.

If no pattern prefix is specified, Selenium assumes that it's a "glob" pattern.

Selenium Recording Problems

Why doesn't everything get recorded?

- Not every event will be recorded by Selenium IDE.
- Usually the ones that won't be recorded are those that involve complex HTML (Hyper Text Markup Language) and/or AJAX (Asynchronous JavaScript and XML)

Careful while testing HTTPS events

Why doesn't event triggered when I select something from auto-complete history?

- Auto-Complete does not trigger Javascript event
- No event triggered means Selenium IDE cannot record it
- Work Around: Manually type the input, instead of selecting it from auto-complete

EXERCISES

1. What are the three categories into which the Selenium commands are divided?
2. What is the difference between Accessors and Assertions?
3. Where can we use the "waitFor..." set of commands?
4. What is the need the pattern matching? What are the various syntax for pattern matching?

11

Selenium Commands — SELENESE

Selenese Commands

Selenese is the language of Selenium IDE and it is pure HTML. However you should not try to compare it to the traditional programming languages or look for the features that they have. Selenese doesn't include any conditional "if" statements or "for" loops, or, in general, there isn't any way to reuse code (with functions or subroutines). However there are some "flow control" user extensions available that provide support for "if/goto" statements in HTML Selenese. You can search for them on internet and try them out.

The lack of these features is not the drawbacks of Selenese as the HTML, but Selenese is about simplicity. Turning HTML Selenese into a full-blown scripting language, with all the advantages that would bring, would still undermine its simplicity. If one needs to write a full blown program then there are options to export the HTML Selenese to high level language of your choice and run it in Selenium RC.

Now let's look at the Selenese language.

In Selenese we have predefined set of commands.

Each command call is one line in the test table of the form:

Command	Target	Value
open	http://www.yahoo.com/	
type	p	energy efficient

A command is what tells Selenium what to do. Selenium commands come in three 'flavors': Actions, Accessors and Assertions.

- **Actions** – Command the browser to do something
- **Accessors** – Store/retrieve data from selenium variables
- **Asserts** – Verify that the browser is in a certain state

Actions are commands that generally manipulate the state of the application. They do things like "click this link" and "select that option". If an Action fails, or has an error, the execution of the current test is stopped.

Many Actions can be called with the "AndWait" suffix, e.g. "clickAndWait". This suffix tells Selenium that the action will cause the browser to make a call to the server, and that Selenium should wait for a new page to load.

Accessors examine the state of the application and store the results in variables, e.g. "storeTitle". They are also used to automatically generate Assertions.

Assertions are like Accessors, but they verify that the state of the application conforms to what is expected. Examples include "make sure the page title is X" and "verify that this checkbox is checked".

All Selenium Assertions can be used in 3 modes: "assert", "verify", and "waitFor". For example, you can "assertText", "verifyText" and "waitForText".

When an "assert" fails, the test is aborted. When a "verify" fails, the test will continue execution, logging the failure. This allows a single "assert" to ensure that the application is on the correct page, followed by a bunch of "verify" assertions to test form field values, labels, etc.

Example:

"waitFor" commands wait for some condition to become true (which can be useful for testing Ajax applications). They will succeed immediately if the condition is already true. However, they will fail and halt the test if the condition does not become true within the current timeout setting (see the setTimeout action below).

Example:

Element Locators tell Selenium which HTML element a command refers to. Many commands require an Element Locator as the "target" attribute. Examples of Element Locators include "elementId" and "document.forms[0].element". These are described more clearly in the further chapters.

Patterns are used for various reasons, e.g. to specify the expected value of an input field, or identify a select option. Selenium supports various types of pattern, including regular-expressions, all of which are described in more detail in the further chapters.

Variable Substitution

You can store any value into a variable using selenium accessors.

Variable substitution provides a simple way to include a previously stored variable in a command parameter.

If you give the variable name as intAmount. To use the variable anywhere else use ${intAmount}. This will substitute the actual value in the place of ${intAmount}.

Use echo ${intAmount} to display the values in the Log.

Any of the selenium accessors can be used to store a value.

Some of the key accessors are:

storeText, storeValue, storeCookie, storeAlert and storeEval

Let's try this out:

1. Download Helloworld.html from http://www.qaagility.com/downloads/SeleniumBook/. Open the file in Firefox
2. Create a test case by opening Firefox → Tools → Selenium IDE (by default it is in Recording mode)
3. Update the base URL of Selenium IDE with the URL in the Firefox address
4. Click on the link "Click here to enter your name", when prompter for your name, enter your name.

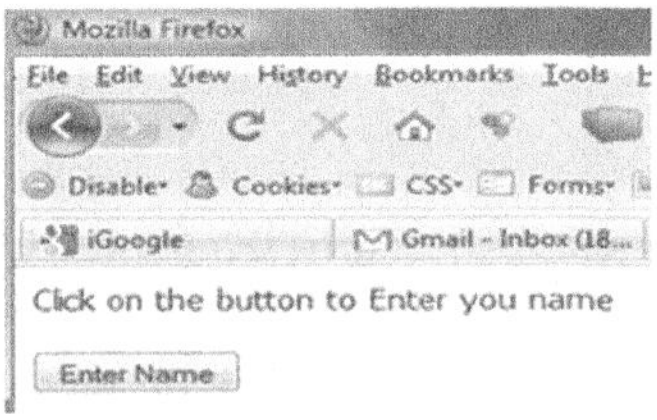

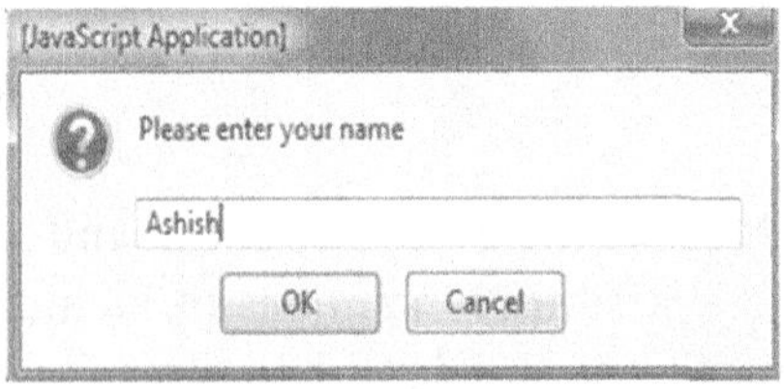

5. Your name will be displayed in next line.
6. Add the line for the assertText to check the name that you entered, and then stop the recording in Selenium IDE.
7. Rerun the test case in Selenium IDE

Your test case would look like as shown in the figure below:

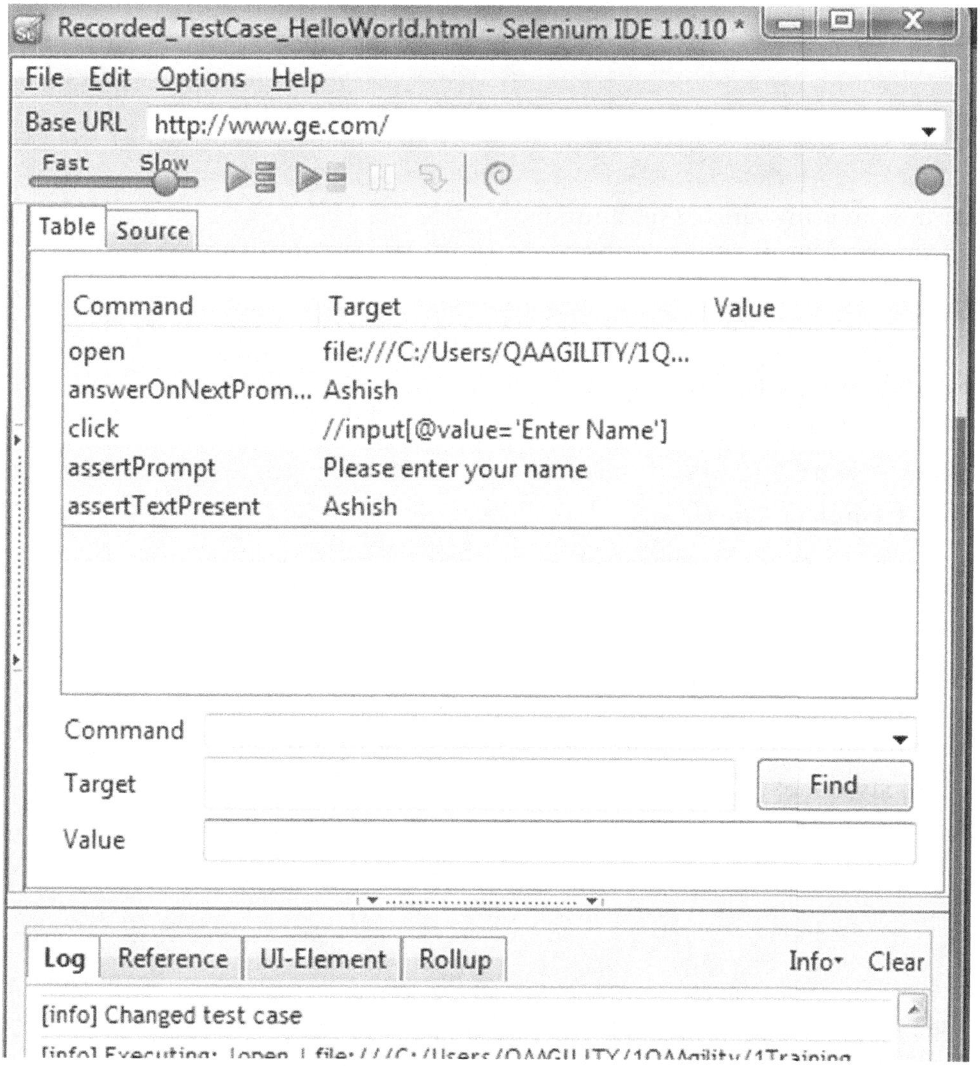

1. Try to run multiple time and make sure your test case is passed without any failures.
2. Now save the test case as "Recorded_TestCase_HelloWorld.html"
3. Double click and open the "Recorded_TestCase_HelloWorld.html" either in IE or Firefox.

4. You can see all the commands in an HTML table as below

TC_CheckPrompts_Init	
open	file:///C:/Selenium-Examples/Day3/Ex/HelloWorld.html
answerOnNextPrompt	Ashish
click	//input[@value='Enter Name']
assertPrompt	Please enter your name
assertTextPresent	Ashish

Let's try this out using variable substitution

1. Now we'll try to do the same exercise using variable substitution
2. In the Selenium IDE, select "answerOnNextPrompt", Right Click and Select a new command
3. Select the command "store"
4. Target "Ashish"
5. Value "vName"
6. Store | Ashish | vName

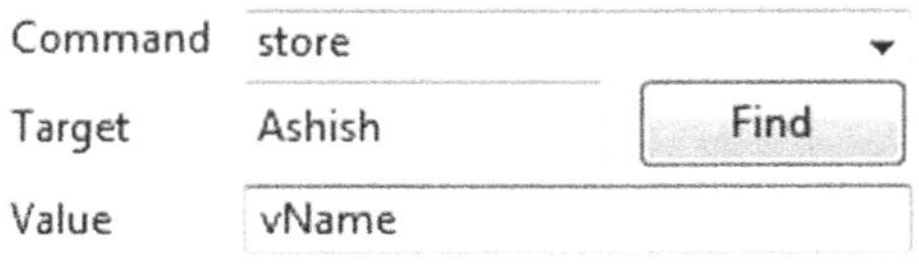

7. Underneath insert a new command and provide the below values
8. echo | ${vName}

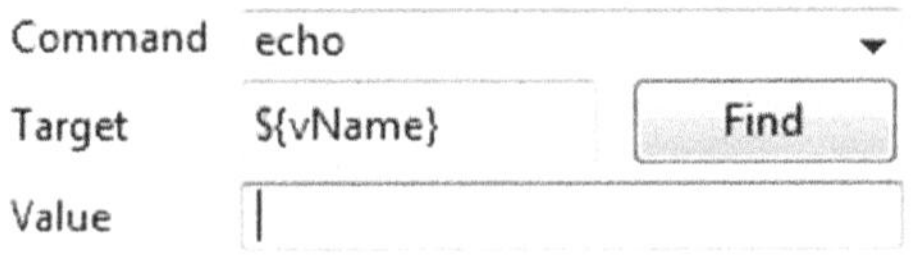

9. Right click and copy the "echo" command, and paste before the assertText command line
10. Now your test would look like below

See how the ${vName} is used in multiple places

Recorded_TestCase_HelloWorld_Modified		
open	file:///C:/Selenium-Examples/Day3/Ex/HelloWorld.html	
store	Ashish	vName
echo	${vName}	
answerOnNextPrompt	${vName}	
click	xpath=/html/body/input	
assertPrompt	Please enter your name	
echo	${vName}	
assertTextPresent	${vName}	

See how the ${vName} is used in multiple places

Now let's have a look at the commands and the log entries

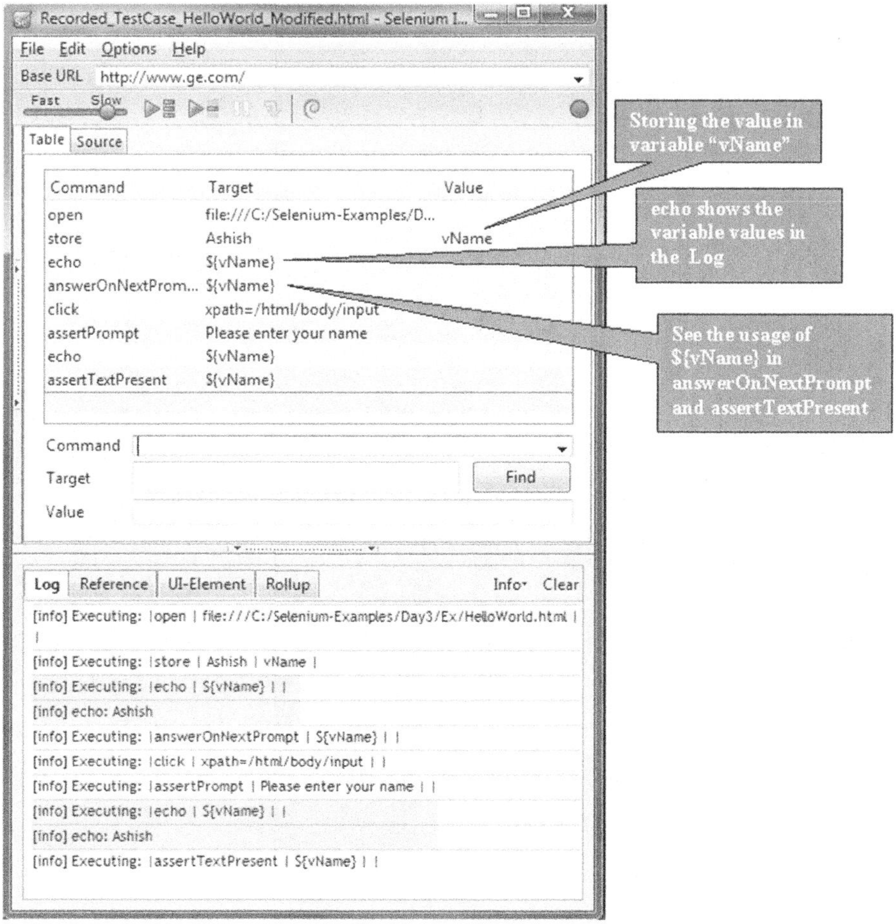

storedVars

All the variables are internally stored in a map named "storedVars". You can also imagine it as storing values as arrays for Selenese.

storedVars allows you to access the ${varName} using the "varName" key within the map.

Using storedVars you can reference the values within Javascript Evaluation code.

What is a Map?

Maps provide a more general way of storing elements. An object that maps keys to values. A map cannot contain duplicate keys (duplicate variable names); The Map collection type allows to store pairs of elements, termed "keys" and "values", where each key maps to one value. Here Keys refers Selenium variable Names and values refers to their values.

Let's try to see it using example.

1. Open URL: http://mail.yahoo.com
2. Type username: <username>
3. Type password: <passwd>
4. Press Sign In button
5. verifyTextPresent <username>
6. Press SignOut
7. waitForTextNotPresent <username>

Your recorded test case will look like this

TC_Yahoo_sVars		
open	http://mail.yahoo.com	
type	username	romila1974
type	passwd	•••••••
clickAndWait	.save	
assertTextPresent	romila1974	
click	link=Sign Out	
waitForTextNotPresent	romila1974	

Please use caution as the password will not be encrypted

Change your Test case to something like this

TC_Yahoo_sVars_Modified		
open	http://mail.yahoo.com	
store	romila1974	vUName
store	•••••••	vUPass
type	username	javascript{storedVars['vUName']}
type	passwd	javascript{storedVars['vUPass']}
clickAndWait	.save	
assertTextPresent	javascript{storedVars['vUName']}	
click	link=Sign Out	
waitForTextNotPresent	javascript{storedVars['vUName']}	

Notice how storedVars is used for userid and password

Why use variables in test scripts?

Javascript Evaluation

JavaScript evaluation allows full power of JavaScript code in constructing the Command Parameter

JavaScript snippet can be given using the following syntax.

- Javascript { <code snippet goes here> }
- Javascript keyword is optional
- The code given is treated as a JavaScript code and executed.
- storedVars Map can be used to access the previously stored variables
- Variable substitution should be handled carefully within the JavaScript code.

1. You can use any of the following **Eval** commands
   - assertEval, assertNotEval, VerifyEval, verifyNotEval, waitForEval, waitForNotEval, storeEval
2. You can use any of the following **Expression** commands
   - assertExpression, assertNotExpression,verifyExpression, verifyNotExpression, waitForExpression, waitForNotExpression, storeExpression, store and WaitForCondition

Exercises

1. Open a specific URL (http://www.barnesandnoble.com/)
2. Search for a specific text ("Javascript") in #1 page
3. Sort by "Price^{V}"
4. How do you check "Online Price: $$$" is in sorted order?

Answers

- In this case I have decided to check the first two Amounts displayed on that page are in the ascending order.
- The first value is A, the second value is B
- If A <= B then we assume the first two listed prices are in ascending order.
- Now get the third value C
- If B <= C then we assume that A, B and C are in ascending order. (i.e., A <= B <=C)

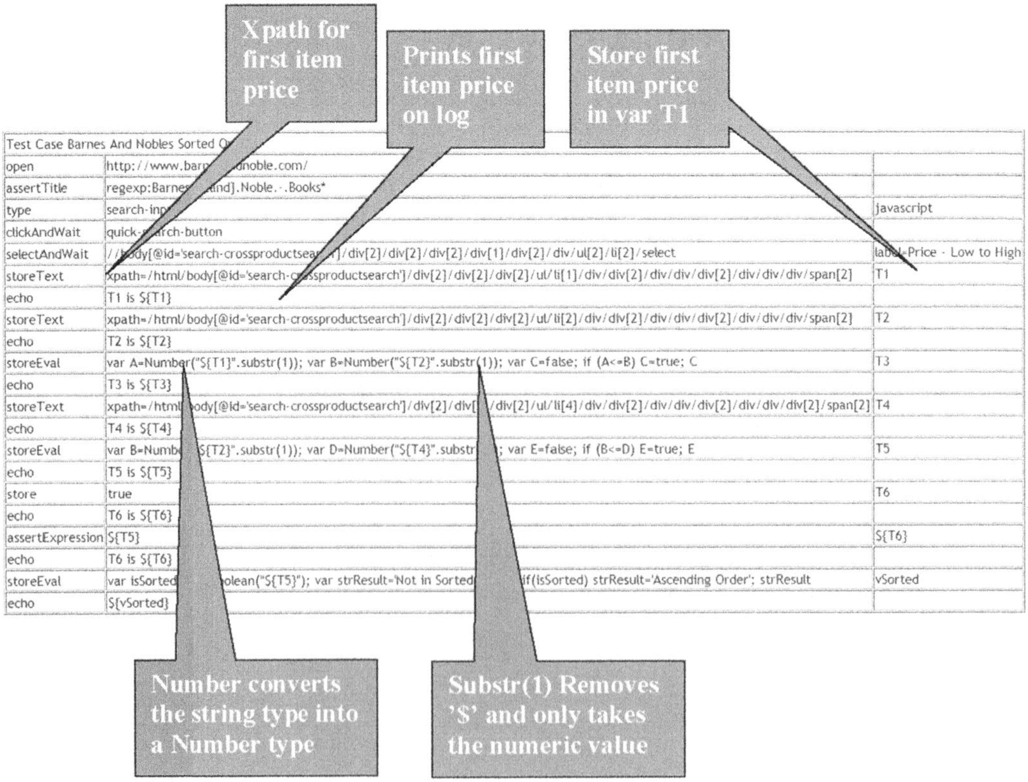

Test Case Barnes And Nobles Sorted O[illegible]		
open	http://www.bar[illegible]noble.com/	
assertTitle	regexp:Barne[illegible]and].Noble.·.Books*	
type	search-inp[illegible]	javascript
clickAndWait	quick-[illegible]rch-button	
selectAndWait	//[illegible]dy[@id='search-crossproductsea[illegible]]/div[2]/div[2]/div[2]/div[1]/div[2]/div/ul[2]/li[2]/select	lab[illegible]=Price - Low to High
storeText	xpath=/html/body[@id='search-c[illegible]ssproductsearch']/div[2]/div[2]/div[2]/ul/li[1]/div/div[2]/div/div/div[2]/div/div/div/span[2]	T1
echo	T1 is ${T1}	
storeText	xpath=/html/body[@id='search-crossproductsearch']/div[2]/div[2]/div[2]/ul/li[2]/div/div[2]/div/div/div[2]/div/div/div/span[2]	T2
echo	T2 is ${T2}	
storeEval	var A=Number("${T1}".substr(1)); var B=Number("${T2}".substr(1)); var C=false; if (A<=B) C=true; C	T3
echo	T3 is ${T3}	
storeText	xpath=/html[illegible]ody[@id='search-crossproductsearch']/div[2]/div[illegible]/div[2]/ul/li[4]/div/div[2]/div/div/div[2]/div/div/div[2]/span[2]	T4
echo	T4 is ${T4}	
storeEval	var B=Numb[illegible]${T2}".substr(1)); var D=Number("${T4}".substr[illegible]; var E=false; if (B<=D) E=true; E	T5
echo	T5 is ${T5}	
store	true	T6
echo	T6 is ${T6}	
assertExpression	${T5}	${T6}
echo	T6 is ${T6}	
storeEval	var isSorted[illegible]olean("${T5}"); var strResult='Not in Sorted[illegible]if(isSorted) strResult='Ascending Order'; strResult	vSorted
echo	${vSorted}	

Handling Alerts

- storeAlert(seleniumVariableName)
  - Checks for JavaScript Alert, stores the alert message. If no alert generated then throws an exception.
  - Getting an alert has the same effect as manually clicking OK.
  - If an alert is generated but you do not get/verify it, then the next Selenium action will fail.
  - JavaScript alerts will NOT pop up a visible alert dialog.
  - Selenium does NOT support JavaScript alerts that are generated in a page's onload() event handler. In this case a visible dialog WILL be generated and Selenium will hang until someone manually clicks OK.
- Returns:
  - The message of the most recent JavaScript alert.
- Other Alert commands are:
  - assertAlert (pattern), assertNotAlert (pattern), verifyAlert (pattern)
  - verifyNotAlert (pattern), waitForAlert (pattern),waitForNotAlert (pattern)

AlertPresent

- verifyAlertPresent()
  - The best way to check the alerts are using this command
  - This command never throws an exception
- Returns:
  - True or False.
- Other AlertPresent Commands are:
  - storeAlertPresent(seleniumVariableName)
  - assertAlertPresent()
  - assertAlertNotPresent()
  - verifyAlertNotPresent()
  - waitForAlertPresent()
  - waitForAlertNotPresent()

On load Alert will not be sensed by Selenium. You need to manually press "Ok" to continue the test.

Example:

Browser Navigation

- goBack and goBackAndWait are the two commands simulates a user clicking on the "back" button of the browser.
- Download the SelectAWebSite.html from http://www.qaagility.com/downloads/SeleniumBook/
- Record the test as listed below:
  - Select Google, after going to Google assertTitle then go back
  - Select QAAgility, after going to QAAgility assertTitle then go back
  - Select Microsoft, after going to MicroSoft assertTitle then go back
  - Select Yahoo, after going to MicroSoft assertTitle then go back
- Run the test
  - Why it fails?
  - How do you fix it?

Recorded Test Case SelectAWebSite	
open	file:///C:/Users/QAAGILITY/1QAAgility/1Training/Selenium/Content/Day3/Ex/SelectAWebSite.html
clickAndWait	link=link
assertTitle	Google
clickAndWait	//a[@href='http://www.qaagility.com']
assertTitle	QAAgility Technologies
clickAndWait	//a[@href='http://www.microsoft.com']
assertTitle	Microsoft Corporation
clickAndWait	//a[@href='http://www.yahoo.com']
assertTitle	Yahoo! India

Reviewed Test Case SelectAWebSite	
open	file:///C:/Users/QAAGILITY/1QAAgility/1Training/Selenium/Content/Day3/Ex/SelectAWebSite.html
clickAndWait	link=link
assertTitle	Google
goBackAndWait	
clickAndWait	//a[@href='http://www.qaagility.com']
assertTitle	QAAgility Technologies
goBackAndWait	
clickAndWait	//a[@href='http://www.microsoft.com']
assertTitle	Microsoft Corporation
goBackAndWait	
clickAndWait	//a[@href='http://www.yahoo.com']
assertTitle	Yahoo! India
goBack	

Try with added command goBackAndWait

Handling Pop-Ups

- waitForPopUp (windowID,timeout) and selectWindow (windowID) are the two commands allows you to test the Popup Windows.
- selectWindow selects a specific Popup, use null to select Parent window.
- Download the Ex1.html, Ex2.html, Ex3.html , CreatePopUps.html from http://www.qaagility.com/downloads/SeleniumBook/ and Open CreatePopUps.html in Firefox browser
- Record the test as listed below:
  - Click Create Windows button
  - Select win1, click the button "Click and get the Welcome Message", minimize win1
  - Select win3, select any option, press "Submit" button
  - Go back to the parent window, press "close button"
- Run the test
  - Is it failing?
  - How do you fix it?

Reviewed Test Case Popup		
open	file:///C:/Users/QAAGILITY/1QAAgility/1Training/Selenium/Content/Day3/Ex/CreatePopUps.html	
click	winBut	
waitForPopUp	win1	30000
waitForPopUp	win2	30000
waitForPopUp	win3	30000
selectWindow	name=win1	
click	acpro_inp0	
assertAlert	Welcome you all Test Automators!	
selectWindow	name=win3	
click	acpro_inp0	
assertAlert	Your time is good!	
selectWindow	null	
click	winBut2	

Navigator Properties

➢ To get Browser information, you can use navigator object
- The common properties of navigator object is like
  - ➤ appName
  - ➤ appCodeName
  - ➤ appEnabled
  - ➤ JavaEnabled
  - ➤ language
  - ➤ cookieEnabled
  - ➤ navigator.userAgent
  - ➤ navigator.plugins
  - ➤ navigator.platform
  - ➤ navigator.mimeTypes
- The common properties of browserVersion object is like
  - ➤ browserVersion.name
  - ➤ browserVersion.browser

    - browserVersion.isFirefox

- Download "TestCaseNavigatorProperties.html" from http://www.qaagility.com/downloads/SeleniumBook/
- Run the Test Case
- Look at the Selenium IDE Log
- You can See all the Navigator Properties

<table>
<tr><td colspan="3">Test Case Navigator Properties</td></tr>
<tr><td>echo</td><td>javascript{navigator.appName}</td><td></td></tr>
<tr><td>echo</td><td>javascript{navigator.appCodeName}</td><td></td></tr>
<tr><td>echo</td><td>javascript{navigator.appVersion}</td><td></td></tr>
<tr><td>echo</td><td>javascript{navigator.javaEnabled()}</td><td></td></tr>
<tr><td>echo</td><td>javascript{navigator.language}</td><td></td></tr>
<tr><td>echo</td><td>javascript{navigator.cookieEnabled}</td><td></td></tr>
<tr><td>echo</td><td>javascript{navigator.userAgent}</td><td></td></tr>
<tr><td>echo</td><td>javascript{navigator.platform.length}</td><td></td></tr>
<tr><td>echo</td><td>javascript{navigator.mimeTypes.length}</td><td></td></tr>
<tr><td>echo</td><td>javascript{browserVersion.name}</td><td></td></tr>
<tr><td>echo</td><td>javascript{browserVersion.browser}</td><td></td></tr>
<tr><td>echo</td><td>javascript{browserVersion.isFirefox}</td><td></td></tr>
<tr><td>storeEval</td><td>var jLen=navigator.plugins.length; jStr=jLen+"Plugin(s)"+"<br>"+"Name | Filename | description"+"<br>"; for(var i=0; i<jLen; i++) {jStr+=navigator.plugins[i].name+" | "+navigator.plugins[i].filename+" | "+navigator.plugins[i].description+"<br>";}</td><td>selPlugIn</td></tr>
<tr><td>echo</td><td>${selPlugIn}</td><td></td></tr>
</table>

Create a string to display the object properties

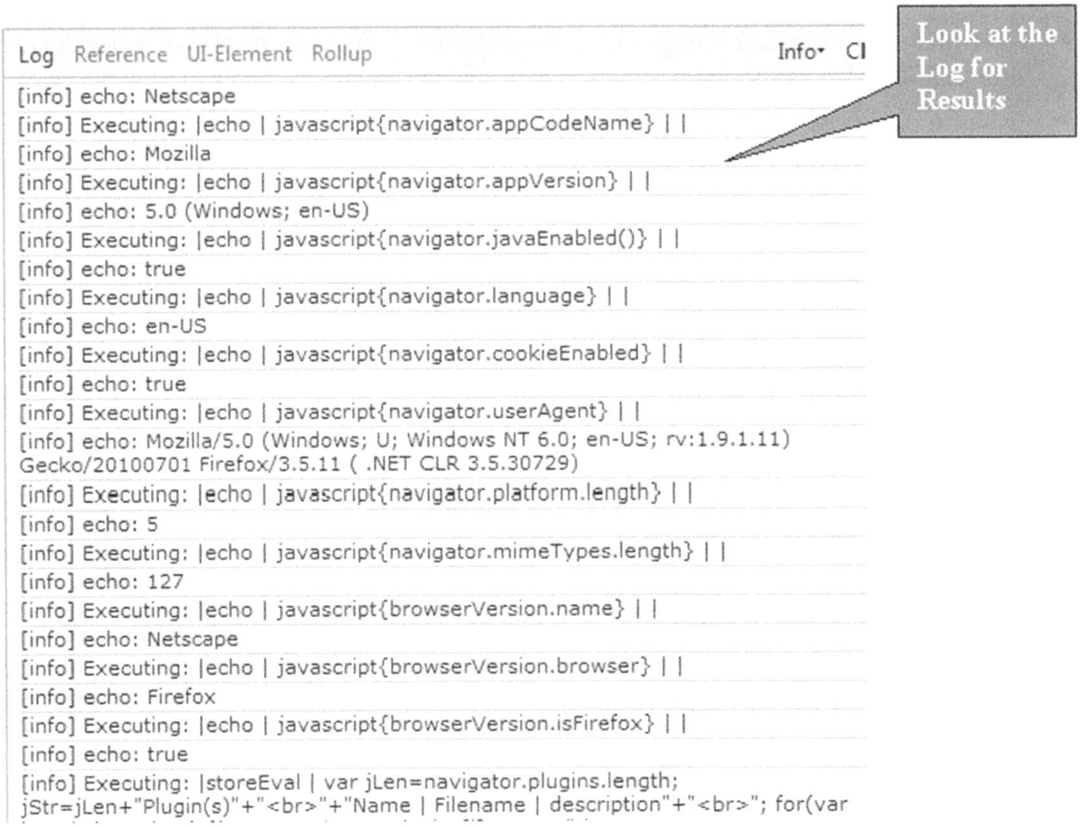

EXERCISES

- **Create a test case with the following steps:**
  1. Open http://www.devry-degrees.com
  2. At the bottom of the page, you will see 4 footer links
  3. Click a link at a time, this will create a popup
  4. verifyTitle on the Popped Up window
  5. Close the Popup
  6. Click on the next link in the parent window, this will create a popup
  7. verifyTitle on the Popped Up window
  8. Close the Popup, Continue the same for all the 4 links

12

PATTERN MATCHING

Patterns frequently occur in the Selenium tests. There are several commands in Selenium that take the pattern parameter. These enable you to match various content types on a web page – links, text, elements. There are mainly three types of patterns you can use in your tests: globs, exact and regular expressions.

Globs

Globs or the verb Globbing is familiar to most people who have ever used file matching patterns. If you have ever searched for a file in Linux or DOS using a line like *.exe or photos*, then you have used globs. But globbing in Selenium is not as rich as the one in Linux – it supports only three special characters: *, ? and [ ].

* matches any number of characters, by any we mean 'nothing', 'a single character' or 'many characters'.

? , matches a single character.

[ ] , called a character class, lets you match any single character found within the brackets. e.g

[0-9] matches any digit

[a-zA-Z] matches any alphabet, regardless of case

To specify a glob in a selenium command, prefix the pattern with the glob: string. For example if you would like to search for the texts color or colour then you can use the colo*r glob as shown below.

Command	*Target*	*Value*
clickAndWait	link=search	
verifyValue	glob: colo*r	

However you are free to eliminate the glob: prefix and only specify the text pattern because globbing patterns are the default in Selenium.

Example:

If you have dropdown combo box then you can use global pattern matching

```
<select id="combo">
<option id="v1" value="option1">First Dropdown Value</option>
<option selected="selected" id="v2" value="option2">Second Dropdown Value</option>
<option id="v3" value="option3">Third Dropdown Value</option>
</select>
```

To select the dropdown option and verify like this:

assertEquals("Second *", selenium.getSelectedLabel("combo"));

Regular Expression Patterns

Of the three types of patterns, Regular Expressions are the one that are the most useful. Selenium supports the complete set of RegEx patterns that Javascript supports. So now you are not limited by the *,? And [] globbing patterns. To use RegEx patterns you need to prefix each RegEx with either regexp: or regexpi:, the latter being case-insensitive.

For example the following will test if a input field with the id 'name' contains the string 'javascript', 'JavaScript' or 'Javascript'.

Command	*Target*	*Value*
clickAndWait	link=search	
verifyValue	id=name	regexp:[Jj]ava([Ss]cript)

Below are a few common regular expression patterns:

- Date

  regexp:(0[1-9]|1[012])[- /.](0[1-9]|[12][0-9]|3[01])[- /.](19|20)\d\d

  This will match a date in 'mm/dd/yyyy' format with any of the '-', '/', '.' as separators.

- Email

  regexpi:^[A-Z0-9+_.-]+@[A-Z0-9.-]+$

  This will match a generic email address.

- Zip Code

  regexp:^[0-9]{5}(?:-[0-9]{4})?$

  This will match a ZIP code (U.S. postal code), allowing both the five-digit and nine-digit (ZIP + 4) formats.

- Social Security Number

  regexp:^(?!000|666)(?:[0-6][0-9]{2}|7(?:[0-6][0-9]|7[0-2]))-?(?!00)[0-9]{2}-(?!0000)[0-9]{4}$

  This will match U.S Social Security numbers in the in the AAA-GG-SSSS format.
- URL

  regexp:^(https?|ftp|file)://.+$

  This will match almost any url.

Example:

```
<select id="combo">
<option id="v1" value="option1">First Dropdown Value</option>
<option selected="selected" id="v2" value="option2">Second Dropdown Value</option>
<option id="v3" value="option3">Third Dropdown Value</option>
</select>
```

To select the dropdown option and verify like this:

assertEquals("regexp:Second .*", selenium.getSelectedLabel("combo"));

Exact Patterns

Patterns with the prefix 'exact:' will match the given text as it is. For example if you give the search pattern as below, then it will match a glob pattern '*' or '*.java'.

Command	*Target*	*Value*
clickAndWait	link=search	
verifyValue	glob: *.java	

But if you want an exact match with the value string, i.e. without the glob operator doing its work then you use the 'exact' pattern as below. In this example the '*' (asterisk) will work as a normal character rather than a pattern-matching wildcard character.

Command	*Target*	*Value*
clickAndWait	link=search	
verifyValue	exact: *.java	

Example:

```
<select id="combo">
<option id="v1" value="option1">First Dropdown Value</option>
```

```
<option selected="selected" id="v2" value="option2">Second Dropdown Value</option>
<option id="v3" value="option3">Third Dropdown Value</option>
</select>
```

To select the dropdown option and verify like this:

assertEquals("exact:Second Dropdown Value", selenium.getSelectedLabel("combo"));

In conclusion the glob: and the exact: patterns are the subsets of the Regular Expression pattern matcher. Everything you can do with glob: or exact: you can accomplish with RegExp.

Selenium Commands

A command is what tells Selenium what to do.

Selenium commands are broken down into 3 types:

- **Actions** – Command the browser to do something
- **Accessors** – Store/retrieve data from selenium variables
- **Asserts** – Verify that the browser is in a certain state

Actions

Actions are commands that generally manipulate the state of the application.

They do things like "click this link" and "select that option".

If an Action fails, or has an error, the execution of the current test is stopped.

Many Actions can be called with the "AndWait" suffix, e.g. "clickAndWait".

Action suffix tells Selenium that the action will cause the browser to make a call to the server, and that Selenium should wait for a new page to load.

Accessors

Accessors examine the state of the application and store the results in variables, e.g. "storeTitle".

They are also used to automatically generate Assertions.

Asserts

Assertions are like Accessors, but they verify that the state of the application conforms to what is expected.

- Examples include "make sure the page title is X" and "verify that this checkbox is checked".

All Selenium Assertions can be used in 3 modes: "assert", "verify", and "waitFor".

- Example include, "assertText","verifyText" and "waitForText".

When an "assert" fails, the test is aborted. When a "verify" fails, the test will continue execution, logging the failure.

This allows a single "assert" to ensure that the application is on the correct page, followed by a bunch of "verify" assertions to test form field values, labels, etc.

"waitFor" commands wait for some condition to become true (which can be useful for testing Ajax applications).

Selenium Parameters

Two types of Selenium Parameters

- **Locators** – Used to find elements in html trees
- **Pattern Matchers** – Used to verify values

Lots of locator types. Some examples are:

- Id based,
- X-Path based, DOM Based
- CSS selector based

Pattern matchers are typically exact matches or regular expressions

Selenium Element Locators

Element Locators tell Selenium which HTML element a command refers to.

Many commands require an Element Locator as the "target" attribute.

- Examples of Element Locator's include "elementId" and "document.forms[0].element".
- The format of a locator is: locatorType=argument.

To locate elements use identifier, id, name, DOM, CSS, XPath, and link. Without an explicit locator prefix, Selenium uses the following default strategies:

- DOM, for locators starting with "document."
- XPath, for locators starting with "//"
- identifier, otherwise

Selenium Element Filter

Element filters can be used with a locator to refine a list of candidate elements.

They are currently used only in the 'name' element-locator. Filters look much like locators, i.e.

- filterType=argument

Supported element-filters are:

- Based on their values match elements. It is useful for refining a list of similarly-named toggle-buttons.
  - value=patternValue
- Selects a single element based on its position in the list (starting from zero).
  - index=indexValue

Selenium String Match Patterns

Various Pattern syntaxes are available for matching string values:

- glob:patternValue: "Glob" is a limited regular expression syntax. Similar to DOS command-line wildcards. In a glob pattern, "*" represents any sequence of characters, and "?" represents any single character. Glob patterns match against the entire string.
- regexp:regexpValue: Match a string using a regular-expression. The full power of JavaScript regular-expression is available.
- exact:stringValue: Match a string value exactly, without using any wildcards.

If no pattern prefix is specified, Selenium assumes that it's a "glob" pattern.

EXERCISES

1. I have a dropdown with values: Large Size, Medium Size, Small Size. How can I use regular expression to pick the second value from the list?
2. What is the difference between "Glob" and "Exact" keywords of pattern matching?
3. For questions one, if I wish to make my pattern matching independent of the case, how will the regular expression look like?
4. What will be regular expression for match any vowel?
5. Make regular expression for match any whitespace (space, tab, newline, carriage return, form feed)?

13

Element Locators

A big part of implementing your browser based automation solution effectively is choosing locators wisely. There are various locators that Selenium's commands support to locate elements on the page to interact with. Using the right locator ensures your tests are faster, more reliable or has lower maintenance over releases. This chapter explains how and when to use these locators.

Simply put, locators are a way to tell selenium which specific element we want it to act on. All the visible elements of a web application are reflected in the Document Object Model (DOM) in HTML, and they can be addressed in various ways: the directions from the root of the document to the element using XPath; unique identifiers; or characteristics possessed by the elements, such as class names, attributes, or link text. Some examples of these addressing options are shown in the Navigation Options illustration below. The navigation using XPath could be much slower than using IDs; and IDs should be unique. Let's look at this in details in the sections below.

Selenium Element Locators

Element Locators tell Selenium which HTML element a command refers to. What do we mean by this? Suppose we want to click on a link on the webpage then we need to supply the details regarding that link to the 'click' command in the target field. Please see the command reference for 'click':

Click (locator)

Arguments:

- locator - an element locator

  Clicks on a link, button, checkbox or radio button. If the click action causes a new page to load (like a link usually does), call waitForPageToLoad.

For e.g. in the page below, if we need to click on the 'Gmail' link then we need to give the details regarding that link to the 'click' command.

In this case we will use the name of the link to locate the object. So we will put 'link=Gmail' in the target field of the command, please see below:

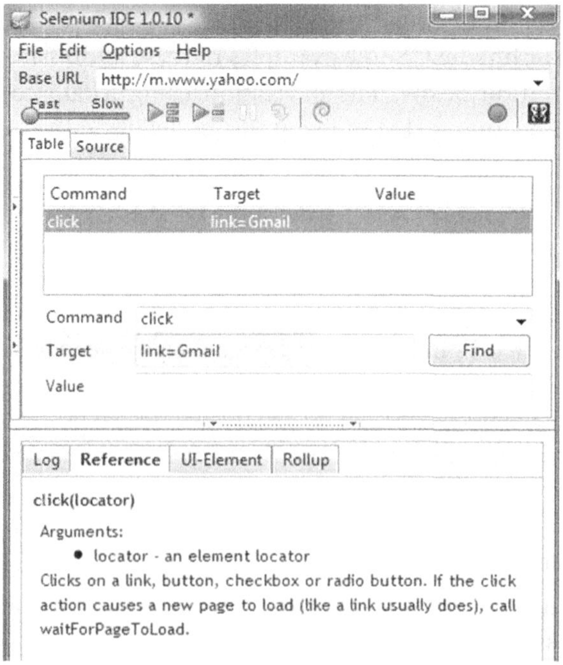

Now if you click on the 'Find' button next the target field, you will notice that it will highlight the link in green box, as below:

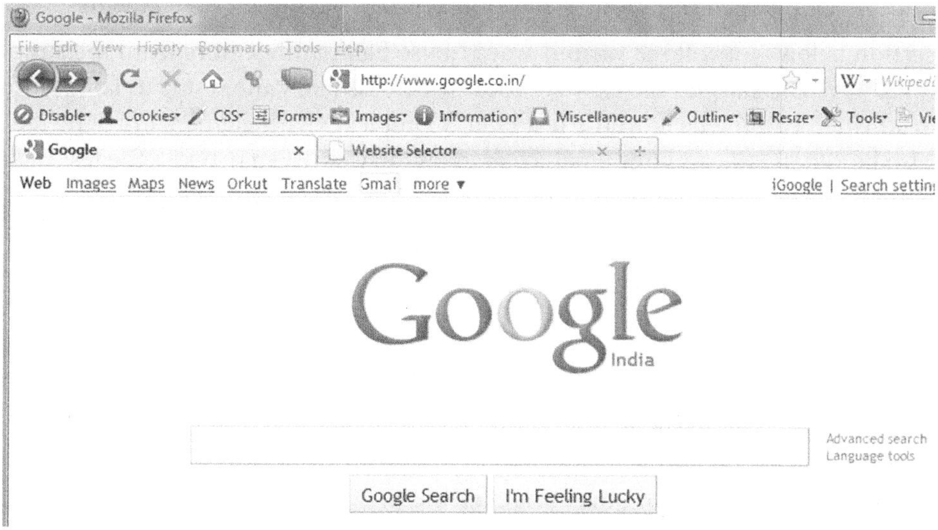

This will tell us that our locator is working fine. Now if you execute the command, it will click on the link and the Gmail page will be launched.

We could use this approach to locate the object using name, however what can we do when the link name is not unique. Please download the following example (SelectAWebSite.html) from http://www.qaagility.com/downloads/SeleniumBook/ and open it in FireFox browser.

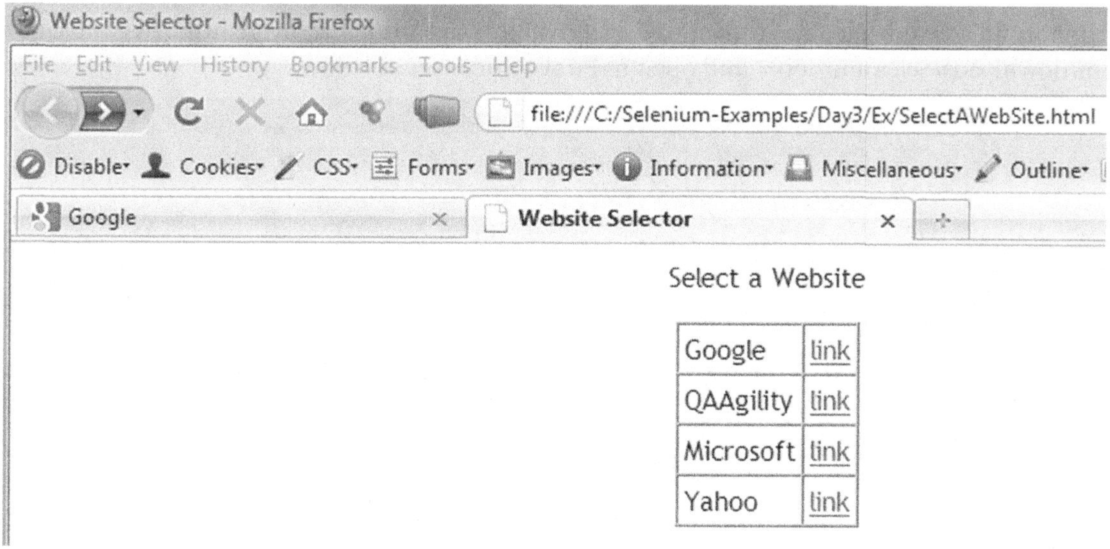

Here our approach will not work as all the links have same name 'link' so if we call command *click | link=link* then it will always launch the first link.

So how do we handle such situation? Let's look at other ways to locate elements.

In the section below you will see various ways to use Element Locators from the simplest to the most complex way. The simpler the element locator the less likely the test is to fail in future, and it is easy to read when coming back to the test later. Complex XPath elements may be required, but they may also be very fragile and one small change on the website may break the test in future.

Note: This does not cover speed of locating the elements, there are many other blog posts about that – XPath may be slower, but sometimes it is the only way.

1. Direct Reference

We can use the direct references to the HTML element via the Name or, the ID. We saw the example of this in the section above where we located the object using the link name. This is the most straightforward way of finding the correct element.

ID=win_button (NOTE IN THIS CASE, "ID =" IS NOT EVEN REQUIRED)

NAME=name_desc

VALUE=Click

LINK=link_gmail

Let's use the tool Firebug (Firebug) to view the internals of the web page and create strategy to locate web elements. Please refer to Chapter 4 for more details in installation of Firebug.

If not already downloaded, download HelloWorldDay3.html file from http://www.qaagility.com/downloads/SeleniumBook/ and open in FireFox browser as below.

Click on the Firebug icon in the status bar, this will open the Firebug window as the horizontal pan.

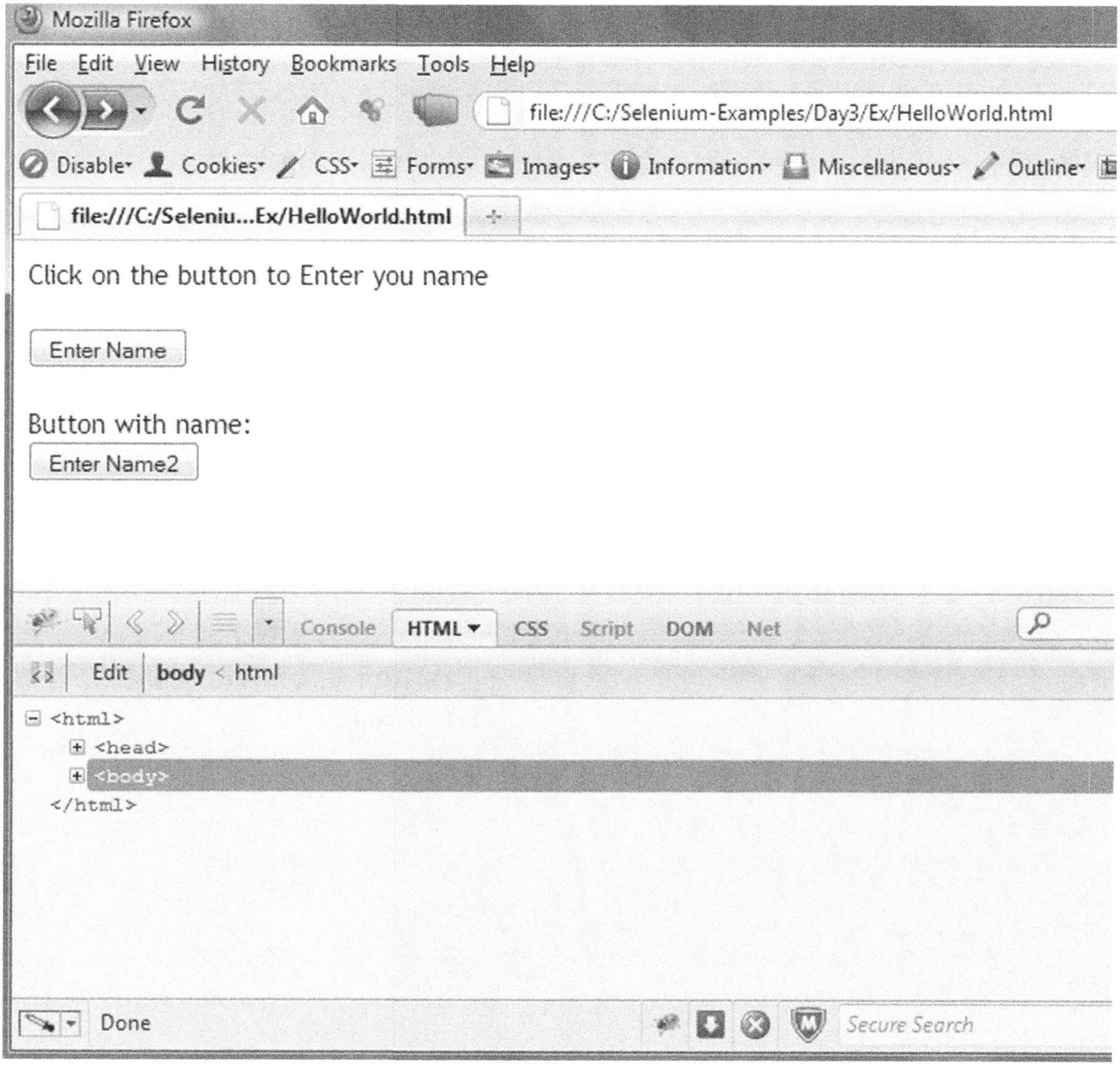

You can expand the collapsed HTML code in the main window of firebug to review the web page code. It should be simple enough to review this web page as it is simple, however when you have a complex web application page then it would be difficult to find the object that you wish to locate using Selenium. We use the Element Inspector feature of Firebug.

Click on the icon, it is used to inspect any element on the webpage and take the mouse over to the object that you want to inspect. This will expand the HTML page source and will highlight the code responsible for the object. Please see below:

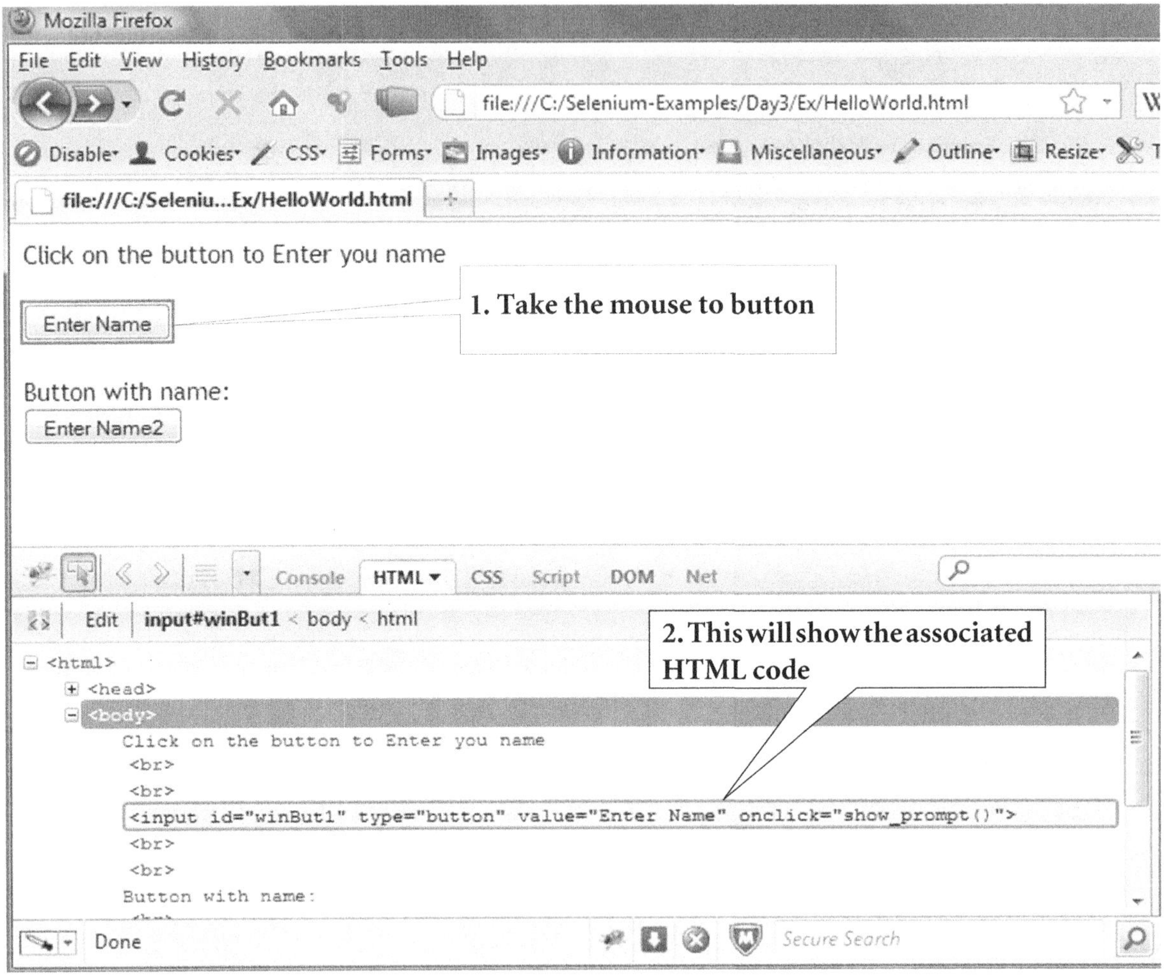

This gives you the information regarding the web element and you can use this information to locate these objects as required in your Selenium tests.

Using ID to locate object using IDE

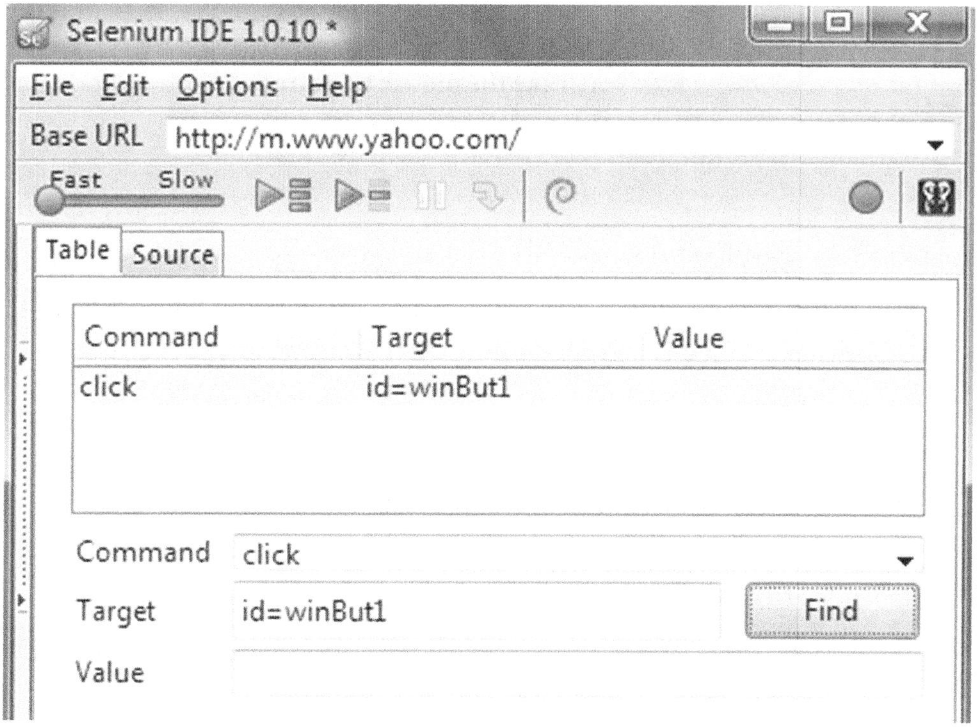

Click on the 'Find' button to ensure that the correct object gets highlighted in green border. If the 'Find' button works then any command that uses this object locator would also work. As in this case, running the command 'click' would find the button 'Enter Name' and click on it.

Using Name to locate object using IDE

Inspect the second button to find the code associated with it to get the object name, as below:

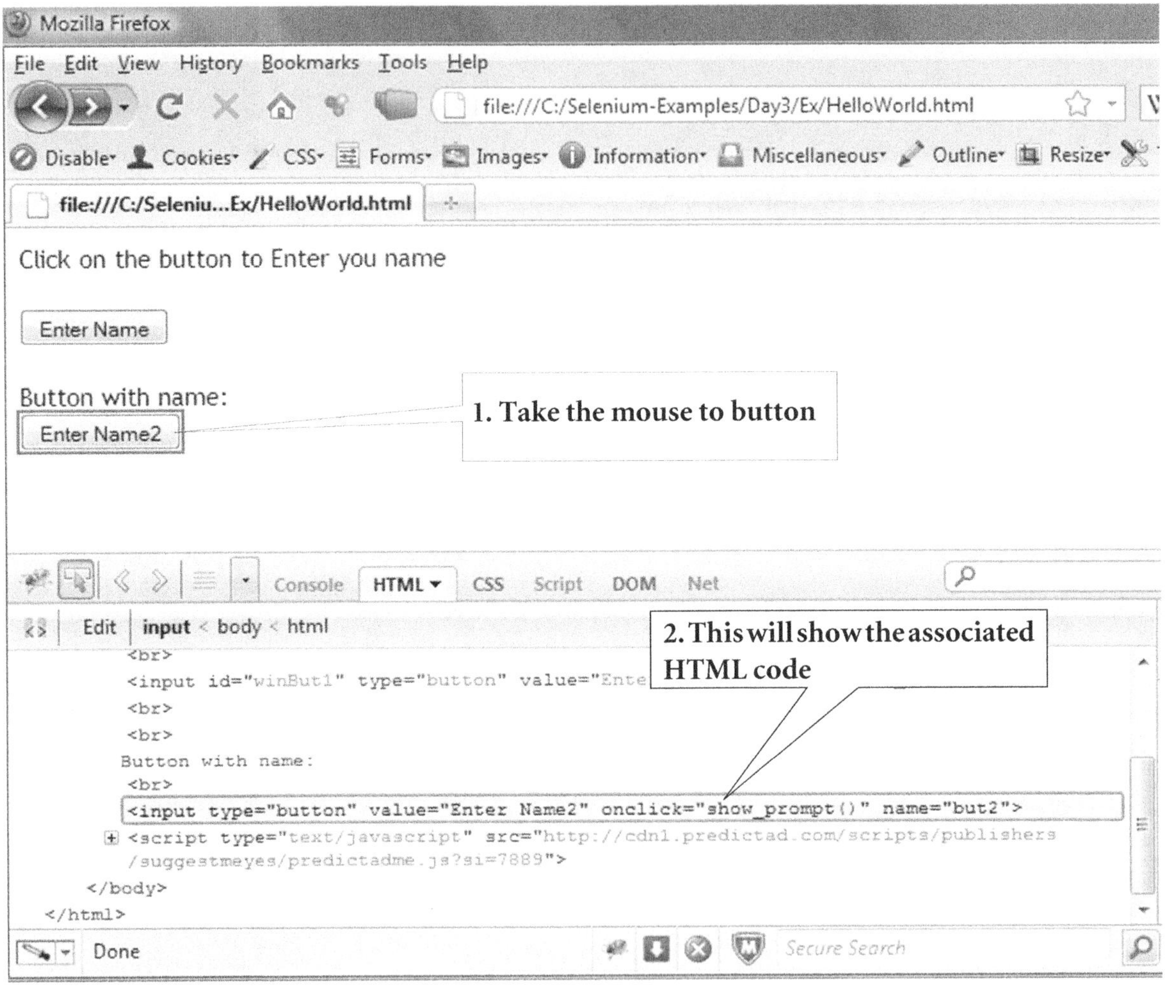

We can see that the name of the object (button) is 'but2'.

Use the following locator using object name to find the button using IDE as below. As a good practice always use the 'Find' button on IDE next to the target field to ensure you got the locator correct.

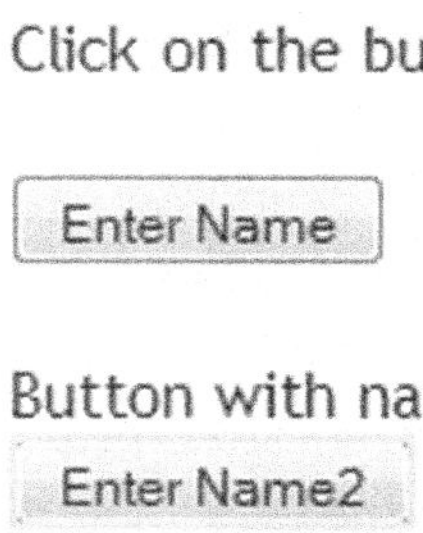

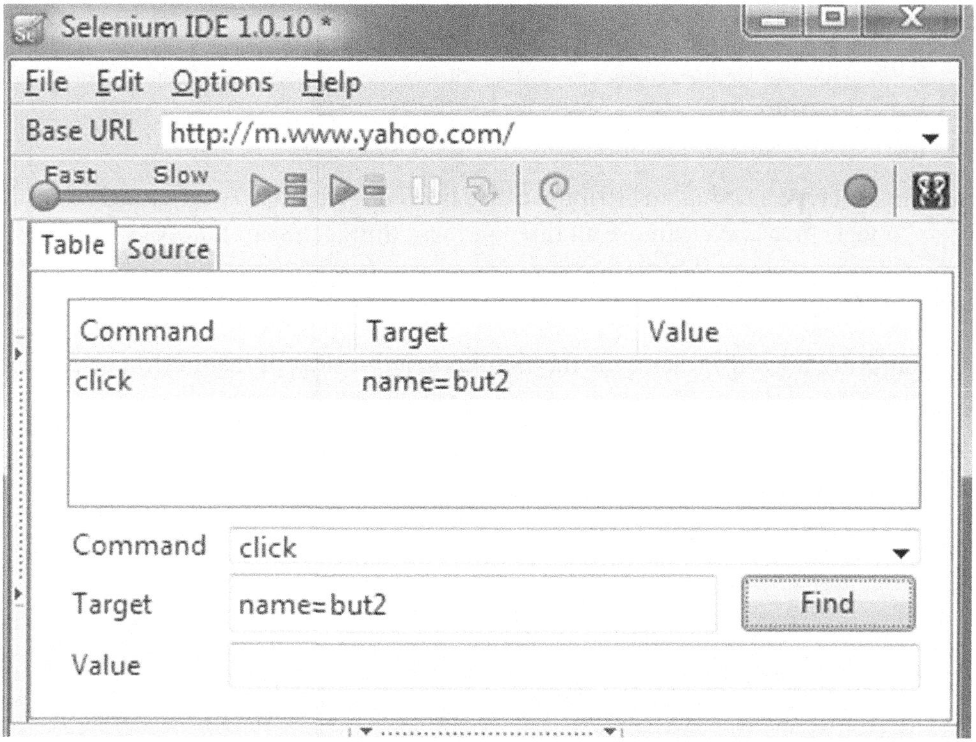

2. XPath References

XPath is a short way of referencing an element on a web page. It stand for XML path, when the HTML page is rendered on a browser, the various web elements are stored under the tags. We can have an address to those elements using these tags.

In selenium it is used for identifying a html element that does not have an easy, unique identifier such as id, name, text.

You can also optimize the full length XPath to a shorter address which uses the address by the relative address to the web elements. It searches the web page, top to bottom, looking for elements that match the criteria.

Let's talk about html. Here is an example element: <a href=http://www.google.com>google link</a>. This will show up on the page as a text link displaying the words "google link" and it will take you to www.google.com.

For each web element there are three main parts:

- the type
- the attributes, and
- the text.

Our element is of type a. It has an attribute called href equal to http://www.google.com and it has text equal to "google link". We can use all three of these things to search for our elements.

Nodes in XPath

Let's understand the idea of nodes, and the familial relationship of html elements. Look at this example code:

```
<div title="Section1">
  <td name="Search">
    <tr class="Yahoo">Yahoo Search</tr>
    <tr class="Google">Google Search</tr>
  </td>
</div>
```

Do you notice the </div> at the bottom? That means the td and tr elements are contained within the div. These other elements are considered descendants of the div. The td is a child, and the tr is a grandchild (and so on and so forth). The two tr elements are considered siblings. This is vital, as XPath uses these relationships to find your element

So suppose I wanted to find the google item. Any of the following expressions will work:

```
//tr[@class='Google']
/div/td/tr[2]
//div[@title="Section1"]//tr[text()="Google Search"]
```

So let's analyse these expressions. We start at the top element (also known as a node). The // means to search all descendants, / means to just look at the current element's children. So //div means look through all descendants for a div element. The brackets [] specify something about that element. So we can look for an attribute with the @ symbol, or look for text with the text () function. We can chain as many of these together as we can.

Here is a quick reference:

- // search all descendant elements
- / search all child elements
- [] The predicate (specifies something about the element you are looking for)
- @ Specifies an element attribute. (For example, @title)
- text() Gets the text of the element.
- . specifies the current node (useful when you want to look for an element's children in the predicate)
- .. specifies the parent node
- contains() Use this in the predicate if you can't do a full string match on an attribute or text() value.

Xpath - Structure

XPath is an optimum way to locate your elements, considering the ease of use against possibility of breaking. Few "experts" in selenium consider that XPath is bad, it's slow, and it needs to be avoided at all costs. This is bit of an exaggeration and generalisation, we need to take an educated judgment as to using XPath based upon the need of the situation. Ultimately we need to reference an item in the most clean and concise method possible. So if an item has a unique id or name, you should use that and avoid an XPath expression. However, there are so many times when the element you're trying to locate does not have a unique identifier, and you need to find it.

The problem with XPath is the way most XPath generating programs work. They generate a string of absolute locators a million miles long. So something like this:

/html/body[@id='sc']/div[2]/div[2]/div[3]/ul/li[1]/div/table/tbody/tr/td/p/a[3]

This might be accurate however you do NOT want to use XPath like this as this is highly dependent upon the structure of the web page and can break even with slight modification to it. The resulting paths can be brittle for a fully qualified path like above and it will break if any elements are added in the tree, and different browsers may insert things like tbody's in different places. This style of XPath expression should be your very LAST resort on locating an element. But what is the alternative? Start with the parent.

First off, I strongly recommend the use of // instead of /. It may be slightly slower locating an element, but it allows you to construct a much more transparent, and reliable XPath expression.

So something like this would be a more appropriate XPath from the above example: //div[@class='object1']/a. This looks through the entire page for a div with attribute "class" equal to "object1". It then looks for a child <a> element. This is fine as long as there is only one div with class=object1. However, class is not a unique identifier, and it's quite possible there is more than one item on the page that matches our expression. What is the solution? Add another parent.

//td[@title='Row1']//div[@class='object1']/a. Neither title nor class are unique, but hopefully the combination of both should be. However, maybe not.

If you can't find a parent or grandparent to start with that is unique, you can also try a sibling node. Suppose we have a table where nothing has attributes. We want to type into the text field in an adjacent row to a link. We can find the link, because the link text is unique. But we can't find the text field without resorting to some caveman XPath expression. The easiest way to do this is to start with the parent node, and in the predicate (the []) look for a child node, then select another node. For example:

```
//tr[.//a[text()="book1"]]//input
```

This expression select a row, looks for a descendant link with text "book1", then selects any descendant input. You have to use the period inside to select the current node.

Simple XPath

Relatively straightforward to compose and read later down the track.

//td[text()='My Cell Contents'] (the first table cell with the specified text)

//td[normalize-space(text())='My Cell Contents'] (for finding text that is surrounded by spaces).

//p[contains(text(), 'My Para Contents')]

//div(@class='MyClass')

//input[contains(@id, 'myTextField')]

Complex XPath

These may be necessary if there are no unique ID's or names in elements nearby the element you need to click on. As mentioned above, try not to use the fully qualified or the raw XPath that Selenium records with, but refine the XPath to be a bit more robust and readable in future.

/html/body/div[1]/div[5]/div/table/tbody/tr/td/p/a[3] (An example bad XPath - it will break as soon as the page layout changes a bit)

//td[contains(text()),'My Label']/following-sibling::td[2]/input (an un-named input box that has a known label 2 table cells away from it).

You can validate your generated XPaths using the $x function of Firebug. For example, you can build the XPath for the "Google Search" and "I am feeling lucky" button on Google website as below:

```
XPath = /html/body/center/form/table/tbody/tr/td[2]/span/span/input
```

You can verify the XPath by putting it in the $x() function of Firebug in the Console tab as shown below. This will give you the matching Web Elements in the next line, when you hover the mouse over them, it takes you to the derived web elements from the XPath.

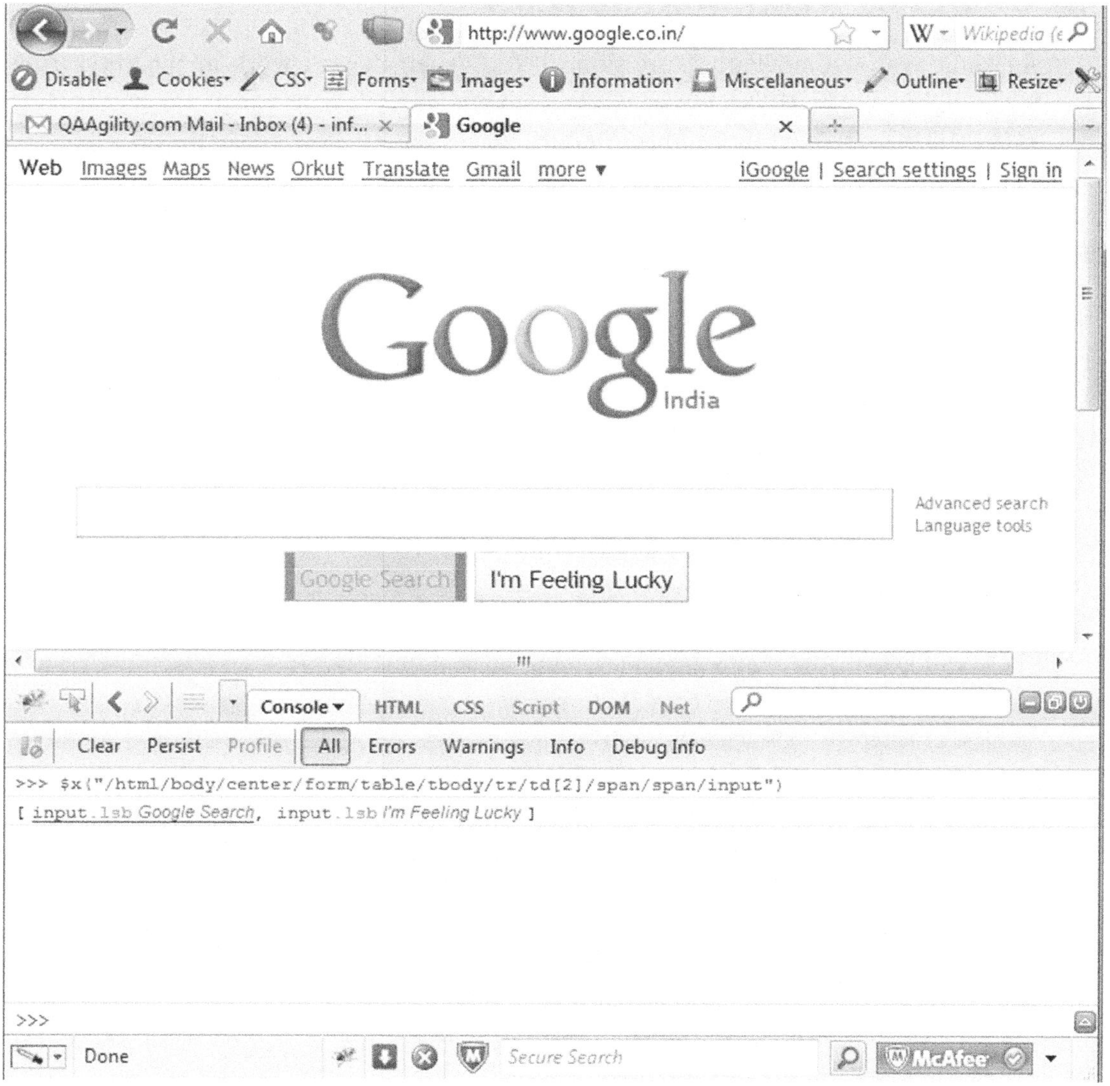

Notes

1. Set selectors [1] [2] etc are numbered from 1, not 0
2. If you use multiple classes on an element (e.g. <div class="foo bar">) you can use //div[contains(@class, "foo")] to find matching elements.

3. Don't forget that id's can't start with numbers.
4. Don't forget that <a> elements have name's not id's.

Why won't this XPath work in IE6?!

1. for some reason the XPath expression id('foo')/span doesn't work in IE6. Try: //div[@id='foo']/span instead.
2. //div[5][@class="foo"] (select the fifth div with class foo that occurs in the document tree) doesn't work in IE6. Try /descendant::div[@class="foo"][5] instead.

Using Regular Expressions in xpath

Here is an example where I have used regular expressions in xpath.

This includes a code sample that demonstrates how you can use the starts-with XPath string function to implement this requirement.

Here is my HTML source code:

```
<h1 id="c100Item_P100">Abrasion Resistance</h1>
<h1 id="c100Item_P101">Access Panels</h1>
<h1 id="c100Item_P102">Access Solutions</h1>
<h1 id="c100Item_P103">Accessories</h1>
<h1 id="c100Item_P104">Acoustic Performance</h1>
<h1 id="c100Item_P105">Affordable Playground Equipment</h1>
<h1 id="c100Item_P106">Aged Care Facilities</h1>
<h1 id="c100Item_P107">Aggregates</h1>
<h1 id="c100Item_P108">Air Circulation</h1>
<h1 id="c100Item_P109">Air Conditioning Filter Cleaning</h1>
<h1 id="c100Item_P110">Air Conditioning Maintenance</h1>
<h1 id="c100Item_P111">Air Conditioning Services</h1>
<h1 id="c100Item_P112">Air Flow</h1>
<h1 id="c100Item_P113">Air Fresheners</h1>
<h1 id="c100Item_P114">Air Movement</h1>
<h1 id="c100Item_P115">Alarm Monitoring</h1>
<h1 id="c100Item_P116">Alfresco</h1>
<h1 id="c100Item_P117">Alternative Waterproofing</h1>
<h1 id="c100Item_P118">Aluminium Composite</h1>
<h1 id="c100Item_P119">Amplifiers</h1>
<h1 id="c100Item_P120">Anodising</h1>
<h1 id="c100Item_P121">Anti Slip</h1>
<h1 id="c100Item_P122">Anti Vandal</h1>
```

```
<h1 id="c100Item_P123">Anti-graffiti</h1>
<h1 id="c100Item_P124">Anti-Rust</h1>
<h1 id="c100Item_P125">Apartments</h1>
<h1 id="c100Item_P126">Appliances</h1>
```

Here is the verifyElement command in Java to verify for the xpath element.

```
verifyTrue(selenium.isElementPresent("//*[starts-with(@id, \"c100Item_P\")]"));
```

3. CSS Path

In general terms, CSS locators are suppose to be faster than XPath and they are more readable. Also, it would make more sense to use CSS if you are testing a website based on jQuery as CSS is jQuery's locating strategy. Let's see some advanced CSS rules and pseudo-classes that will help you move your XPath locators to CSS, a native approach on all browsers.

Next Sibling

Let's see how we can navigate lists of elements, such as forms or ul items. The next sibling will tell selenium to find the next adjacent element on the page that's inside the same parent. Let's take an example using a form to select the field after username.

```
<form>
<input id="id_inp2" class="username"></input>
<input id="id_inp3" class="alias"></input>
<input value="435435435-7a3e-23f4-af1d-a83b5fe03f4d" name="vid" type="hidden"><input value="FL_
d10dr3e3" name="fl_cid" type="hidden"></form>
```

Let's write a css selector that will choose the input field after "username". This will select the "alias" input, or will select a different element if the form is reordered.

```
css=form input.username + input
```

Attribute Values

If you don't care about the ordering of child elements, you can use an attribute selector in selenium to choose elements based on any attribute value. A good example would be choosing the 'username' element of the form without adding a class.

```
<form>
<input id="id_inp6" name="username"></input>
<input id="id_inp7" name="password"></input>
<input name="continue" type="button"></input>
```

```
<input name="cancel" type="button"></input>
<input value="435435435-7a3e-23f4-af1d-a83b5fe03f4d" name="vid" type="hidden"><input value="FL_d10dr3e3" name="fl_cid" type="hidden"></form>
```

We can easily select the username element without adding a class or an id to the element.

```
css=form input[name='username']
```

We can even chain filters to be more specific with our selections.

```
css=input[name='continue'][type='button']
```

Here Selenium will act on the input field with name="continue" and type="button"

Choosing a Specific Match

CSS selectors in Selenium allow us to navigate lists with more finesse than that the above methods. If we have an ul and we want to select its fourth li element without regard to any other elements, we should use nth-child or nth-of-type.

```
<ul id="recordlist">
<p>Heading</p>
<li>Cat</li>
<li>Dog</li>
<li>Car</li>
<li>Goat</li>
</ul>
```

If we want to select the fourth li element (Goat) in this list, we can use the nth-of-type, which will find the fourth li in the list.

```
css=ul#recordlist li:nth-of-type(4)
```

On the other hand, if we want to get the fourth element only if it is a li element, we can use a filtered nth-child which will select (Car) in this case.

```
css=ul#recordlist li:nth-child(4)
```

Note, if you don't specify a child type for nth-child it will allow you to select the fourth child without regard to type. This may be useful in testing css layout in selenium.

```
css=ul#recordlist *:nth-child(4)
```

Sub-string matches

CSS in Selenium has an interesting feature of allowing partial string matches using ^=, $=, or *=. I'll define them, then show an example of each:

^= Match a prefix

$= Match a suffix

*= Match a substring

```
css=a[id^='id_prefix_']
```

A link with an "id" that starts with the text "id_prefix_"

```
css=a[id$='_id_sufix']
```

A link with an "id" that ends with the text "_id_sufix"

```
css=a[id*='id_pattern']
```

A link with an "id" that contains the text "id_pattern"

Matching by Inner Text

And last, one of the more useful pseudo-classes, :contains() will match elements with the desired text block:

```
css=a:contains('Log Out')
```

This will find the log out button on your page no matter where it's located.

Note: Elements may have more than one class, however you don't need to list them all. Only specify enough to unambiguously locate the element. You can chain classes by separating them will a period.

Readability Compared to XPath

XPath	*CSS*
//input[@id="myId"]	input#myId
//input[@class="myClass"]	input.myClass
//input[@name="myName"]	input[name=myName]
//*[@id="myId"]	#myId
//table[@id="myId"]//tr[@class="myClass"]//td[3]	table#myId tr.myClass td:nth(3)

Limitation of CSS Locators

The only thing that I don't like with CSS locators is that indexing specific sibling elements is more verbose—it must be done with nth-child():

```
.content .sidebar:nth-child(1) a
```

With XPath you can use a simple pair of brackets:

```
//div[@class='content']/div[@class='sidebar'][1]/a
```

It would be really nice if CSS selectors had the same bracket-style indexing syntax as XPath. (Of course, this is a limitation of CSS itself, not Selenium.)

In addition, nth-child() is a little more brittle in that it isn't constrained to the current selection scope. For example, assume you have markup like so:

```
<div class="content">
  <div class="something_else">...</div>
  <div class="sidebar">...</div>
</div>
```

There is now a non-sidebar sibling <div> appearing before the sidebar <div>. In this case, there will be no element that matches *.sidebar:nth-child(1)*—the sidebar is matched by *.sidebar:nth-child(2)*. This means that adding additional unrelated mark-up to your page can break your tests if you're using CSS locators. If you were using the XPath locators in this case, the indexing of the element in question would remain constant because the index doesn't refer to children, but to elements matching that specific XPath. (If you added additional sidebar <div>'s the XPath would break as well, but all the same it's still less brittle.)

One final point to note is that there's also a bug in the cssQuery library that prevents nth-child() from working correctly—it's Selenium bug #698. Unfortunately, the patch posted on the bug does not fix the problem for me. Instead, you have to resort to suffixing any nth-child() selector with a child or sibling combinator like so:

```
.content .sidebar:nth-child(1) > a
```

Despite these minor wrinkles, I find that the CSS locators used with Selenium are less verbose in general and lead to faster running tests.

4. Click and Mouse Events

Sometimes to replicate a specific Javascript event that occurs, there are a few tricks that need to be tried. The Javascript may not activate on the selenium Click event. It may actually activated on the Mouse Up Event. There is no way to know this except testing each different scenario (if you don't have access to the developer, who may be able to help).

Some of the useful commands are:

- Click and ClickAt
- MouseDown and MouseDownAt
- MouseUp and MouseUpAt
- MouseMove and MouseMoveAt
- DragDrop (useful for moving slider bars that calls a JavaScript event to change a value when the slider is moved).

You usually need to use these in combination with each other.

e.g. doing a ClickAt, MouseDownAt and MouseUpAt in sequence on the same locator, may actually make the Javascript work, whereas a Click will not.

5. Keyboard and Coordinates

There will be time when all your locators can fail, such situations can occur and we need to have some locator strategy. If all else fails, you may actually have to resort to simulate the key press events on locators to get the right action (or it could very well for filling text into a text field).

Usually the **type** command works fine, but there may be cases where the javascript is called after every single key press and you need to replicate that (e.g. like the Google search box that shows the results after each key stroke). In this case you will need to use **typeKeys** commands.

You can also go to the extreme of KeyDown and KeyUp – rather than the equivalent command of KeyPress as the Javascript may be called on KeyUp. You can use Selenium for keyboard commands to test a website for keyboard only accessibility. This can also be a fantastic use for Selenium and shows just how powerful it is.

In the absolute worst case scenario you could use a **clickAt** event with X,Y coordinates from the top left hand corner of the page.

Fortunately, most of the times such extremely situations do not arise but you need to be prepared for such complex Selenium testing. I have found that even if it takes a while, there is usually a way to find the locator and work with it using one of the tricks listed above.

EXERCISES

1. What are different ways of locating an element other than use of Xpath and CSS?
2. If you had three buttons on the web page in the AUT with unique IDs, would you use Xpath pr CSS path? Why?
3. How does this locator work, css=label:contains(Email:) >> This locates the first label element on the page that has text contents of 'Email:'
4. How does this locator work, xpath=id('register')/input[2] >> This locates the second input element beneath the element with an id value of 'register'
5. Using the regular expression in my locator, xpath=//div[matches(@id,'che.*boxes')] >> This would click the div with 'id=checkboxes', or 'id=cheANYTHINGHEREboxes'

14

Selenium RC Overview

Remember that Selenium consists of

- Selenium IDE
- **Selenium RC**
- Selenium Grid

Let's look at Selenium RC now.

The Selenium RC Server is used for testing complex AJAX-based web user interfaces under a Continuous Integration system.

Selenium RC is used with Selenium Core/Selenium IDE to write tests in programming languages other than the Selenese HTML table format.

The RC server is bundled with Selenium Core and automatically loads it into the browser.

Without using special modes, using Selenium RC test script, one cannot test domain changing web applications or within the same domain to change from insecure (http) page to secure (https) page.

Selenium-RC Architecture

- Selenium Remote Control (RC) is a test tool that allows testers to write automated Web Application User Interface tests in many programming languages against any HTTP website using any mainstream JavaScript-enabled browser.
- Selenium RC comes in two parts.
  - A server which automatically launches and kills browsers, and acts as a HTTP proxy for web requests from them.

- Client libraries for computer languages.

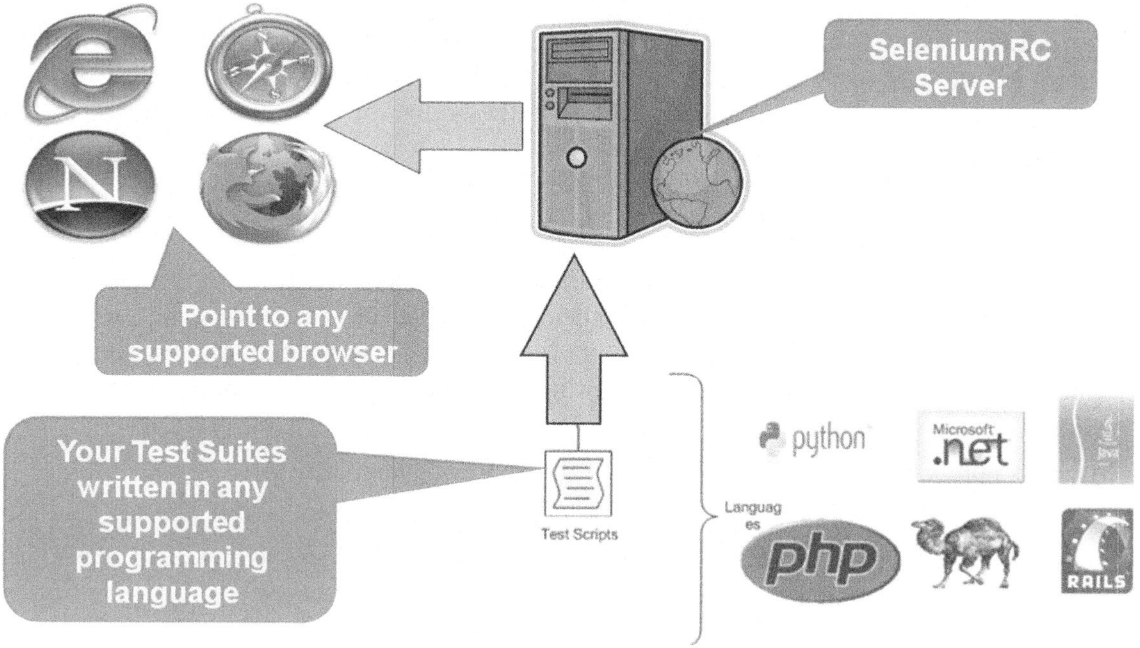

How Selenium acts as proxy and overcomes Same-origin policy:

What is Proxy?

The proxy is a third person in the middle that passes the ball between the two parts. It acts as a "web server" that delivers the AUT to the browser. Being a proxy gives Selenium Server the capability of "lying" about the AUT's real URL.

What is Same-origin Policy?

The main restriction that Selenium faces is the Same Origin Policy. This security restriction is applied by every browser in the market and its objective is to ensure that a site's content will never be accessible by a script from another site. The Same Origin Policy dictates that any code loaded within the browser can only operate within that website's domain. It cannot perform functions on another website. So for example, if the browser loads JavaScript code when it loads www.mysite.com, it cannot run that loaded code against www.mysite2.com–even if that's another of your sites. If this were possible, a script placed on any website you open would be able to read information on your bank account if you had the account page opened on other tab. This is called XSS (Cross-site Scripting).

To work within this policy, Selenium-Core (and its JavaScript commands that make all the magic happen) must be placed in the same origin as the Application Under Test (same URL).

Historically, Selenium-Core was limited by this problem since it was implemented in JavaScript. Selenium RC is not, however, restricted by the Same Origin Policy. Its use of the Selenium Server as a proxy avoids this problem. It, essentially, tells the browser that the browser is working on a single "spoofed" website that the Server provides.

Proxy Injection

The first method Selenium used to avoid the The Same Origin Policy was Proxy Injection. In Proxy Injection Mode, the Selenium Server acts as a client-configured HTTP proxy, that sits between the browser and the Application Under Test. It then masks the AUT under a fictional URL (embedding Selenium-Core and the set of tests and delivering them as if they were coming from the same origin).

As a test suite starts in your favorite language, the following happens:

1. The client/driver establishes a connection with the selenium-RC server.
2. Selenium RC server launches a browser (or reuses an old one) with a URL that injects Selenium-Core's JavaScript into the browser-loaded web page.
3. The client-driver passes a Selenese command to the server.
4. The Server interprets the command and then triggers the corresponding JavaScript execution to execute that command within the browser.
5. Selenium-Core instructs the browser to act on that first instruction, typically opening a page of the AUT.
6. The browser receives the open request and asks for the website's content from the Selenium RC server (set as the HTTP proxy for the browser to use).
7. Selenium RC server communicates with the Web server asking for the page and once it receives it, it sends the page to the browser masking the origin to look like the page comes from the same server as Selenium-Core (this allows Selenium-Core to comply with the Same Origin Policy).
8. The browser receives the web page and renders it in the frame/window reserved for it.

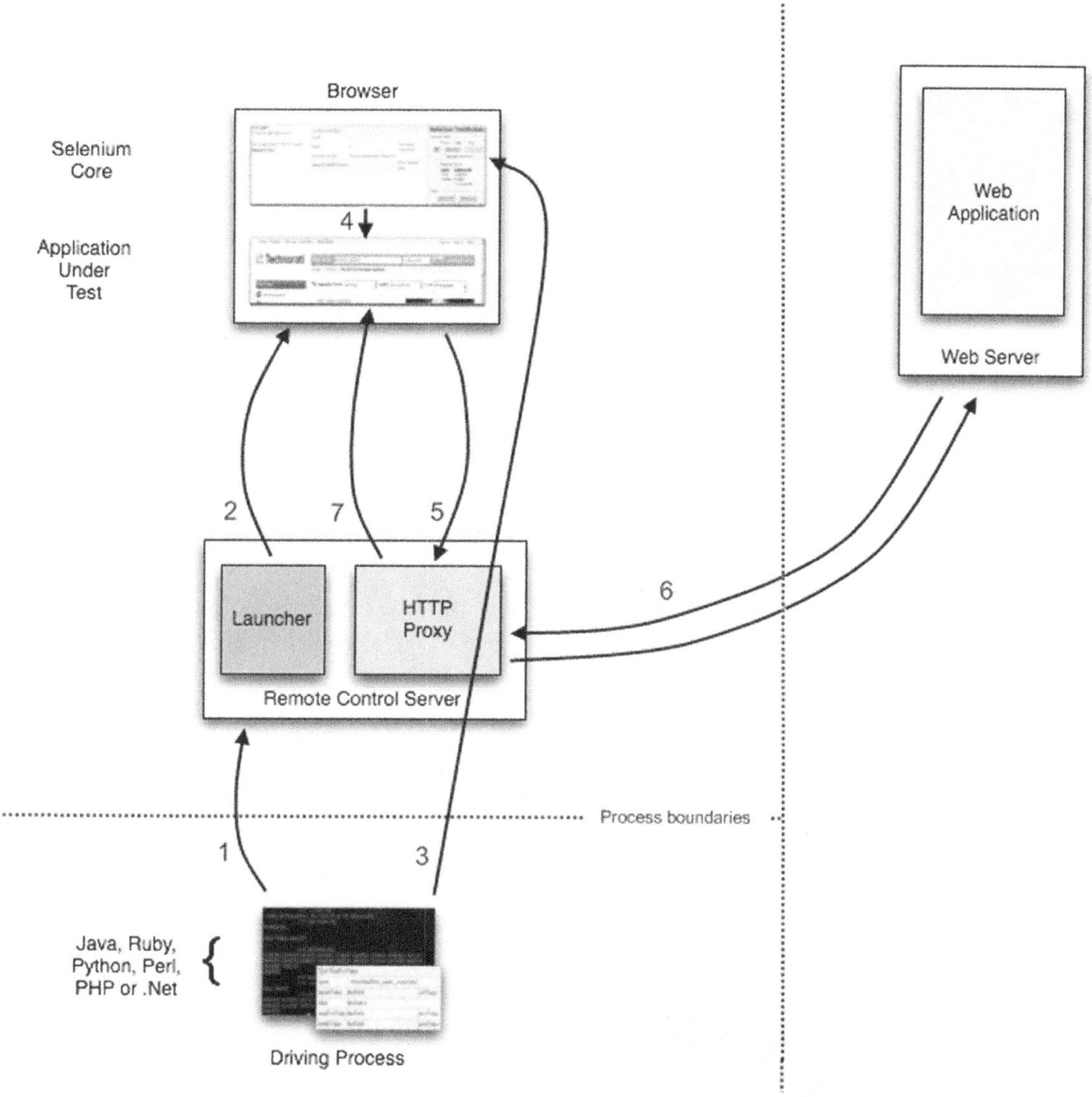

Heightened Privileges Browsers

This workflow in this method is very similar to Proxy Injection but the main difference is that the browsers are launched in a special mode called Heightened Privileges, which allows websites to do things that are not commonly permitted (as doing XSS, or filling file upload inputs and pretty useful stuff for Selenium). By using these browser modes, Selenium Core is able to directly open the AUT and read/interact with its content without having to pass the whole AUT through the Selenium RC server.

Here is the architectural diagram.

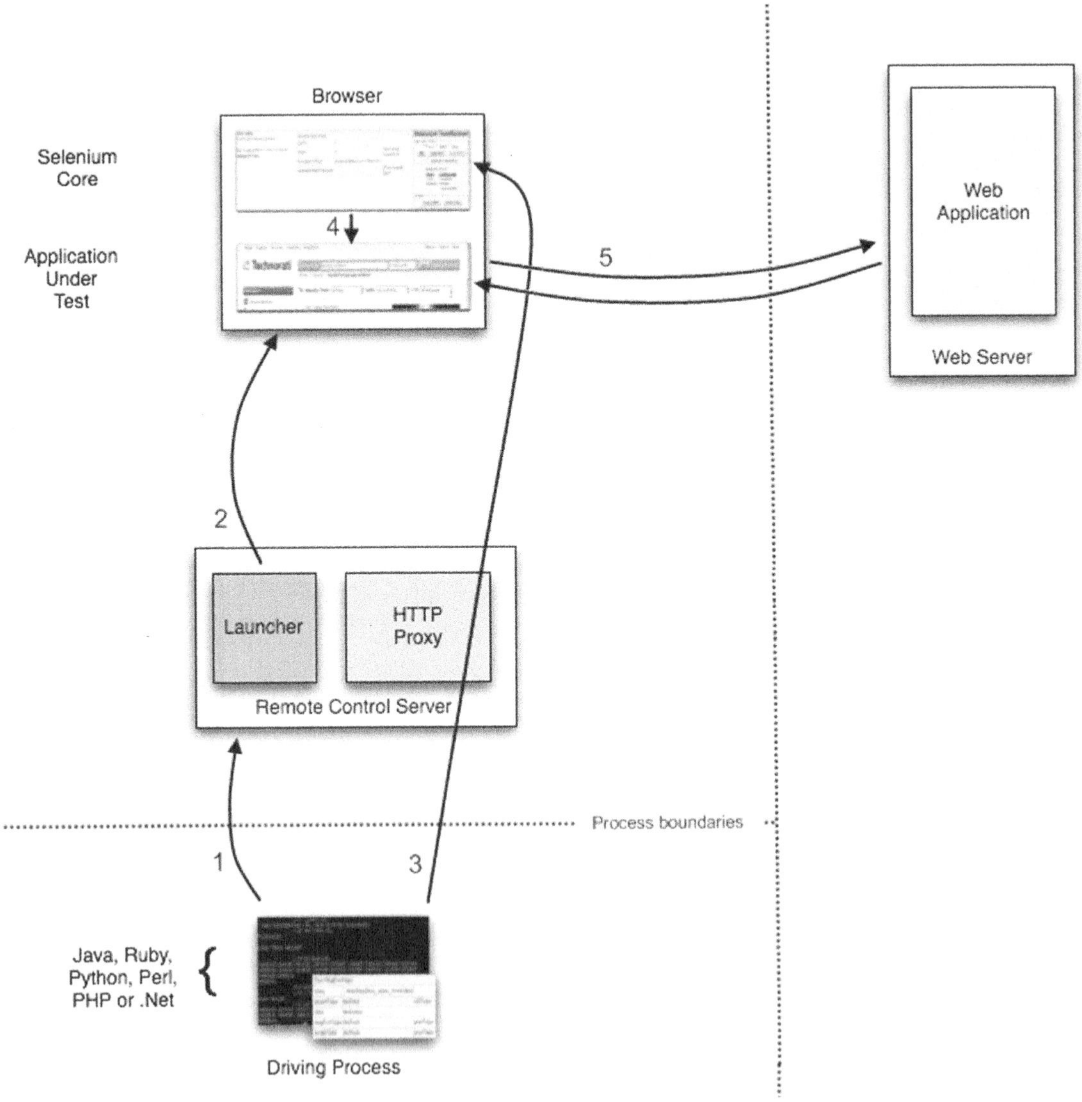

As a test suite starts in your favorite language, the following happens:

1. The client/driver establishes a connection with the selenium-RC server.
2. Selenium RC server launches a browser (or reuses an old one) with a URL that will load Selenium-Core in the web page.

3. Selenium-Core gets the first instruction from the client/driver (via another HTTP request made to the Selenium RC Server).
4. Selenium-Core acts on that first instruction, typically opening a page of the AUT.
5. The browser receives the open request and asks the Web Server for the page. Once the browser receives the web page, renders it in the frame/window reserved for it.

Platforms Supported by Selenium-RC

- Browsers
  - Firefox, IE, Safari and Opera
- Operating Systems
  - Windows, Mac OS X, Linux, and Solaris
- Programming Languages
  - C#, Java, Perl, PHP, Python, and Ruby
- Testing Frameworks
  - Bromine, JUnit & TestNG (Java), NUnit (.Net), RSpec & Test::Unit (Ruby), unittest (Python)

Selenium-RC Command Line Options

Usage: java -jar selenium-server.jar [-interactive] [-options]

port <nnnn>:(default 4444)

the port number the selenium server should use

timeout <nnnn>: (eg: 180)

an integer number of seconds

interactive:

Interactively enter the commands.

multiWindow:

Tests are executed in a separate window and supports web pages with frames.

forcedBrowserMode <browser>: (eg: *iehta)

sets the forced default browser mode (e.g. "*iexplore") for all sessions, no matter what is passed in getNewBrowserSession userExtensions <file>:

indicates a JavaScript file that will be loaded into selenium

browserSessionReuse:

stops re-initialization and spawning of the browser between tests

avoidProxy:

Uses by default proxy for browser request

set this flag to make the browser use proxy only for URLs containing '/selenium-server'

firefoxProfileTemplate <dir>:

By default generates a fresh empty Firefox profile for every test.

Provide a directory to use your profile directory instead.

debug:

Debug mode provides more trace information and used for diagnostics purpose

log:

When enabled writes debug information out to a log file

htmlSuite <browser> <startURL> <suiteFile> <resultFile>:

Provide browser and URL to run a single HTML Selenese Test suite and then exit immediately.

Provide absolute path to the HTML test suite, and HTML results file.

proxyInjectionMode:

A proxy injection mode is a mode where the selenium server acts as a proxy server for all content going to the AUT. Under this mode, multiple domains can be visited.

The following additional flags are supported for proxy injection mode:

- dontInjectRegex <regex>: an optional regular expression that proxy injection mode can use to know when to bypass injection
- userJsInjection <file>: specifies a JavaScript file which will then be injected into all pages userContentTransformation <regex> <replacement>:
- A regular expression which is matched against all test HTML content; the second is a string which will replace matches. These flags can be used any number of times. A simple example of how this could be useful: if you add "-userContentTransformation https http" then all "https" strings in the HTML of the test application will be changed to be "http".

Java system properties:

- Dhttp.proxyHost and -Dhttp.proxyPort

Normally Selenium RC overrides the proxy server configuration, using the Selenium Server as a proxy. Use these options if you need to use your own proxy together with the Selenium Server proxy.

Use the proxy settings like this:

- java -Dhttp.proxyHost=myproxy.com -Dhttp.proxyPort=1234 -jar selenium-server.jar
- HTTP proxy requires authentication, you will also need to set -Dhttp.proxyUser and -Dhttp.proxyPassword, in addition to http.proxyHost and http.proxyPort.
- java -Dhttp.proxyHost=myproxy.com -Dhttp.proxyPort=1234 -Dhttp.proxyUser=joe -Dhttp.proxyPassword=example -jar selenium-server.jar

15

Install and Run Selenium RC

Step One - Download & Install Selenium-Rc

Installing Selenium Remote Control (RC) requires three step process:

- First: Install JRE 1.5 or later version (for execution install JDK)
- Second: Install the Selenium RC
- Third: Install Java Client

Install JDK

- Go to Start . Run . cmd
  - Java – version (*1)
- If you see an older version (< 1.5) it is better to uninstall it

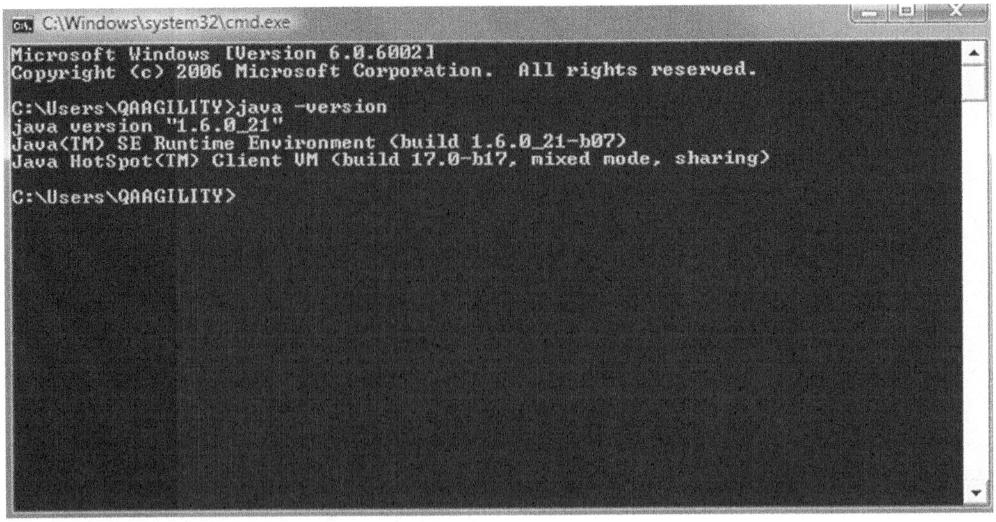

Please refer to Chapter 1 for details on JDK installation.

Install RC

Go to http://code.google.com/p/selenium/downloads/detail?name=selenium-remote-control-1.0.3.zip

Select selenium-remote-control-1.0.3.zip file (*1) link

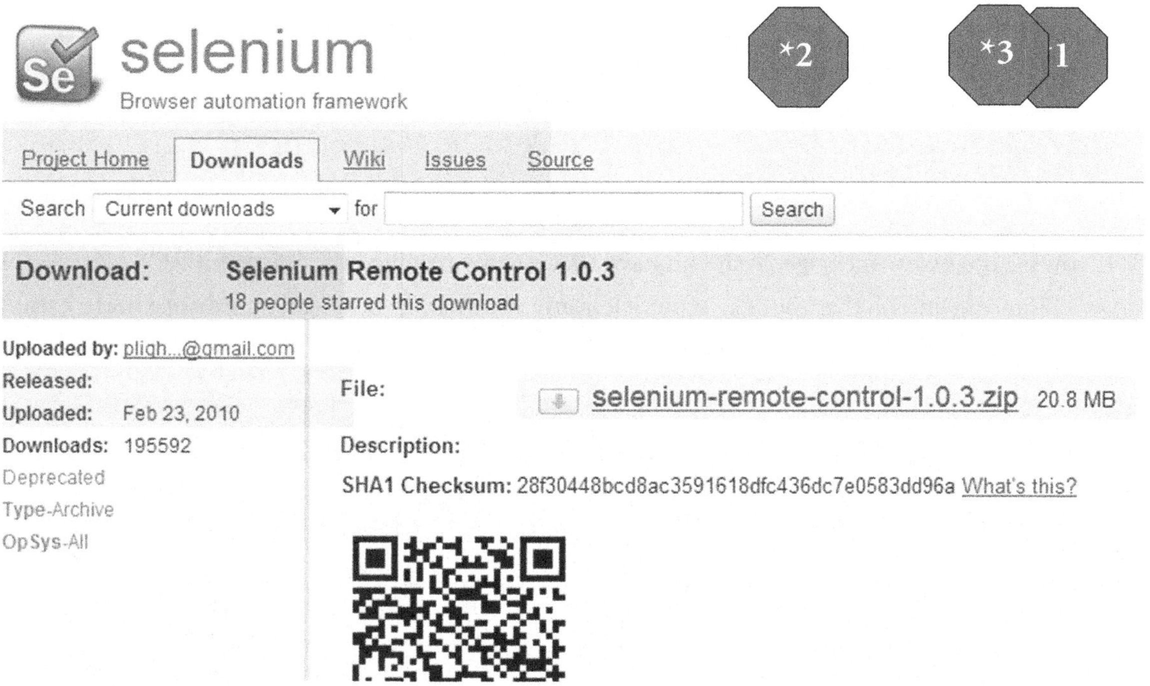

UnZip the selenium-remote-control-1.0.3.zip in C:\ (*3)

Rename the selenium-remote-control-1.0.1 folder into SeleniumRC (optional)

Rename the selenium-java-client-driver-1.0.1 folder into JavaClient (optional)

Rename the selenium-server-1.0.1 into JavaServer (optional)

Overview of the Contents of the Selenium Archive

Step Two - Run Selenium-RC

Open Windows Explorer go to (or to the folder where you have unpacked your selenium-server. jar file)

C:\SeleniumRC\JavaServer

Go to Start → Run → Cmd (enter the following command)

➢ Java -jar selenium-server.jar –interactive

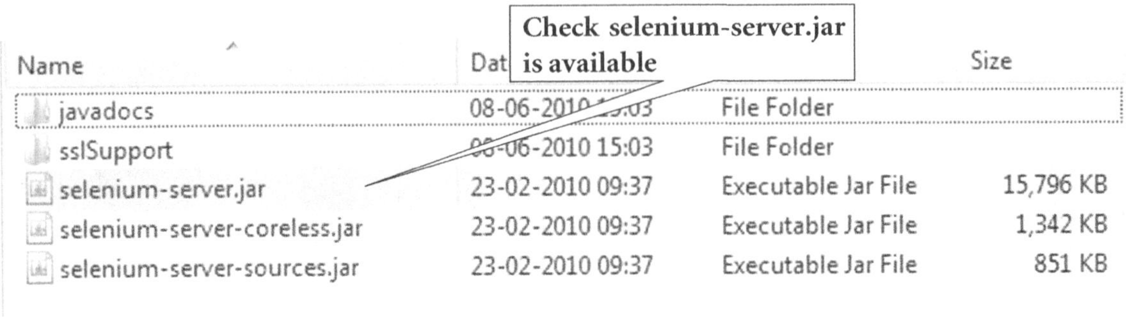

If you see the below message, then you have successfully installed the Selenium RC

➢ Entering interactive mode... type Selenium commands here (e.g: **cmd=open&1=http://www.yahoo.com)**

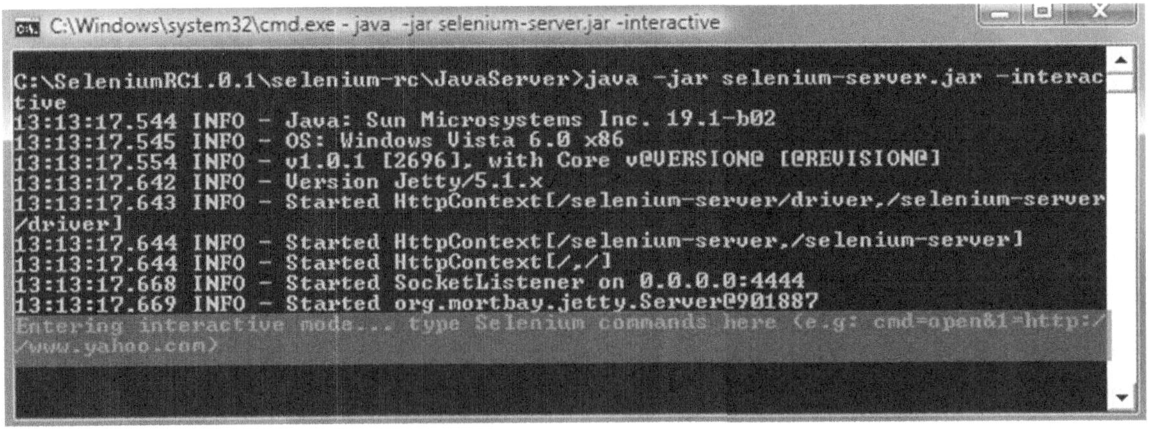

Provide the below command

cmd=getNewBrowserSession&1=*firefox&2=http://www.yahoo.com

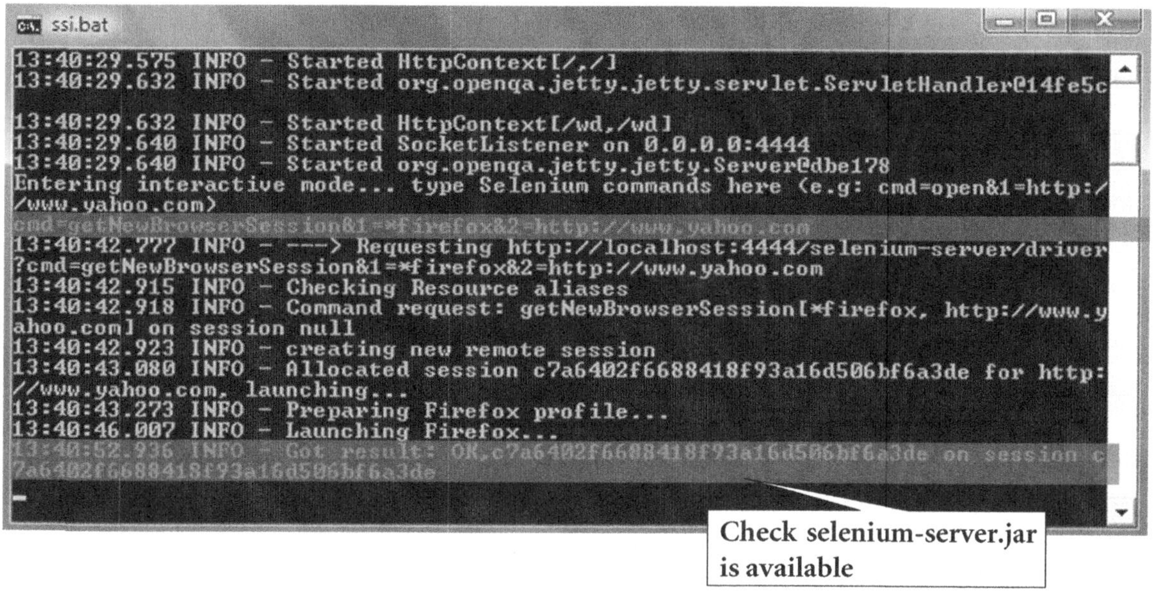

This will launch two windows of Firefox, which will align horizontally.

In your cmd window, go to menu by clicking the left corner, Select Edit → Mark, then select the last two rows, then press Enter.

Now open your Wordpad. Paste the contents

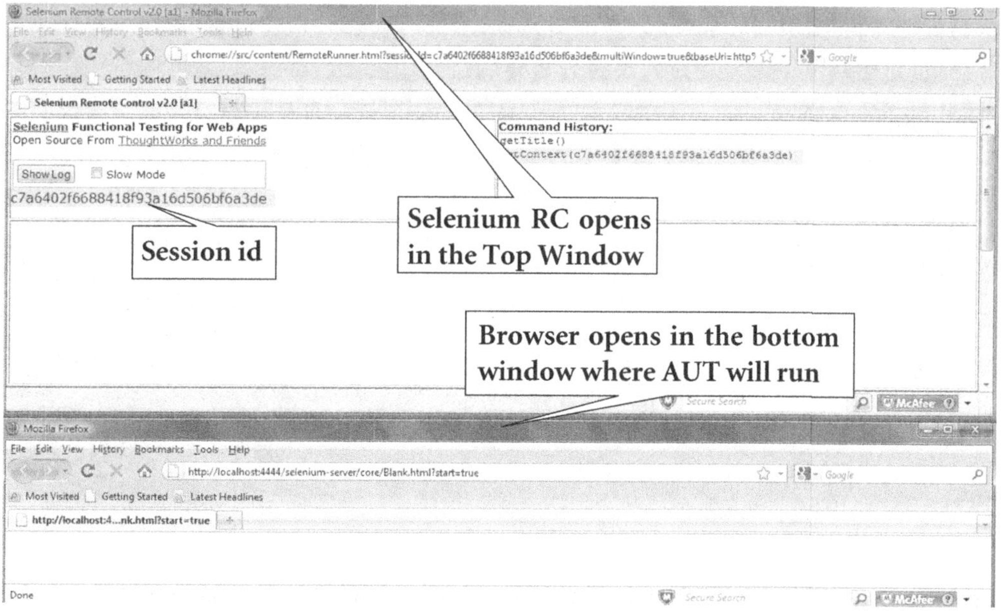

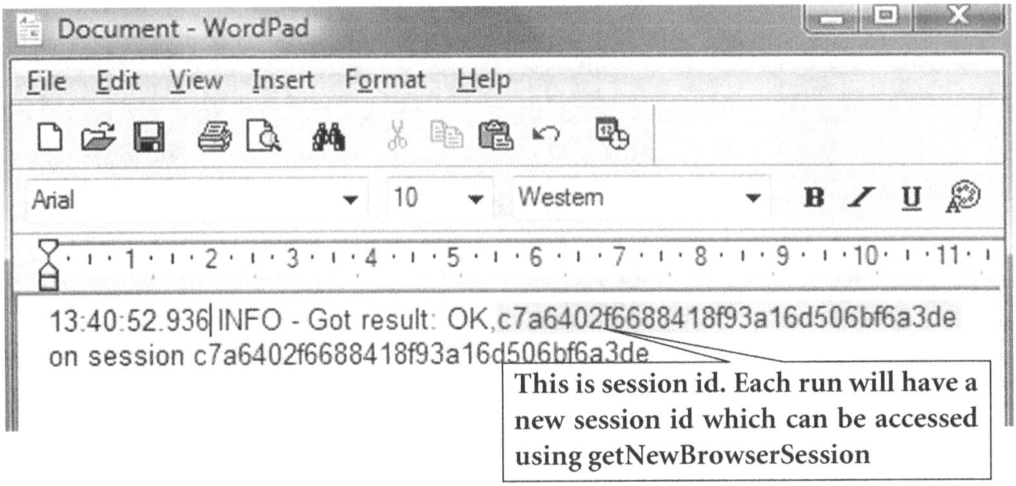

Step Three – Stop The Selenium Server

From the command line

Press Control+C and you will get message INFO-Shutting Down

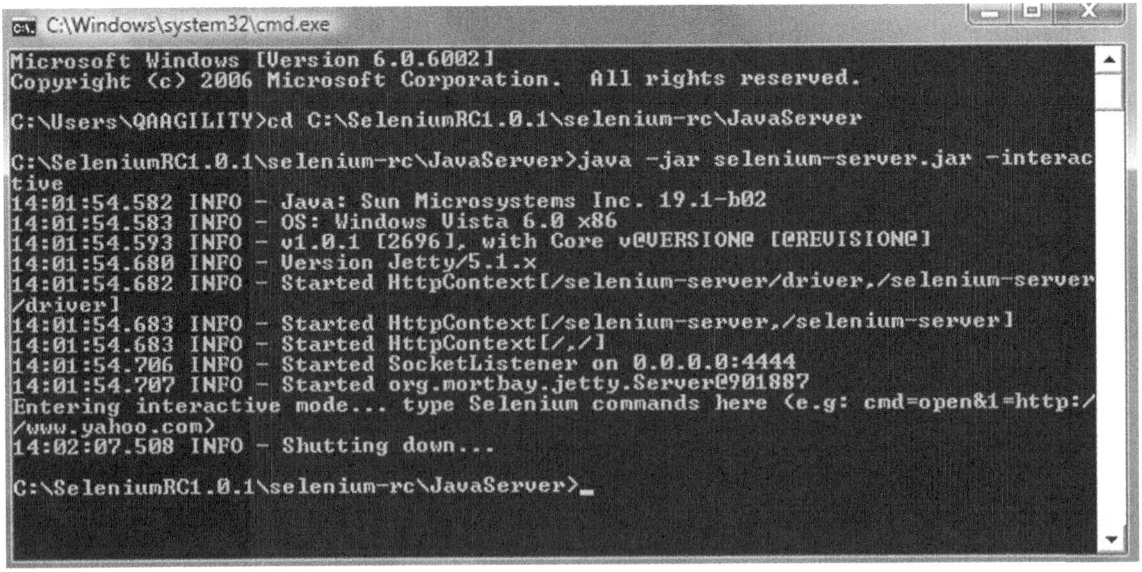

From a browser url

Type **http://localhost:4444/selenium-server/driver/?cmd=shutDownSeleniumServer** in the URL, you will see OKOK on the browser content area.

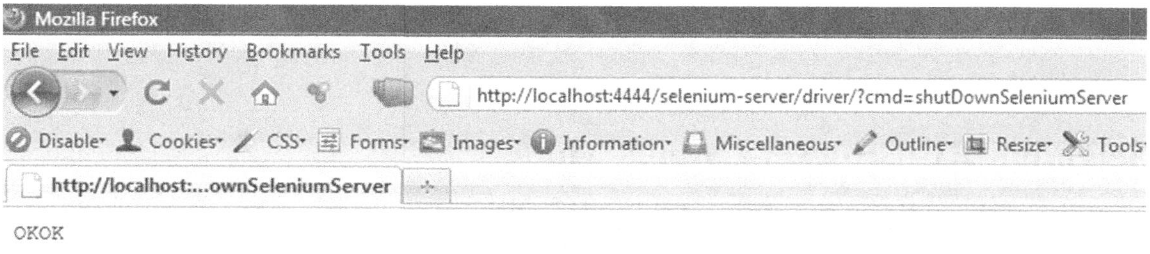

On the RC server side, you will find message on server shutdown

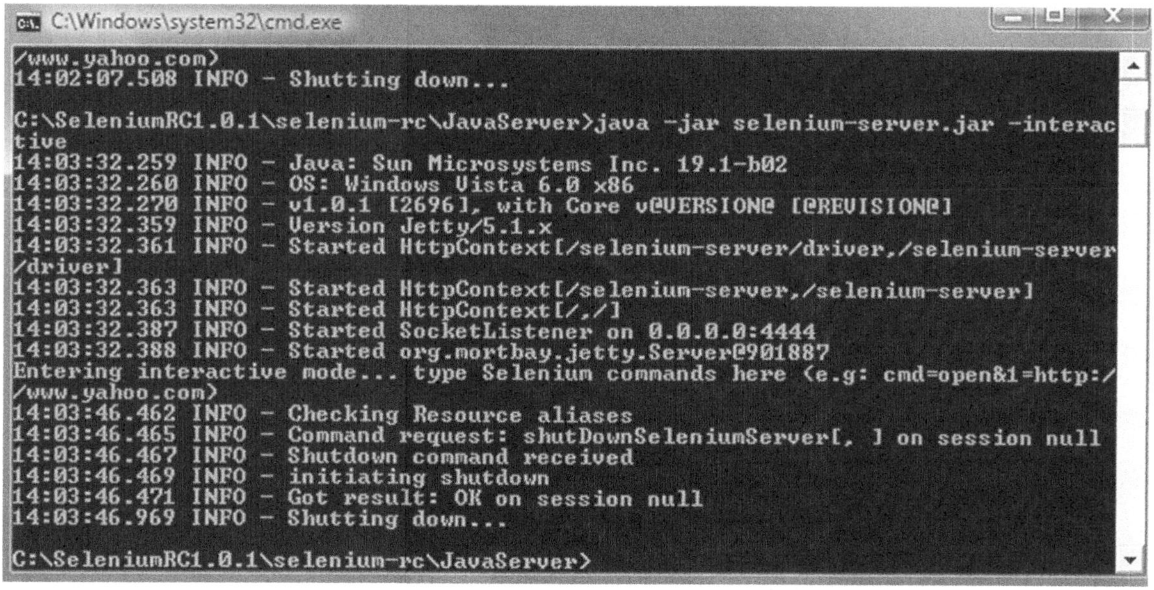

Running Selenium-Rc In Interactive Mode

The "interactive mode (IM)" allow you to run your test case commands on the Selenium Server interactively.

This works like Ruby IRB shell, where you can type the code and see the results immediately. Likewise Selenium Server shows the executed commands results into a browser interactively.

This approach is suited for novice programmers to understand.

To completely automate the test suites, it is best practice to write your tests in a suitable programming language. Not using interactive mode.

Type **exit** to quit from interactive mode

Selenium-RC Browser Launch Mode

Browser Launch Mode	*Description*	*Cross Domain*
*iexplore, *iehta	Internet Explorer in HTA mode	Yes
*iexploreproxy	Internet Explorer HTML mode	No
*firefox, *chrome	Firefox in Chrome mode	Yes
*firefoxproxy	Firefox normal	No
*opera	Opera mode	No
*safari	Safari mode	No
*custom	Custom mode	Dynamic

Parameters for Interactive Mode

During the "interactive mode" one can get the current browser Session ID using the getNewBrowserSession command.

This command accepts two parameters.

Both are mandatory parameters.

First Parameter: Browser Launch mode

Example: *iexplore, *firefox, etc

Second Parameter: URL

Example: http://www.google.com

testComplete command will stop the current session. No longer you can use the same session for further testing after executing this command.

Selenium RC – Interactive Mode Command Line

Interactive mode allows you to execute commands using cmd command

The format of the command is as follows:

cmd={SeleneseCommand}&1={FirstParameter}&2={SecondParameter}&sessionId={sessionID got using getNewBrowserSession}

Example:

cmd=type&1=q&2=energy efficient&sessionId=500b9ffb521d4c67b37e649a7bd5e527

cmd=close&sessionId=500b9ffb521d4c67b37e649a7bd5e527

cmd=waitForTextPresent&1=energy efficiency&sessionId=500b9ffb521d4c67b37e649a7bd5e527

The session ID is optional. Use session ID when you have multiple sessions.

Selenese Command Parameter is mandatory.

Both **&1** and **&2** parameters are optional. If the Selenese command requires these parameter then you may need it.

Example:

For this test, we'll use the example from Chapter 2, TC_GE_EE.html (*1)

First we need to convert this test into interactive mode format.

The converted code is available under the name Test Case Google Search Energy Efficient Interactive Mode No Session ID.txt (*2)

*1

GE Test Case 1		
open	http://www.ge.com/	
type	textToSearch	energy efficient
clickAndWait	searchSubmit	
assertTitle	exact:GE: Search Results	
assertTextPresent	energy efficient	

*2

```
cmd=getNewBrowserSession&1=*firefox&2=http://www.ge.com
cmd=open&1=http://www.ge.com
cmd=type&1=textToSearch&2=energy efficient
cmd=clickAndWait&1=searchSubmit
cmd=assertTitle&1=exact:GE: Search Results
cmd=assertTextPresent&1=energy efficient
cmd=close
cmd=testComplete
```

Closes the AUT Browser

Open your Windows explorer, go to C:\SeleniumRC\JavaServer

Goto Start → Run → cmd

If necessary - change the directory to the location where SeleniumRC is installed.e.g. on the command prompt - type cd "C:\SeleniumRC\JavaServer and then type ssi.bat (*3).

Download ssi.bat file from http://www.qaagility.com/downloads/SeleniumBook/

Or you can type

Java -jar Selenium-server.jar -interactive

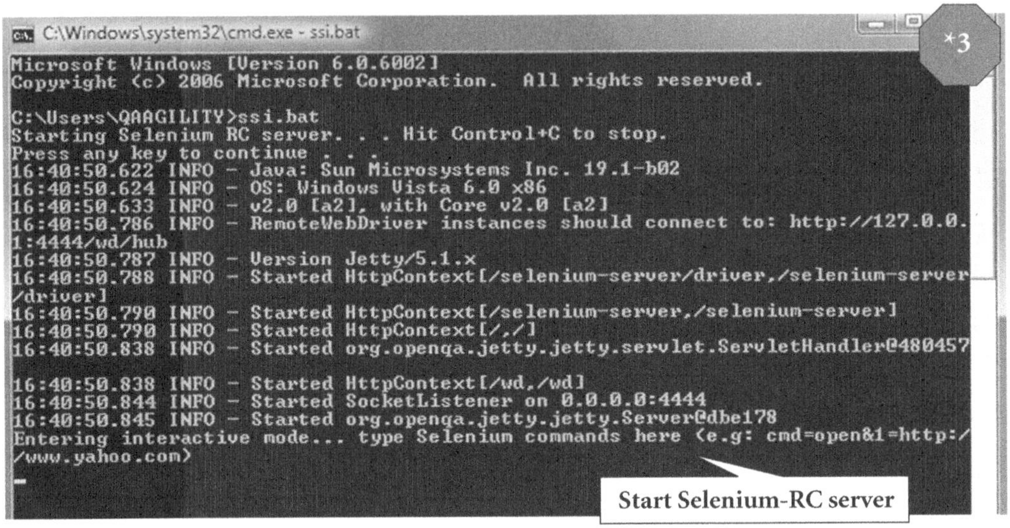

Copy the first line of the code and paste in the interactive mode (*4)

cmd=getNewBrowserSession&1=*firefox&2=http://www.ge.com

Press Enter Key

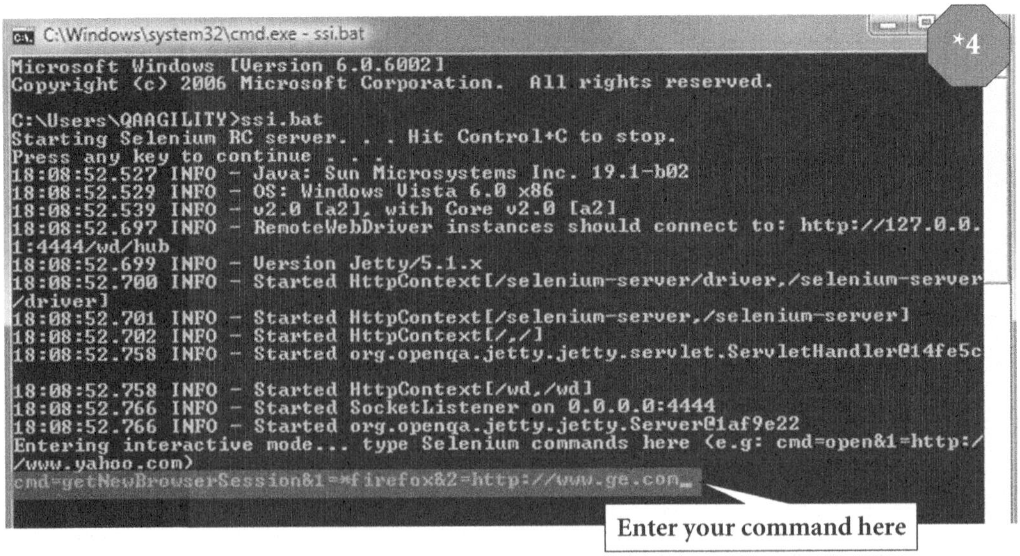

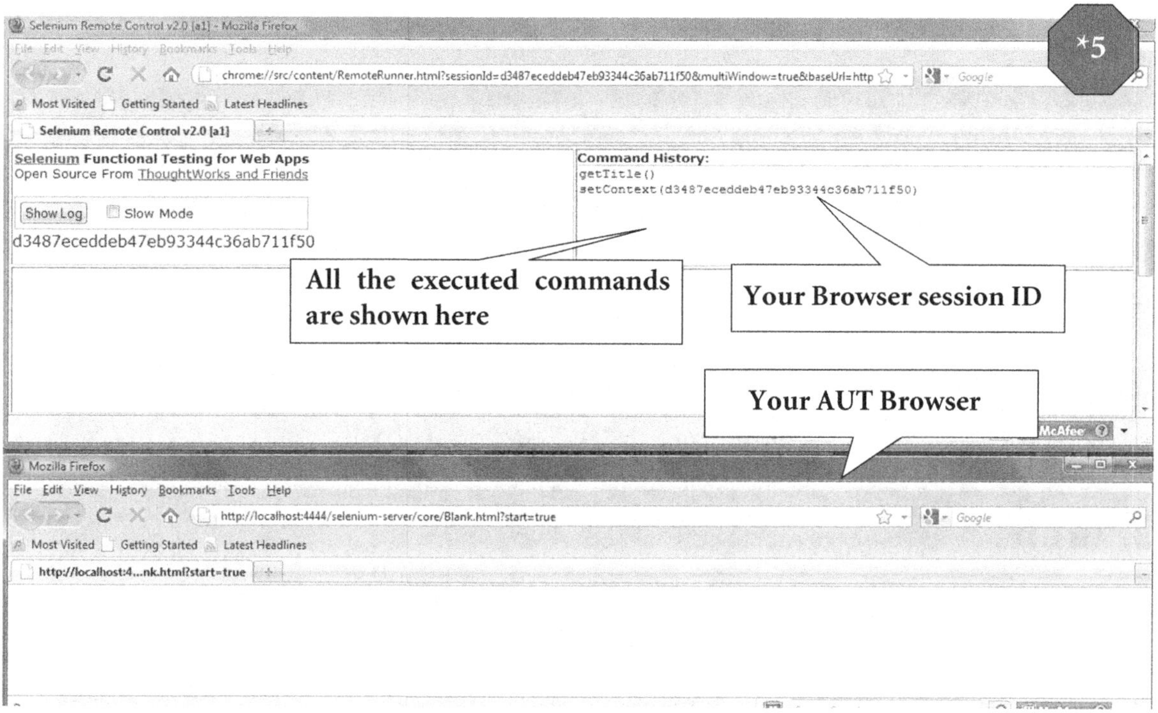

Execute the next lines one by one on IM (*6) until the assert commands

cmd=type&1=textToSearch&2=energy efficient

cmd=clickAndWait&1=searchSubmit

cmd=assertTitle&1=exact:GE: Search Results

cmd=assertTextPresent&1=energy efficient

After finishing each command press Enter Key

C:\Windows\system32\cmd.exe - ssi.bat
*6
//www.ge.com, launching...
18:09:35.121 INFO - Preparing Firefox profile...
18:09:42.270 INFO - Launching Firefox...
18:09:50.320 INFO - Got result: OK,d3487eceddeb47eb93344c36ab711f50 on session d3487eceddeb47eb93344c36ab711f50
cmd=open&1=http://www.ge.com
18:12:19.856 INFO - ---> Requesting http://localhost:4444/selenium-server/driver?cmd=open&1=http://www.ge.com&sessionId=d3487eceddeb47eb93344c36ab711f50
18:12:19.874 INFO - Command request: open[http://www.ge.com,] on session d3487eceddeb47eb93344c36ab711f50
18:12:28.291 INFO - Got result: OK on session d3487eceddeb47eb93344c36ab711f50
cmd=type&1=textToSearch&2=energy efficient
18:12:56.791 INFO - ---> Requesting http://localhost:4444/selenium-server/driver?cmd=type&1=textToSearch&2=energy efficient&sessionId=d3487eceddeb47eb93344c36ab711f50
18:12:56.802 INFO - Command request: type[textToSearch, energy efficient] on session d3487eceddeb47eb93344c36ab711f50
18:12:56.841 INFO - Got result: OK on session d3487eceddeb47eb93344c36ab711f50
cmd=clickAndWait&1=searchSubmit
18:13:17.834 INFO - ---> Requesting http://localhost:4444/selenium-server/driver?cmd=clickAndWait&1=searchSubmit&sessionId=d3487eceddeb47eb93344c36ab711f50
18:13:17.844 INFO - Command request: clickAndWait[searchSubmit,] on session d3487eceddeb47eb93344c36ab711f50
18:13:26.757 INFO - Got result: OK on session d3487eceddeb47eb93344c36ab711f50
cmd=assertTitle&1=exact:GE: Search Results
18:13:39.440 INFO - ---> Requesting http://localhost:4444/selenium-server/driver?cmd=assertTitle&1=exact:GE: Search Results&sessionId=d3487eceddeb47eb93344c36ab711f50
18:13:39.449 INFO - Command request: assertTitle[exact:GE: Search Results,] on session d3487eceddeb47eb93344c36ab711f50
18:13:39.471 INFO - Got result: OK on session d3487eceddeb47eb93344c36ab711f50
cmd=assertTextPresent&1=energy efficient
18:14:02.171 INFO - ---> Requesting http://localhost:4444/selenium-server/driver?cmd=assertTextPresent&1=energy efficient&sessionId=d3487eceddeb47eb93344c36ab711f50
18:14:02.178 INFO - Command request: assertTextPresent[energy efficient,] on session d3487eceddeb47eb93344c36ab711f50
18:14:02.208 INFO - Got result: OK on session d3487eceddeb47eb93344c36ab711f50

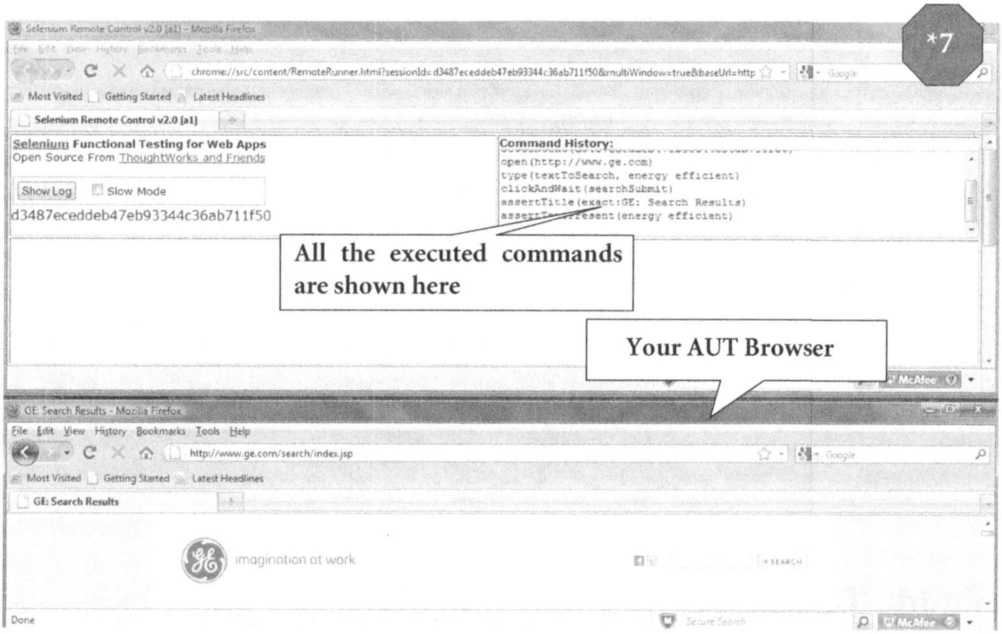

Execute the next two lines one by one in interactive mode (*8)

cmd=close

// Closes the AUT browser

cmd=testComplete

// Stops the current Session and Closes Selenium Command Browser

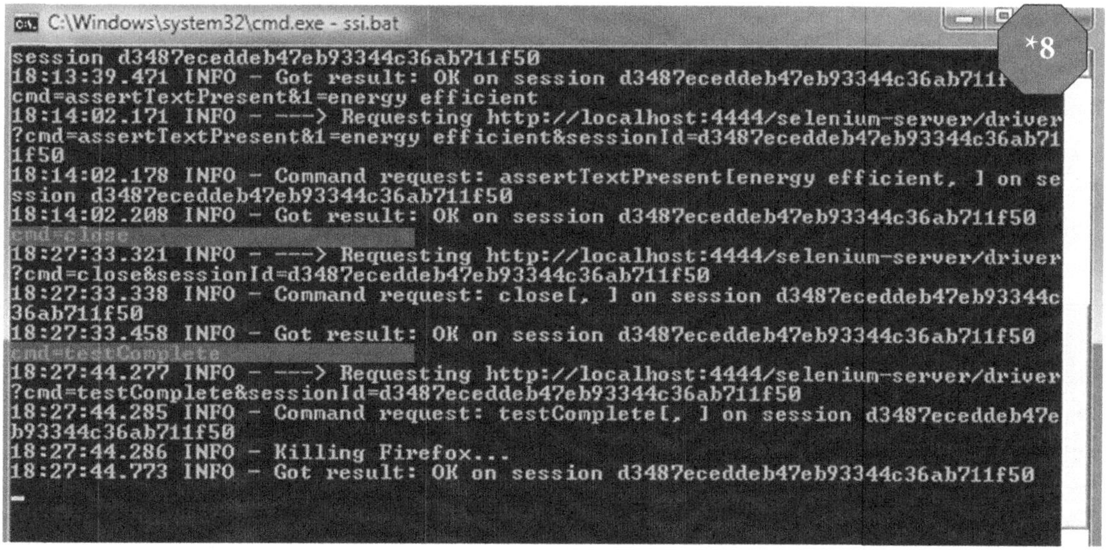

Finally Type Exit to quit from Interactive mode (*9)

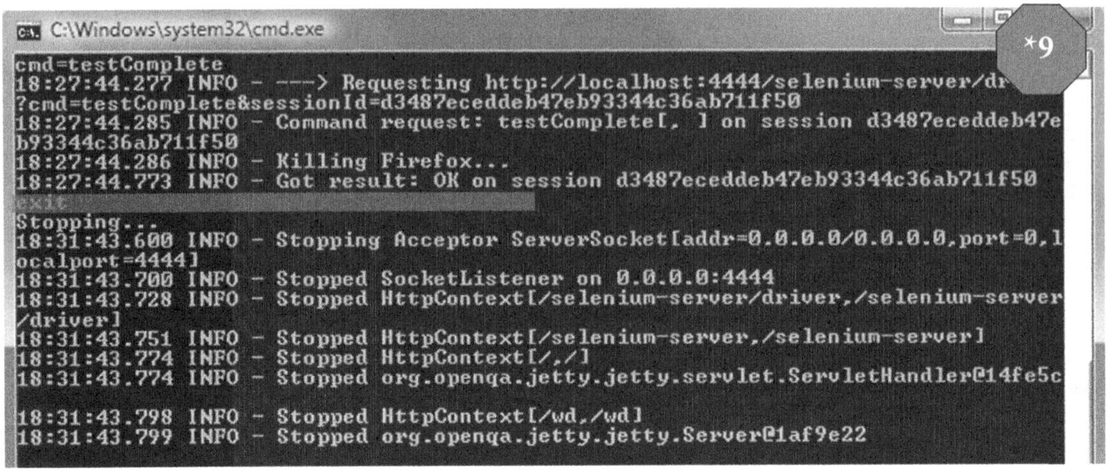

Posting Ide Test Suite Results Using Selenium-Rc

You must have noticed that Selenium IDE does not give any consolidated output reports. The only out that we see is in the form of IDE Logs and Color coding of the commands (Light Green, Dark Green and Red). We can run Selenium-RC in htmlSuite mode to post results as an HTML file. This can work as an acceptable reports that consolidates the actual run time logs, commands snapshots and summary of the Test Suite. The tests need to be run as Test Suite in this mode.

It is actually a command line run options for RC, however as we have eight parameters to pass to the commands line, we can simplify it by using the batch file. Please follow the steps below:

1. Open notepad/wordpad
2. Cut and Paste the below code.
3. Save the batch file with name "GE_TC1.bat"
4. Please ensure that the GE_TS1.html file is stored in C:\EX\GE\GE_TS1.html folder. Download the GE_TS1.html file from the QAAgility site if not created earlier.
5. Please ensure that the following folder exists: C:\EX\GE\FF

```
@echo off
java -jar C:\selenium-rc\selenium-server.jar -htmlSuite "*firefox"
"http://www.ge.com" "C:\Ex\GE\GE_TS1.html"
"C:\Ex\GE\FF\GE_TS1_Result.html"
pause
```

Param 1,2,3 - For launching RC

Param 4 - RC Mode

Param 5 - Browser

Param 6 - Base URL of Test Suite

Param 7 - Test Suite file with full path

Param 8 - Name of the Report html file

Please check:

- ➢ Before running bat file, run Test Suite manually to ensure that it runs and also check the file paths.
- ➢ Also ensure that the folder name used do not have any spaces in them, at times bat files can have issue with that.
- ➢ Please make sure that you have write access to the folder mentioned in param 8.

Now Double click on the GE_TS1.bat file

Command window open and run the test suite (*1)

After completing the test, double click on the "GE_TS1_Result.html" (*2)

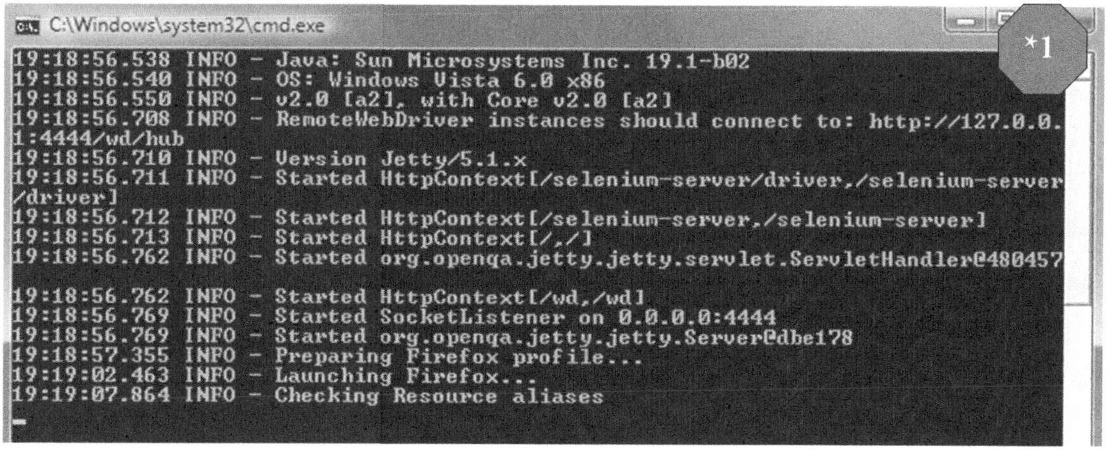

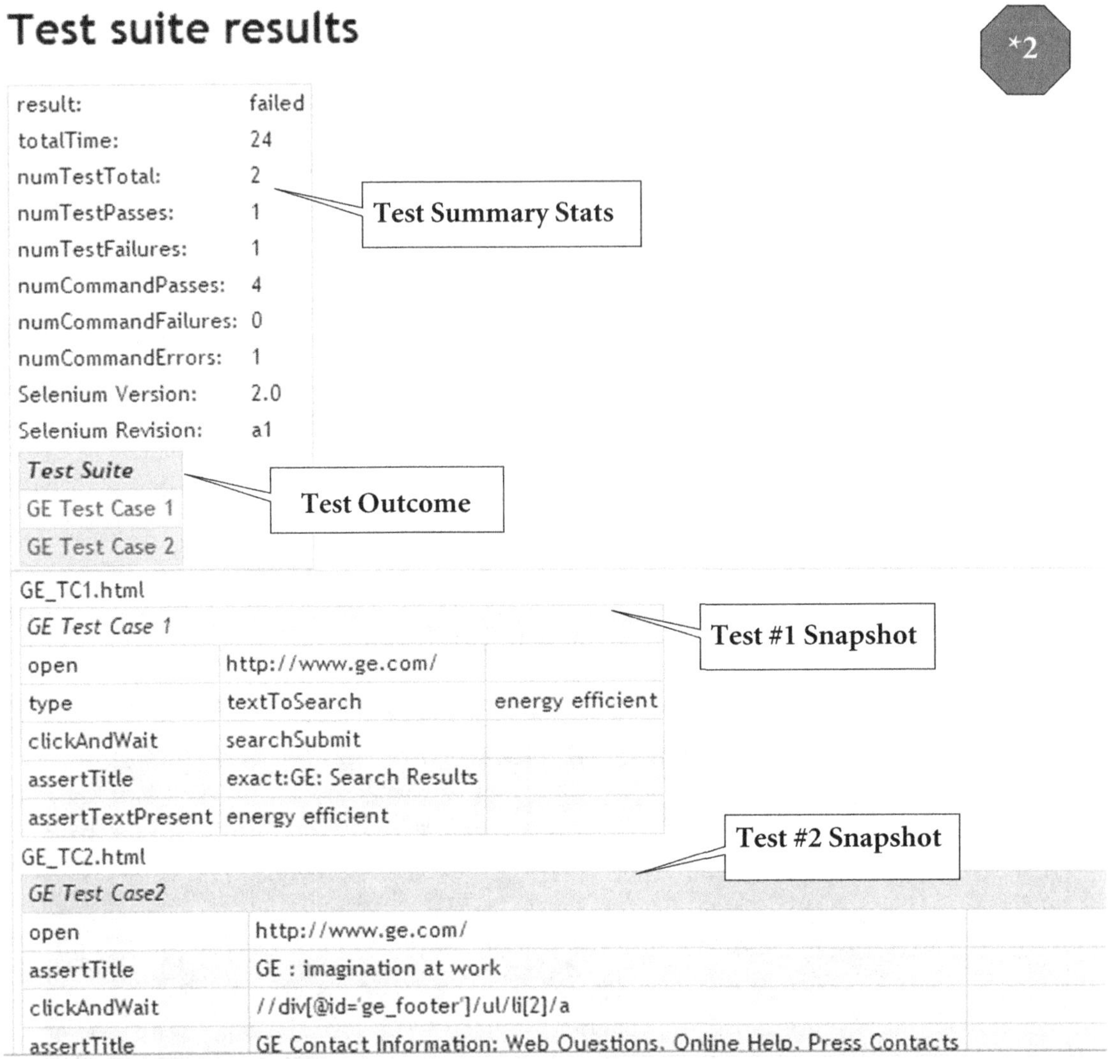

Test suite results

result:	failed
totalTime:	24
numTestTotal:	2
numTestPasses:	1
numTestFailures:	1
numCommandPasses:	4
numCommandFailures:	0
numCommandErrors:	1
Selenium Version:	2.0
Selenium Revision:	a1

Test Suite
GE Test Case 1
GE Test Case 2

GE_TC1.html

GE Test Case 1		
open	http://www.ge.com/	
type	textToSearch	energy efficient
clickAndWait	searchSubmit	
assertTitle	exact:GE: Search Results	
assertTextPresent	energy efficient	

GE_TC2.html

GE Test Case2		
open	http://www.ge.com/	
assertTitle	GE : imagination at work	
clickAndWait	//div[@id='ge_footer']/ul/li[2]/a	
assertTitle	GE Contact Information: Web Questions, Online Help, Press Contacts	

Test Log Snapshot

```
info: Starting test /selenium-server/tests/GE_TC1.html
info: Executing: |open | http://www.ge.com/ |  |
info: onXhrStateChange(): xhr.readyState = 1 method = HEAD time = 1304253012071
info: onXhrStateChange(): xhr.readyState = 1 method = HEAD time = 1304253012071
info: onXhrStateChange(): xhr.readyState = 2 method = HEAD time = 1304253013168
info: onXhrStateChange(): xhr.readyState = 4 method = HEAD time = 1304253013168
info: Executing: |type | textToSearch | energy efficient |
info: Executing: |clickAndWait | searchSubmit |  |
info: Executing: |assertTitle | exact:GE: Search Results |  |
info: Executing: |assertTextPresent | energy efficient |  |
info: Starting test /selenium-server/tests/GE_TC2.html
info: Executing: |open | http://www.ge.com/ |  |
info: onXhrStateChange(): xhr.readyState = 1 method = HEAD time = 1304253027017
info: onXhrStateChange(): xhr.readyState = 1 method = HEAD time = 1304253027018
info: onXhrStateChange(): xhr.readyState = 2 method = HEAD time = 1304253027029
info: onXhrStateChange(): xhr.readyState = 3 method = HEAD time = 1304253027029
info: onXhrStateChange(): xhr.readyState = 4 method = HEAD time = 1304253027029
info: Executing: |assertTitle | GE : imagination at work |  |
info: Executing: |clickAndWait | //div[@id='ge_footer']/ul/li[2]/a |  |
info: Executing: |assertTitle | GE Contact Information: Web Questions, Online Help, Press Contacts |  |
info: Executing: |clickAndWait | link=Feedback and Inquiries |  |
info: Executing: |assertTitle | Feedback & Inquiries : Contact Information : GE |  |
error: Actual value '' did not match 'Feedback & Inquiries : Contact Information : GE'
warn: currentTest.recordFailure: Actual value '' did not match 'Feedback & Inquiries : Contact Information : GE'
```

In order to run the Test in another browser, you need to change the param 5. This is also the only way to make your IDE tests run in various browsers.

EXERCISES

1. How can you run your IDE scripts in browsers other than Firefox?
2. What browsers are supported by Selenium RC?
3. What is interactive mode in RC?
4. How can I avoid launching RC from long command line control?
5. Can I have multiple versions of RC installed on one machine?

16

THE ECLIPSE IDE

Install Eclipse

Eclipse requires an installed Java Runtime. I recommended to use Java 6 (also known as Java 1.6).

Download "Eclipse IDE for Java Developers" from the website Eclipse Downloads http://www.eclipse.org/downloads/ and unpack it to a directory.

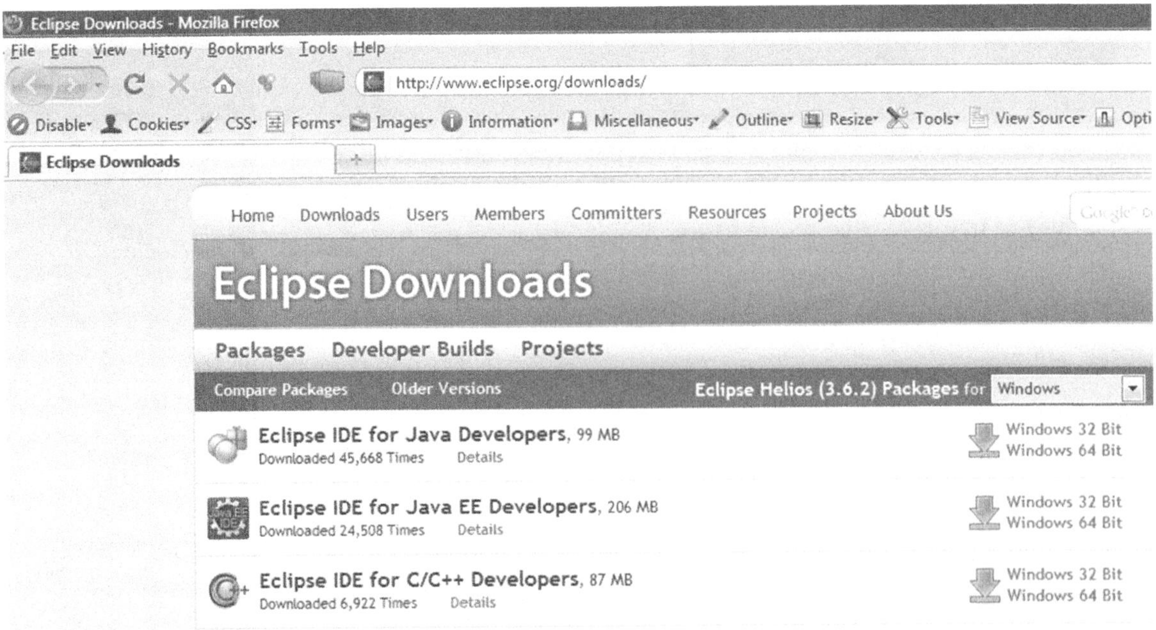

Use a directory path that does not contain spaces in its name as Eclipse sometimes have problems with that. After unpacking the download Eclipse is ready to be used; no additional installation procedure is required.

Run Eclipse

To start Eclipse double-click on the file "eclipse.exe" (Microsoft Windows) or eclipse (Linux / Mac) in the directory you unpacked Eclipse. The system will prompt you for a workspace. The workspace is the place there you store your Java projects (more on workspaces later). Create a directory under C: drive (or where you want to save all your work) as C:\ 1SeleniumWorkspace (you can give any name as you want). Select this directory when you launch eclipse and press Ok.

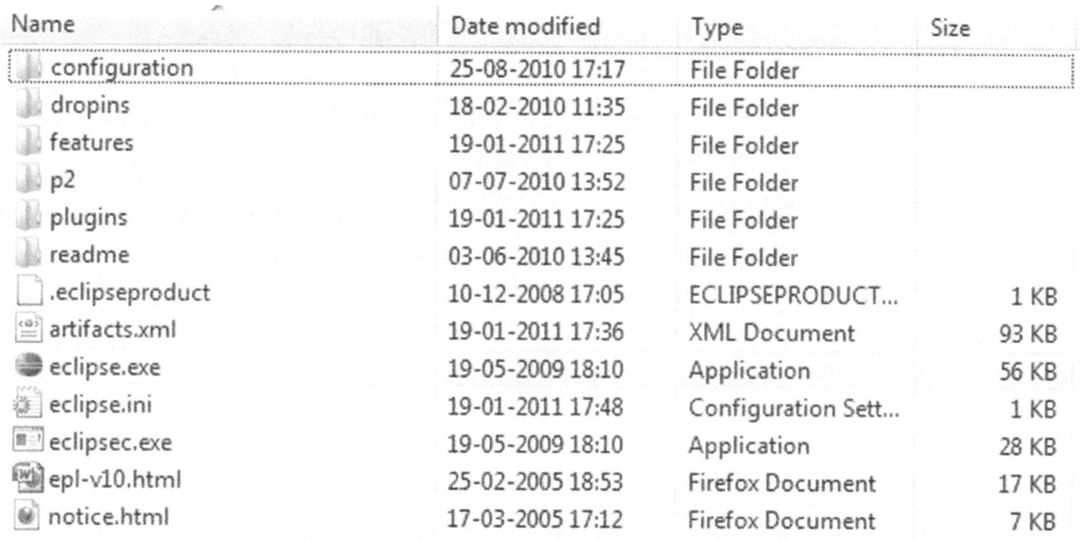

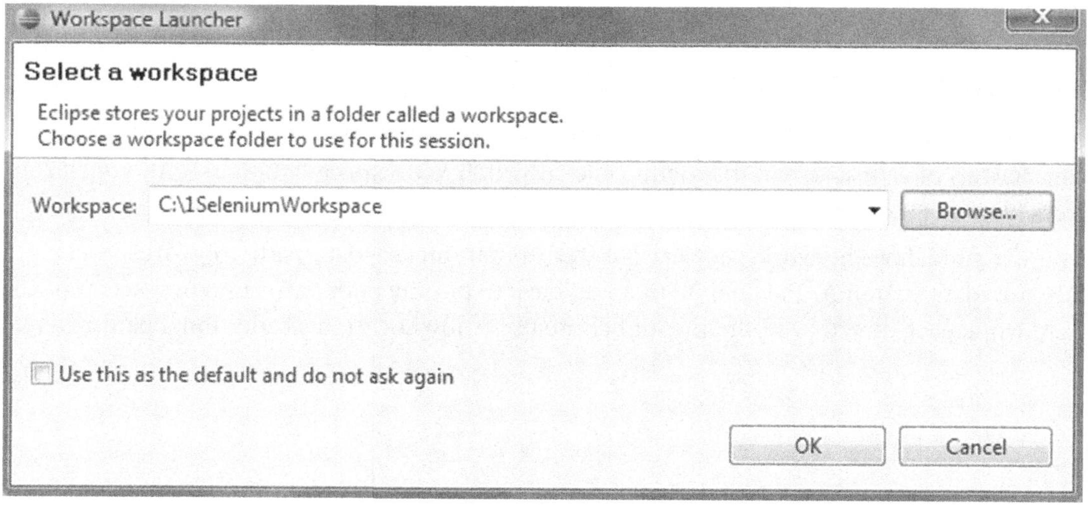

Eclipse will start and show the Welcome page. Close the welcome page by press the "X" besides the "Welcome".

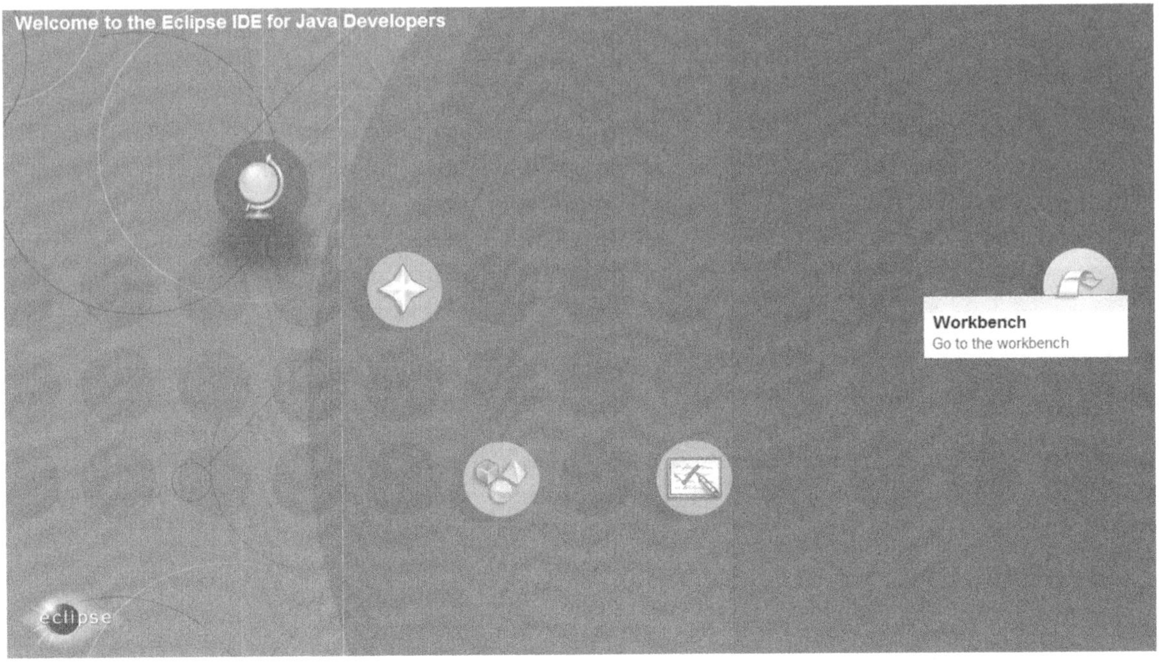

Eclispe Ui Overview

Eclipse provides perspectives, views and editors. Views and editors are grouped into perspectives. All projects are located in a workspace.

Workspace

The workspace is the physical location (file path) you are working in. You can choose the workspace during startup of eclipse or via the menu (File-> Switch Workspace-> Others). All your projects, sources files, images and other artefacts will be stored and saved in your workspace.

You can predefine the workspace via the startup parameter -data path_to_workspace, e.g. "c:\eclipse.exe -data "c:\temp" Please note that you have to put the path name into brackets. To see the current workspace directory in the title of Eclipse use -showLocation as additional parameter.

Perspective

A perspective is a visual container for a set of views and editors. You can change the layout within a perspective (close / open views, editors, change the size, change the position, etc.). Eclipse allows you to switch to another perspective via the menu Window → Open Perspective → Other. For Java development you usually use the "Java Perspective".

Tip

A common problem is that you closed a view and don't know how to re-open this view. You can reset a perpective it to it original state via the menu "Window" -> "Reset Perspective".

Views and Editors

A view is typically used to navigate a hierarchy of information or to open an editor. Changes in a view are directly applied to the underlying data structure. Editors are used to modify elements. Editors can have code completion, undo / redo, etc. To apply the changes in an editor to the underlying resources, e.g. Java source file, you usually have to save.

Create a New Java Project

When you enter the Eclispe IDE after selecting the appropriate workspace (C:\1SeleniumWorkspace), the package explorer window would be blank. Right click on the view and select Java Project

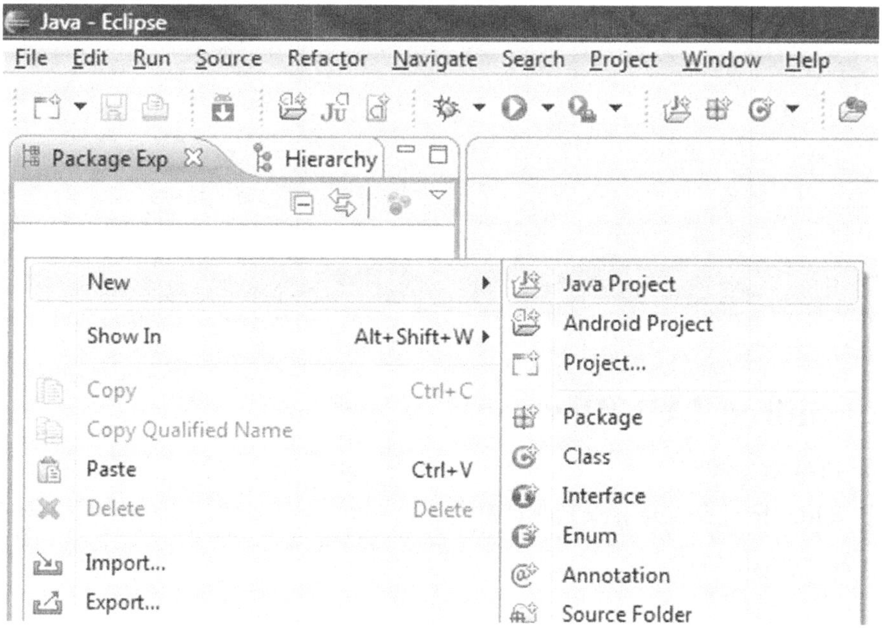

Enter the project name as "SeleniumTestProject"

Click on Next button (*1)

Click on Finish button as the last step to create Java Project.

The project is created and visible in the Package Explorer window. (*2)

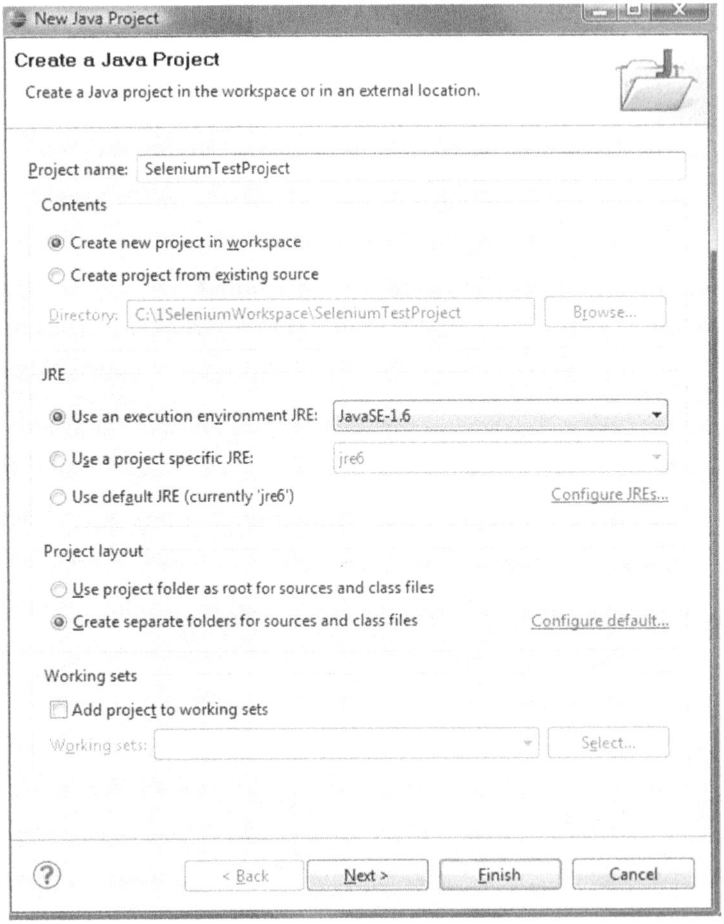

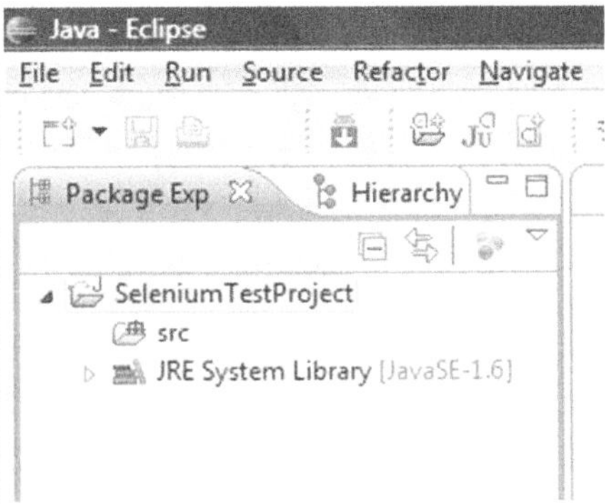

Add the required JAR files

Right click on Project and

Create 'lib' folder for keeping JAR files (*3)

'lib' folder is created (*4)

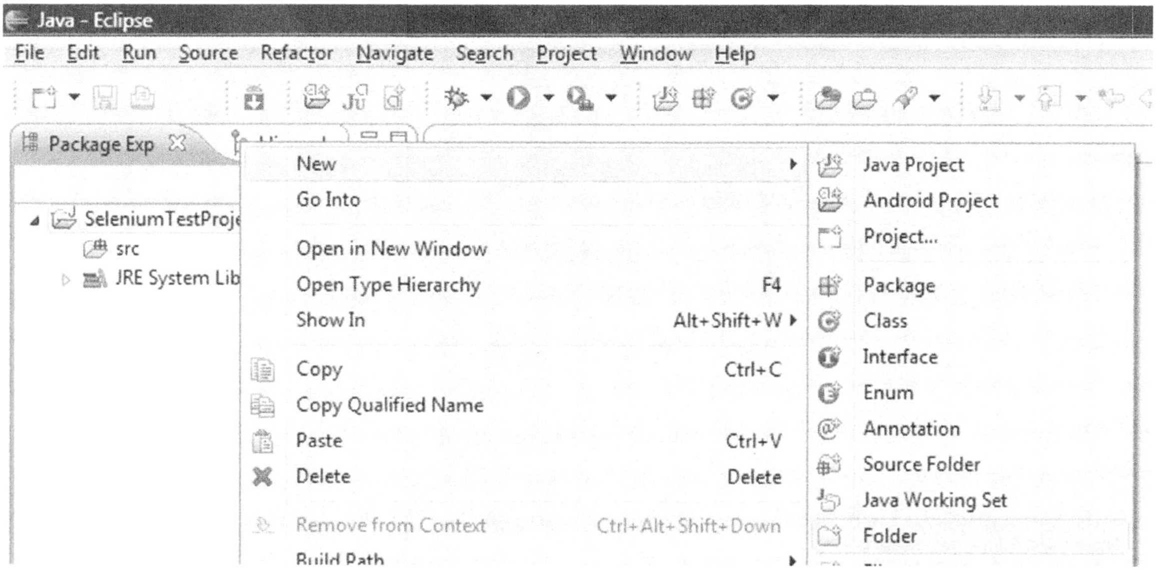
Java - Eclipse
File Edit Run Source Refactor Navigate Search Project Window Help
Package Exp
SeleniumTestProj
src
JRE System Lib
New
Go Into
Open in New Window
Open Type Hierarchy F4
Show In Alt+Shift+W
Copy Ctrl+C
Copy Qualified Name
Paste Ctrl+V
Delete Delete
Remove from Context Ctrl+Alt+Shift+Down
Java Project
Android Project
Project...
Package
Class
Interface
Enum
Annotation
Source Folder
Java Working Set
Folder

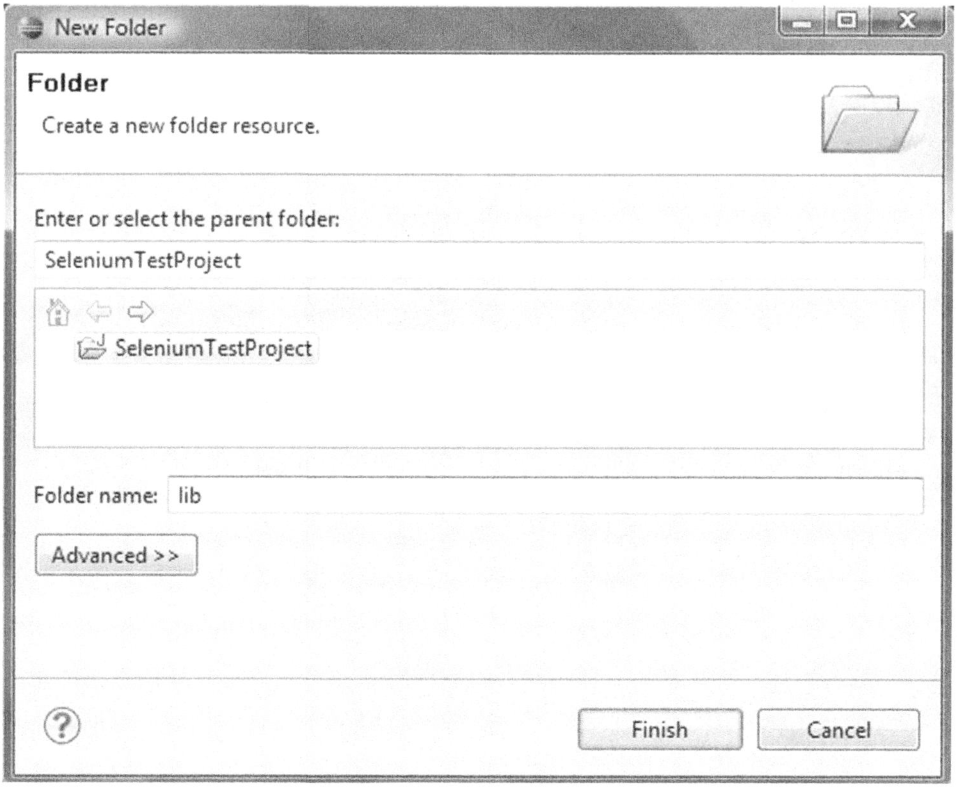
New Folder
Folder
Create a new folder resource.
Enter or select the parent folder:
SeleniumTestProject
SeleniumTestProject
Folder name: lib
Advanced >>
Finish
Cancel

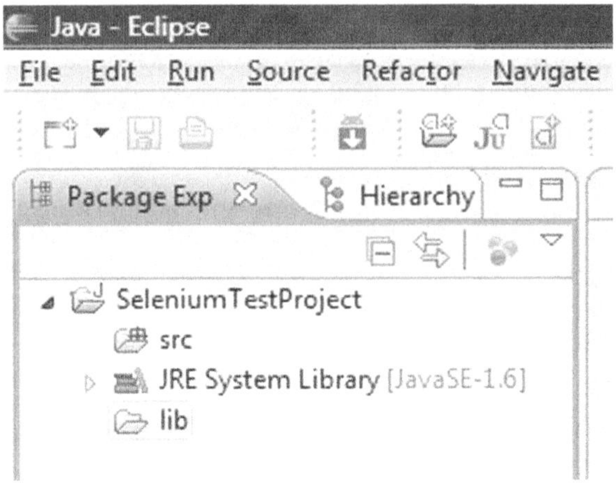

Add the required JAR files to the newly created 'lib' folder. We would need the following JARS:

➢ selenium-server.jar (to be found in folder C:\SeleniumRC1.0.1\selenium-rc\JavaServer if you have renamed the folders as mentioned in Chapter XX)

➢ selenium-java-client-drive.jar (to be found in folder C:\SeleniumRC1.0.1\selenium-rc\JavaClient if you have renamed the folders as mentioned in Chapter XX)

You can simply open the File Explorer and drag and drop the JAR files to the lib folder:

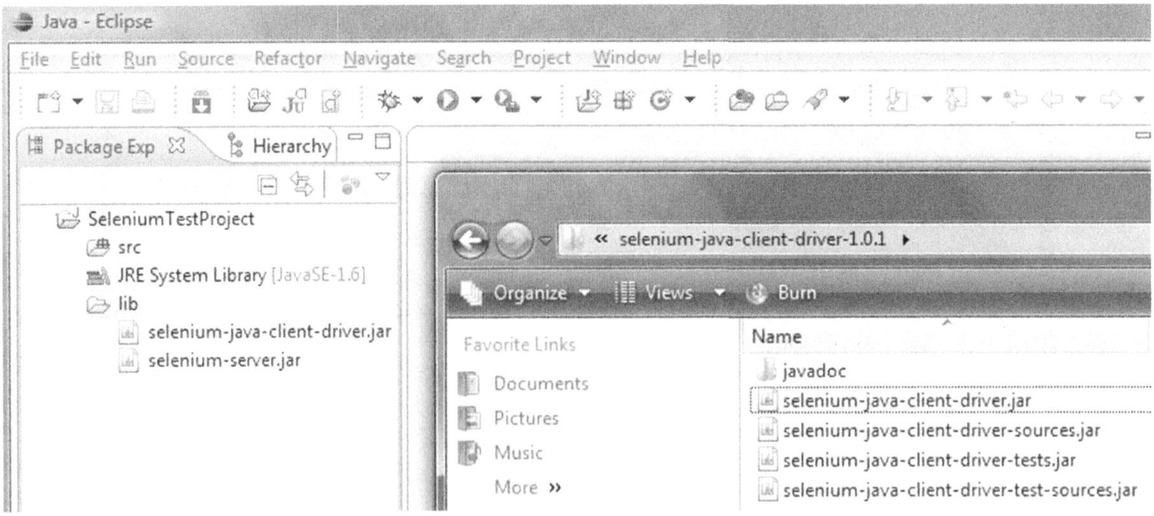

Add JARs to the build-path of the Project

1. Right click Project and Click Properties option
2. Select Java Build Path option and Libraries tab

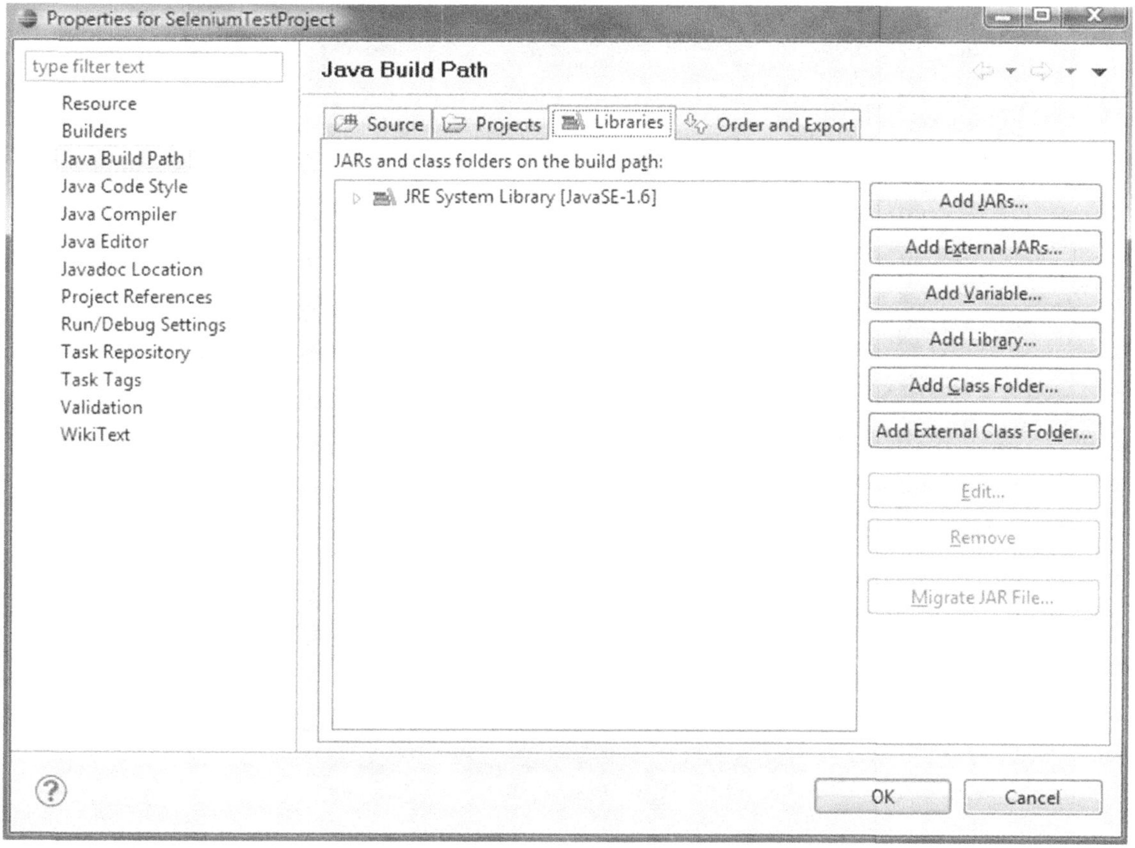

Click "Add JARs.." button and select all the JAR files under 'lib' folder and click OK (*7)

This will add JAR files to the Project classpath (*8)

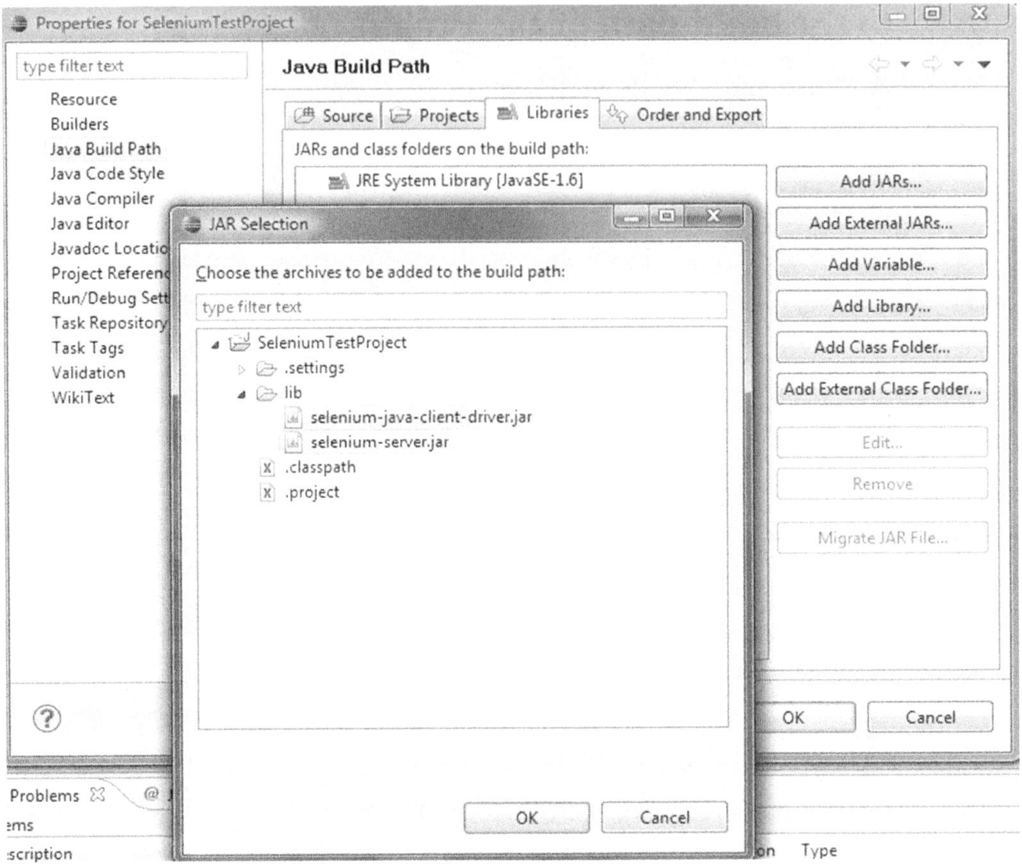
Properties for SeleniumTestProject
type filter text
Resource
Builders
Java Build Path
Java Code Style
Java Compiler
Java Editor
Java Build Path
Source
Projects
Libraries
Order and Export
JARs and class folders on the build path:
JRE System Library [JavaSE-1.6]
Add JARs...
Add External JARs...
Add Variable...
Add Library...
Add Class Folder...
Add External Class Folder...
Edit...
Remove
Migrate JAR File...
JAR Selection
Choose the archives to be added to the build path:
type filter text
SeleniumTestProject
.settings
lib
selenium-java-client-driver.jar
selenium-server.jar
.classpath
.project
OK
Cancel
Problems
Type

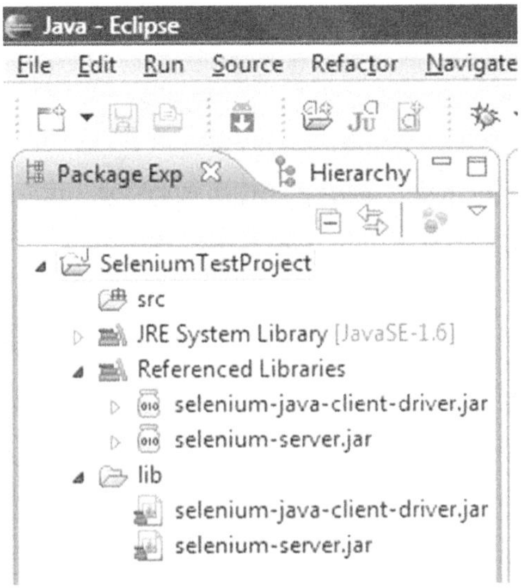
Java - Eclipse
File Edit Run Source Refactor Navigate
Package Exp
Hierarchy
SeleniumTestProject
src
JRE System Library [JavaSE-1.6]
Referenced Libraries
selenium-java-client-driver.jar
selenium-server.jar
lib
selenium-java-client-driver.jar
selenium-server.jar

Create folder for Source files

Create folder in project where we will keep all the Test Scripts and Data

Right Click on project, select New – Source Folder, give name as "test", click Finish.

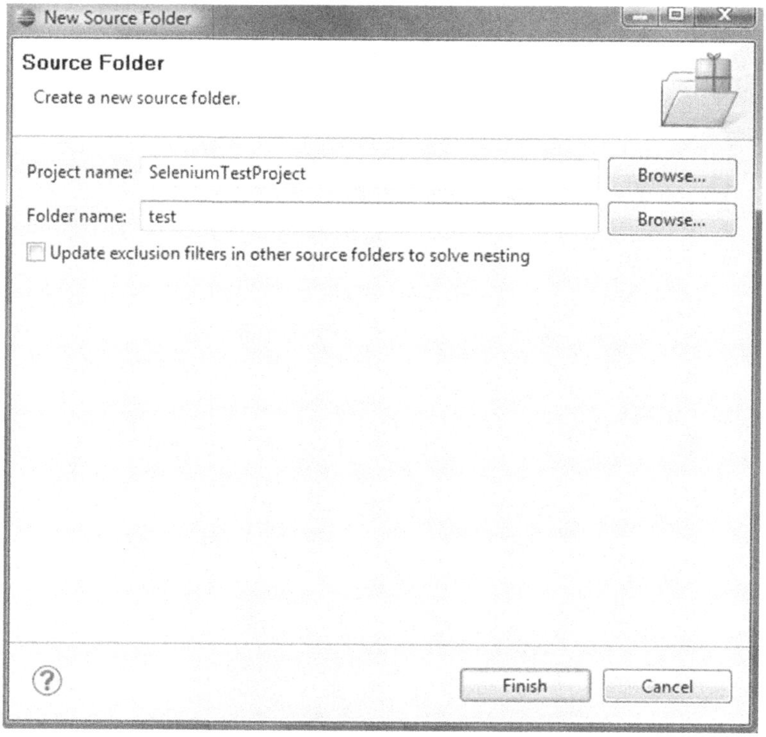

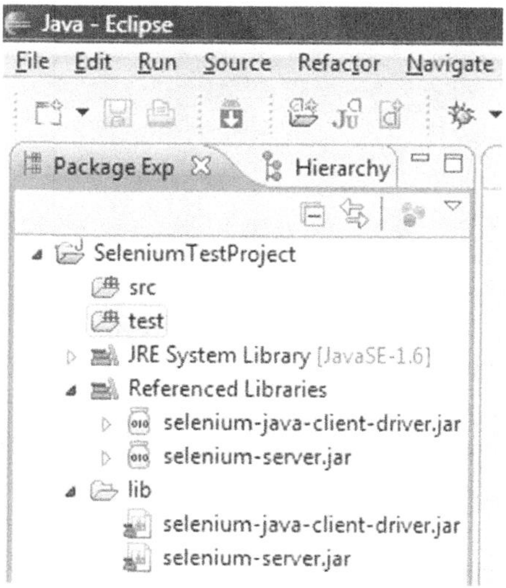

Create folder for scripts

Create a Package within the source folder. Right click on 'test' select New – Package option, name as 'script'. Click on Finish.

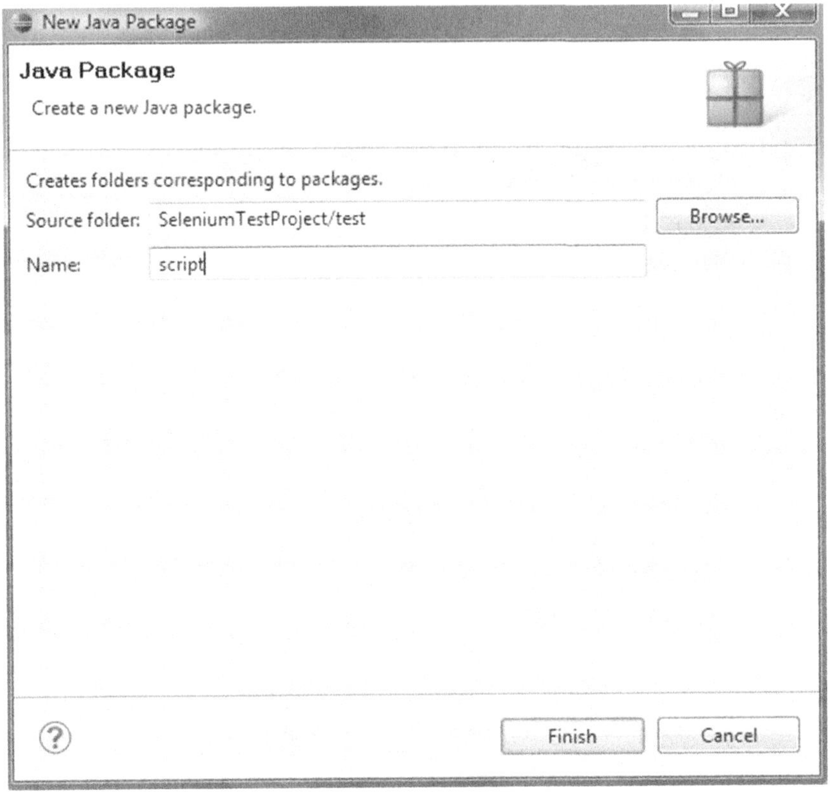

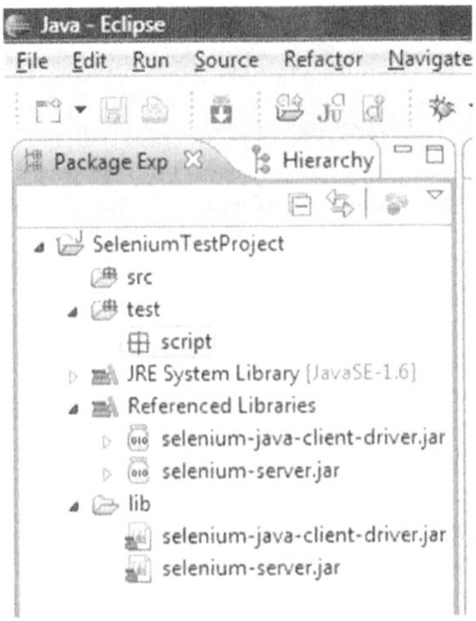

Create Folder for data files

Create folder under the 'test' where we will keep the data files, name as 'data'.

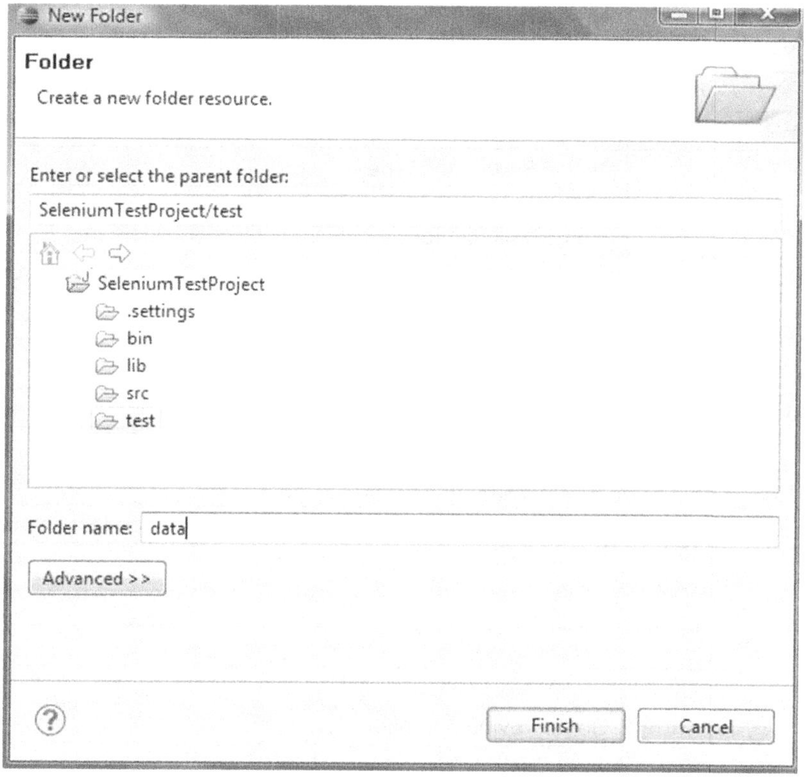

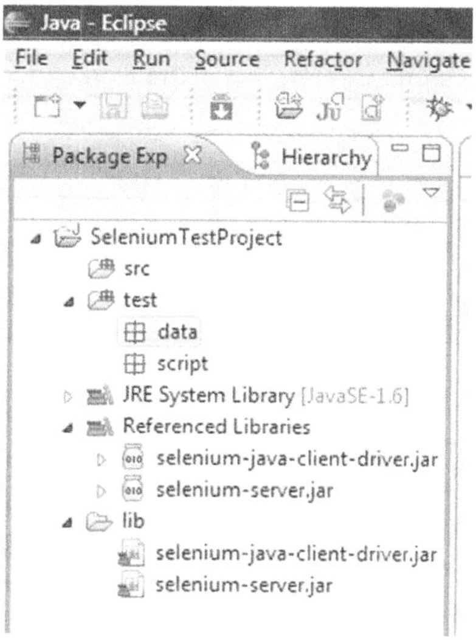

Eclipse Shortcuts

Table 1. Navigation

Shortcut	*Description*
CTRL + SHIFT + R	Open / Search for resources, e.g. files
CTRL + SHIFT + T	Open / Search for Types
CTRL + T	Used on a method or class shows the whole inheritance tree, for example all methods which implement an interface.
STRG + O	In place outline view (displayed in editor), allows to search directly for elements in the selected file via type-ahead
ALT + LEFT ARROW KEY or ALT + RIGHT ARROW KEY	Go to prev/ next editor position in history
Ctrl-PageUp/PageDown	Previous/next tab
F3	Go to declaration of this variable
CTRL + SHIFT + P	Go to matching bracket
CTRL + Q	Go to editor area and position the cursor at the last changed position

Table 2. Search

Shortcut	*Description*
Ctrl + .	Go to next problem
Ctrl + ,	Go to previous problem
F3 on a variable	Goto Declaration of this variable
F4 on a variable	Show type hierarchy
Strg + J , Strg +k	Incremental search, find next
STRG + SHIFT + G	Search for reference in the workspace

Table 3. Run

Shortcut	*Description*
Ctrl F11	Run last launched
Alt + Shift + X - J	Run as Java application

Table 4. Handling the editor

Shortcut	*Description*
CTRL + 1	Quickfix, dependend on cursor position
F12	Focuses the editor (especially helpful if you working with Fast Views

(Contd.)

Table 4. *(Contd.)*

Ctrl + M	Maximize Java editor
CTRL + Shift + F	Format source code
CTRL + Shift + O	Organize the imports/Will import the missing imports.
CTRL + Shift + S	Source generation related operations such as creating getter/setter
CTRL + Q	Last edited position

Table 5. Arrow Keys

Shortcut	*Description*
CTRL + Left	Move one element to the left
CTRL + Right	Move one element to the right
CTRL + ALT + Up/Down	Copy line
ALT + Up / Down	Move line up / down
ALT + SHIFT Up / Down	Select the previous / next syntactical element
ALT + SHIFT Up / Down / Left / Right	Extending / Reducing the selection of the previous / next syntactical element
CTRL + Up / Down	Scroll up / down a line in the editor

Table 6. Delete

Shortcut	*Description*
Ctrl + D	Deletes line
STRG + SHIFT + DELE	Delete until end of line
Ctrl + DELE	Delete next element
Ctrl + BACKSPACE	Delete previous element

Table 7. Variable assignment

Shortcut	*Description*
Ctrl + 2 + L	Assign statement to new local variable
Ctrl + 2 + F	Assign statement to new field

Table 8. Coding

Shortcut	*Description*
Shift + F2	Call the Javadoc for the selected type / class / method
Alt+Shift + N + Letter	Type shortcut for the command, e.g. njc to create a new Java class or npip to create a new Plugin project.
Alt + Shift + Z	Surround block with try and catch

Table 9. Refactoring

Shortcut	*Description*
ALT- SHIFT +R	Rename
ALT- SHIFT +R	Quick refactoring menu
ALT- SHIFT + T	Opens the quick refactoring menu

Table 10. Debugging

Shortcut	*Description*
F11	Debug last run
Ctrl + Shift + B	Toggle breakpoint
F5	Single Step (Down)
F6	Single Step (Jump)
F7	Up

EXERCISES

1. What is the Eclipse platform?
2. What is a project in Eclipse?
3. How can I import a project into Eclipse?
4. What is a plug-in in Eclipse?
5. How does a java program compile in Eclipse/
6. Where can I find the class files?
7. What are the imported Jar files in the class path?

17

Running a Test Using the JUnit Export from Selenium-IDE

Introduction

In this section we are going to export the recorded script in IDE, which is in HTML format to JUnit, and then run it in Eclipse.

Export an IDE script as a JUnit test

Open the script that you want to run in RC in Selenium IDE first.

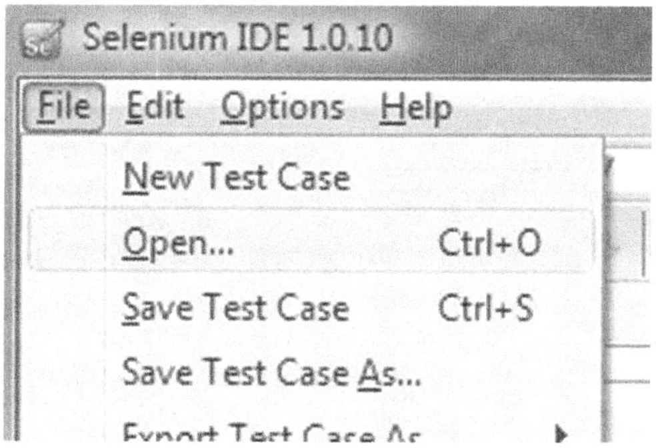

Select TC_GE_EE.html and it will be loaded as below.

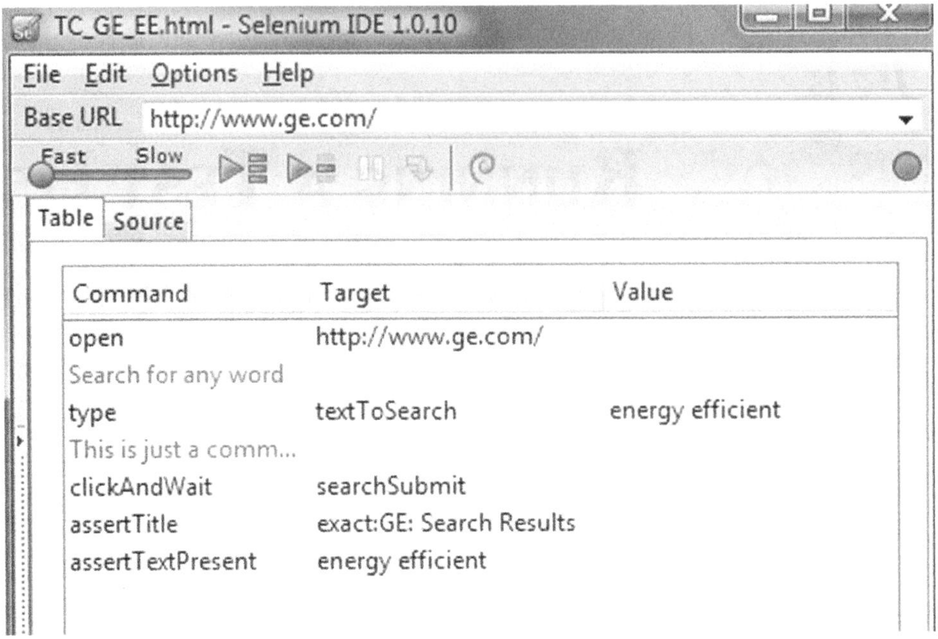

Change the format of the script to JUnit3.

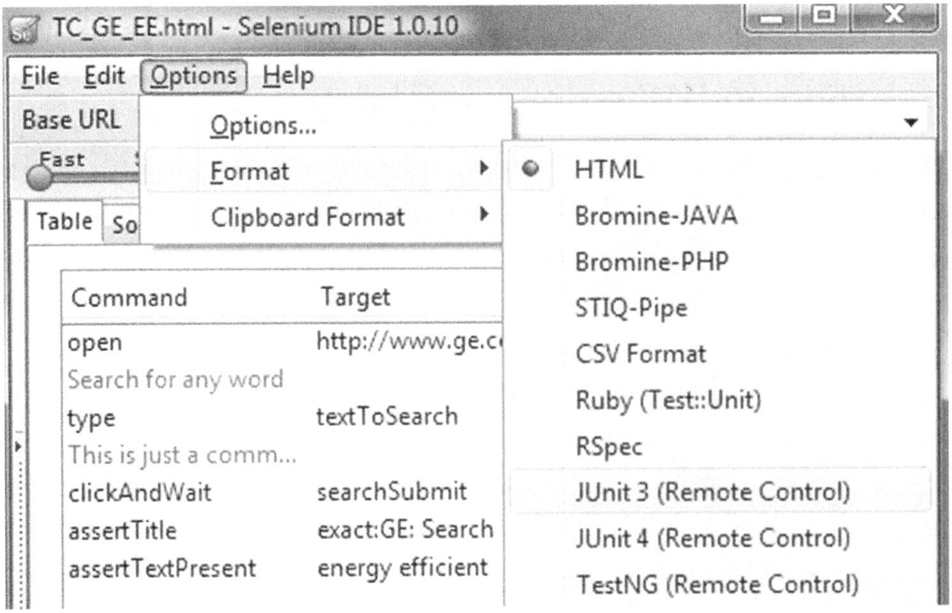

This is open the Source Tab with JUnit code as below.

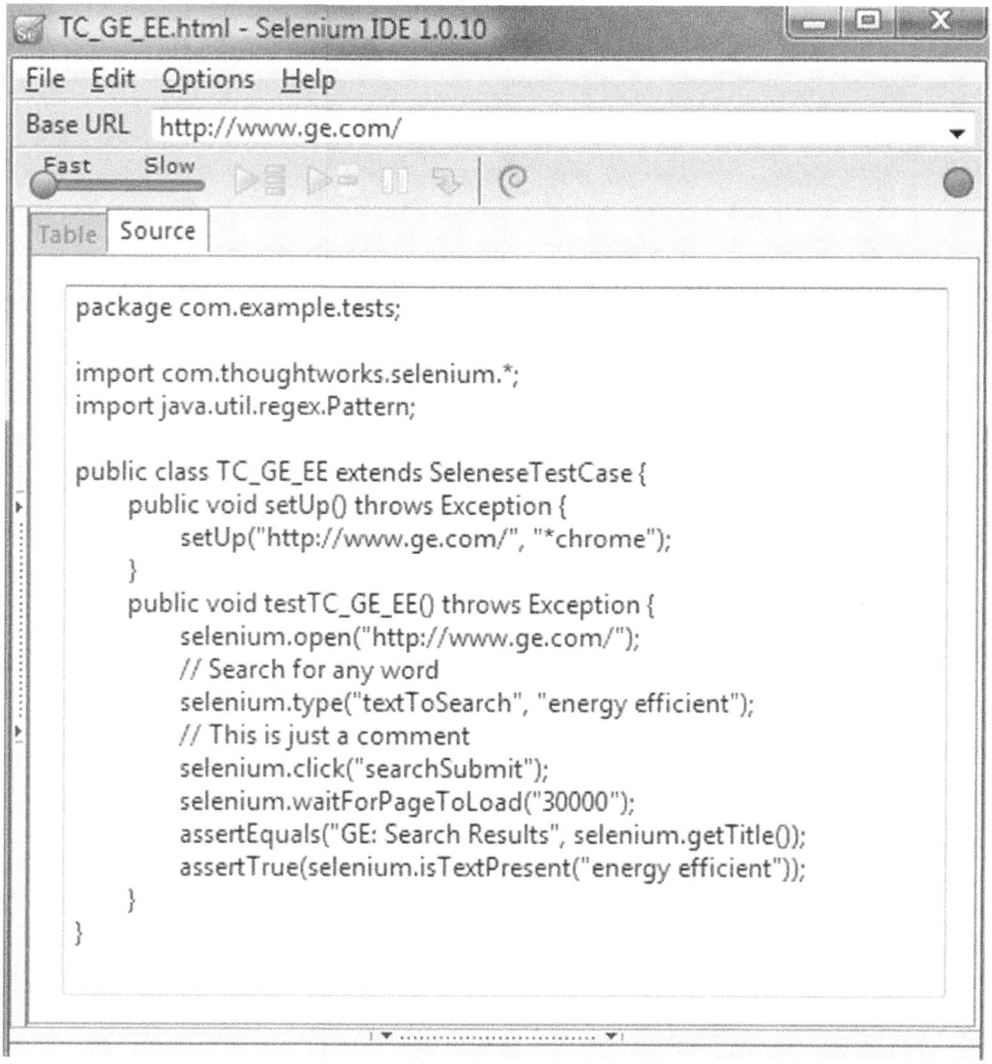

Copy this code and you can save it temporarily as we prepare Eclipse to run this JUnit code.

Create a New Class in Eclipse

All test code for Java needs to created as new class so we will create new class under the selected project. File → New → Class

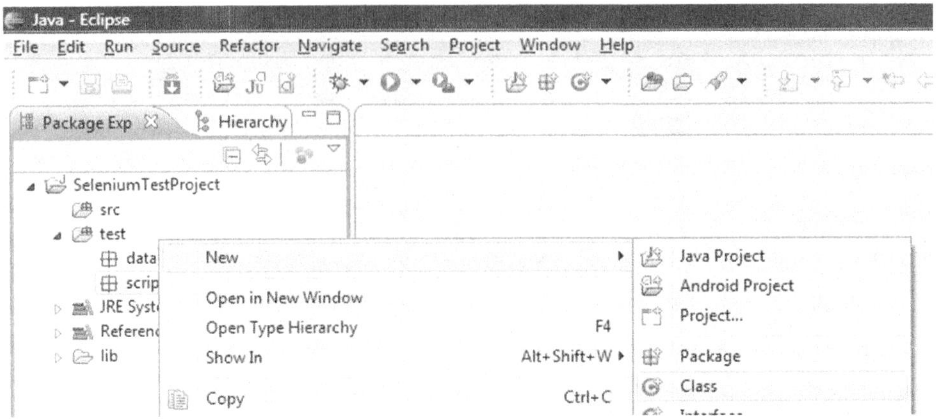

New Class wizard window will appear where provide the name of the Java class, we prefer to keep the name same as what we gave in IDE to avoid confusion later.

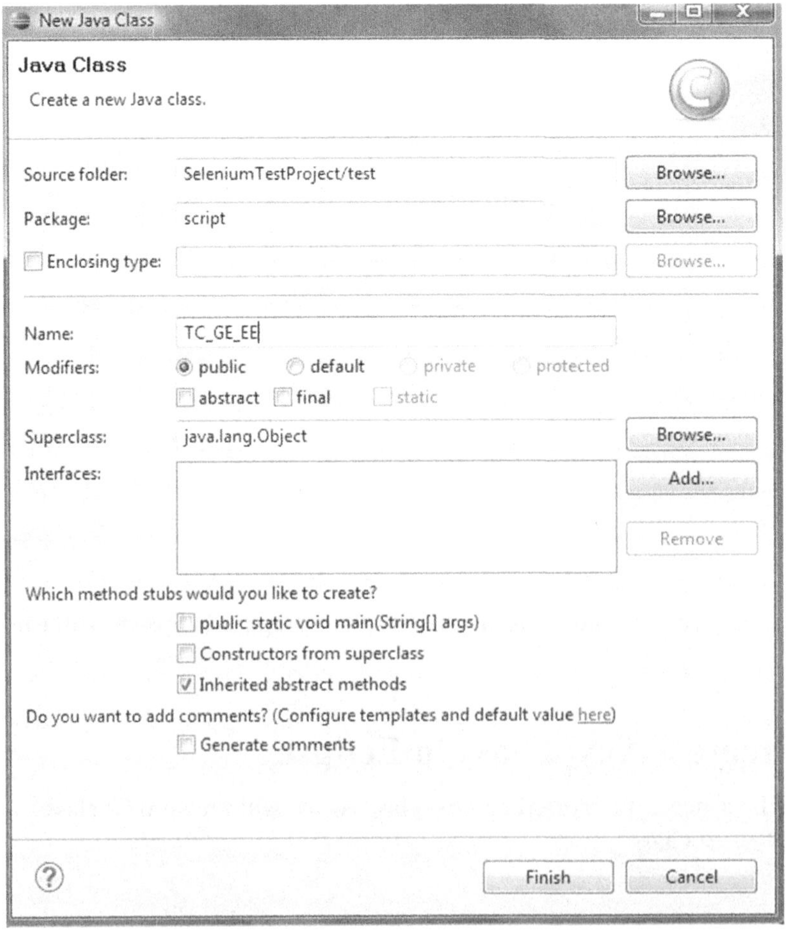

When you press Finish the following empty class will be created with default code as below:

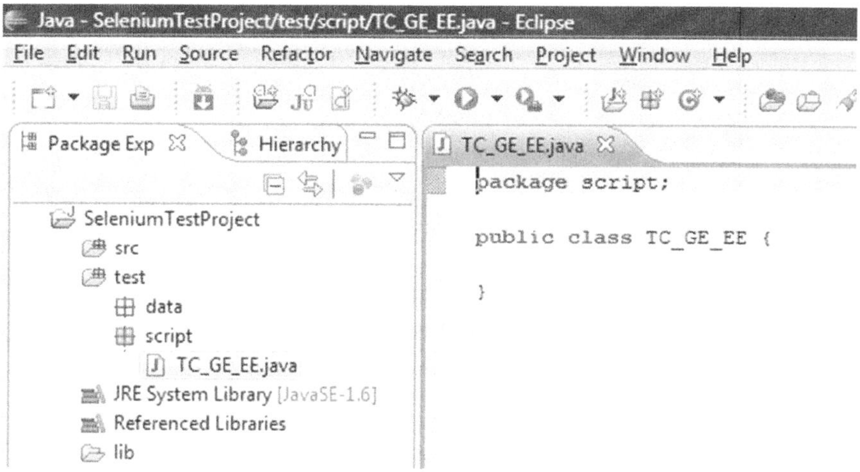

Now we need to add the code from Source tab of IDE to Eclipse.

Overwrite the default content of the Eclipse class file with the copied code from IDE.

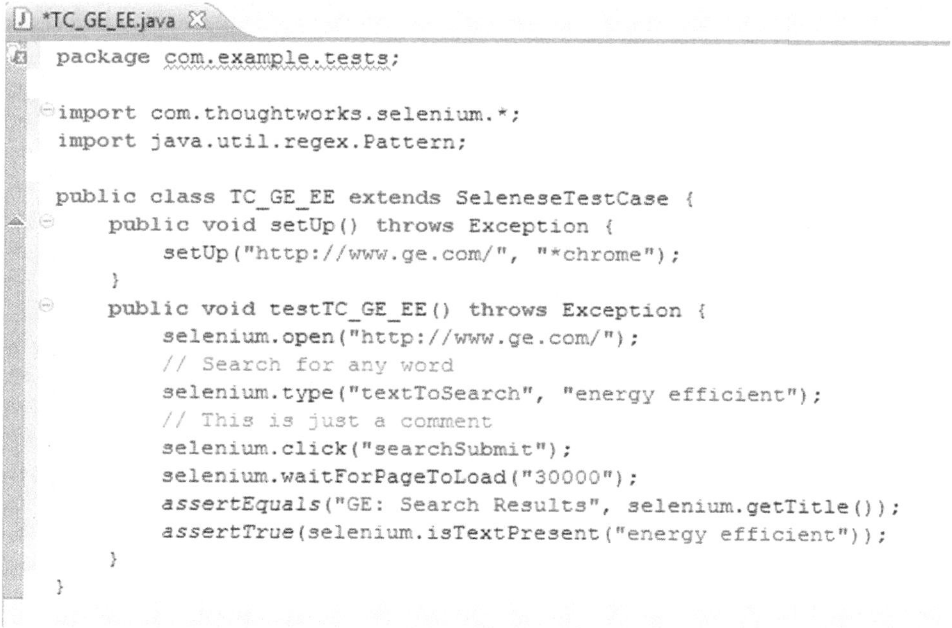

As you can see there is an error displayed in Eclipse with 'x' sign on red color, if you also see a bulb then it means that Eclipse has suggestion to fix it. Just hover your mouse on 'X' and you will see details of the error.

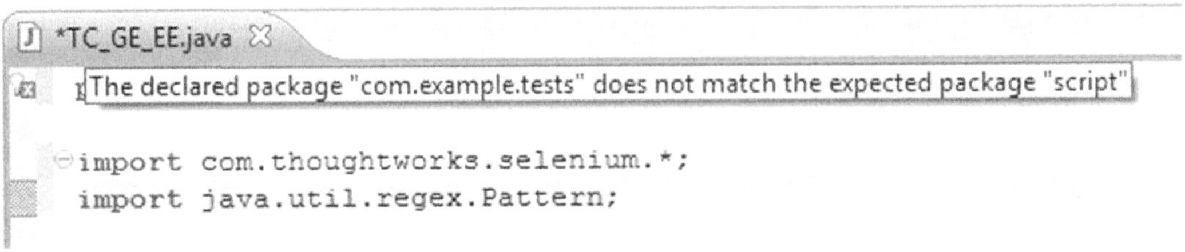

You can see the suggestion to fix the error by clicking on the 'x' sign

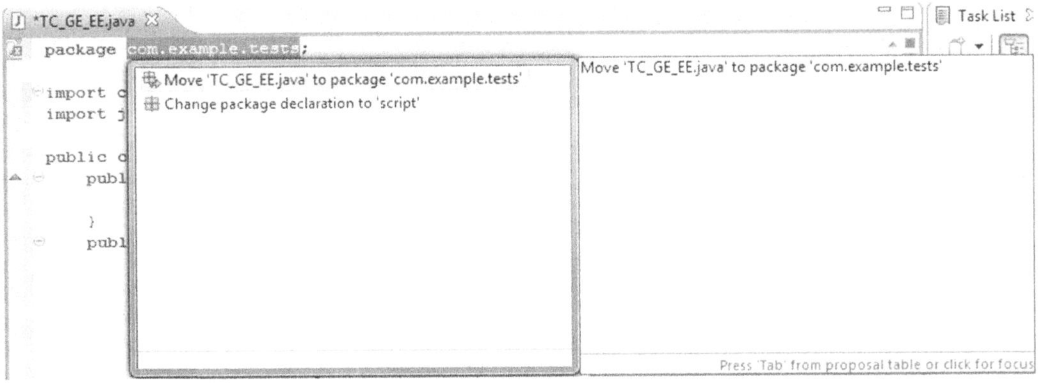

In this case we know that the package name should be 'script' so we select the second option and the script is updated accordingly.

TC_GE_EE.java

```
package script;

import com.thoughtworks.selenium.*;
import java.util.regex.Pattern;

public class TC_GE_EE extends SeleneseTestCase {
    public void setUp() throws Exception {
        setUp("http://www.ge.com/", "*chrome");
    }
    public void testTC_GE_EE() throws Exception {
        selenium.open("http://www.ge.com/");
        // Search for any word
        selenium.type("textToSearch", "energy efficient");
        // This is just a comment
        selenium.click("searchSubmit");
        selenium.waitForPageToLoad("30000");
        assertEquals("GE: Search Results", selenium.getTitle());
        assertTrue(selenium.isTextPresent("energy efficient"));
    }
}
```

Now we don't see any red 'x' however an '!' sign in yellow background is shown. These are warnings and hover your mouse on the '!' sign to see the details.

```
import com.thoughtworks.selenium.*;
The import java.util.regex.Pattern is never used
```

Click on the yellow '!' sign to see the suggestions from Eclipse

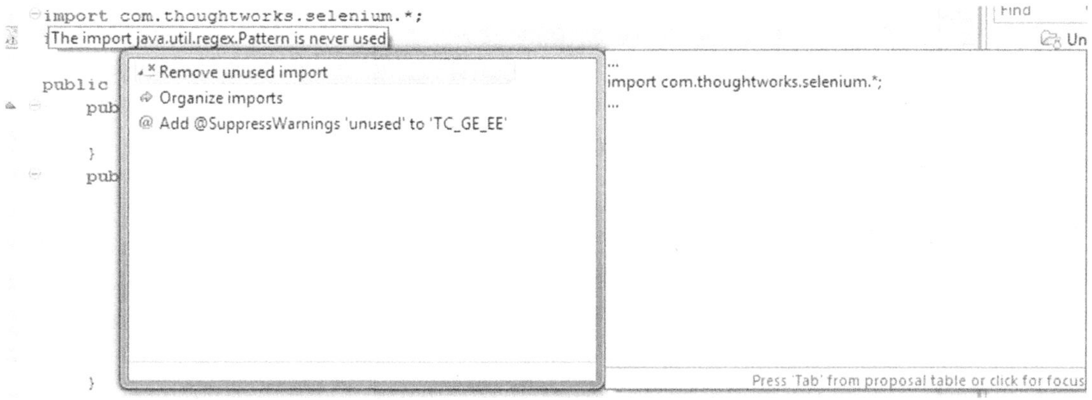

Depending upon what works best for you, you can select the fix for the warning. We suggest you select "Organise imports". The code will be fixed accordingly as below:

```
TC_GE_EE.java
package script;

import com.thoughtworks.selenium.SeleneseTestCase;

public class TC_GE_EE extends SeleneseTestCase {
    public void setUp() throws Exception {
        setUp("http://www.ge.com/", "*chrome");
    }
    public void testTC_GE_EE() throws Exception {
        selenium.open("http://www.ge.com/");
        // Search for any word
        selenium.type("textToSearch", "energy efficient");
        // This is just a comment
        selenium.click("searchSubmit");
        selenium.waitForPageToLoad("30000");
        assertEquals("GE: Search Results", selenium.getTitle());
        assertTrue(selenium.isTextPresent("energy efficient"));
    }
}
```

Now you can save your code by choosing Ctrl+S.

Run the JUnit test

Notice the elements of the class on the package explorer view:

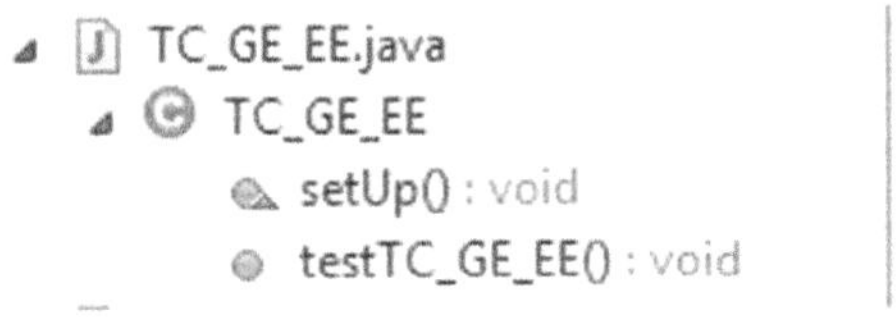

Right click on the file and select Run As → JUnit Test

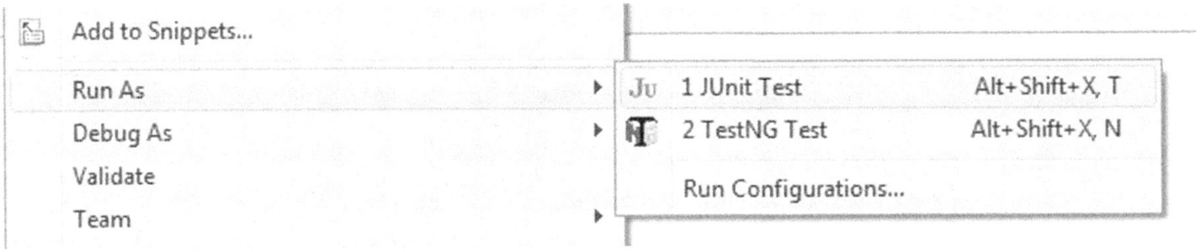

The test does not run and the results are displayed in the JUnit tab and highlighted in red color which indicates error:

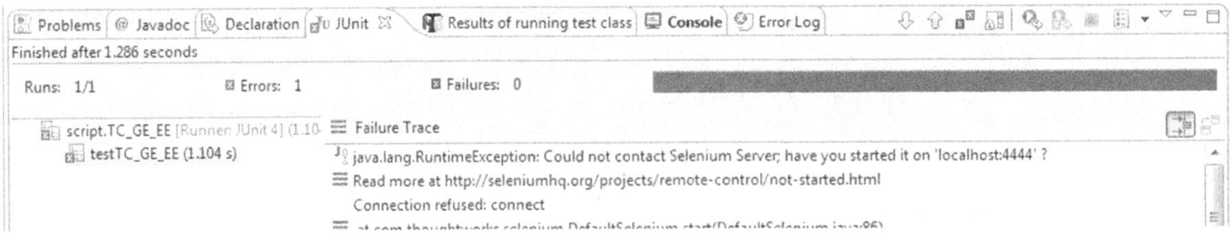

Please evaluate the error and see that the failure trace shows that java.lang.RuntimeException: Could not contact Selenium Server; have you started it on 'localhost:4444' ?

It means that the Selenium Server is not running. Let's start the server and run the test again. The test should launch the two Firefox windows – one for RC and other for AUT.

Seeing the Test Running

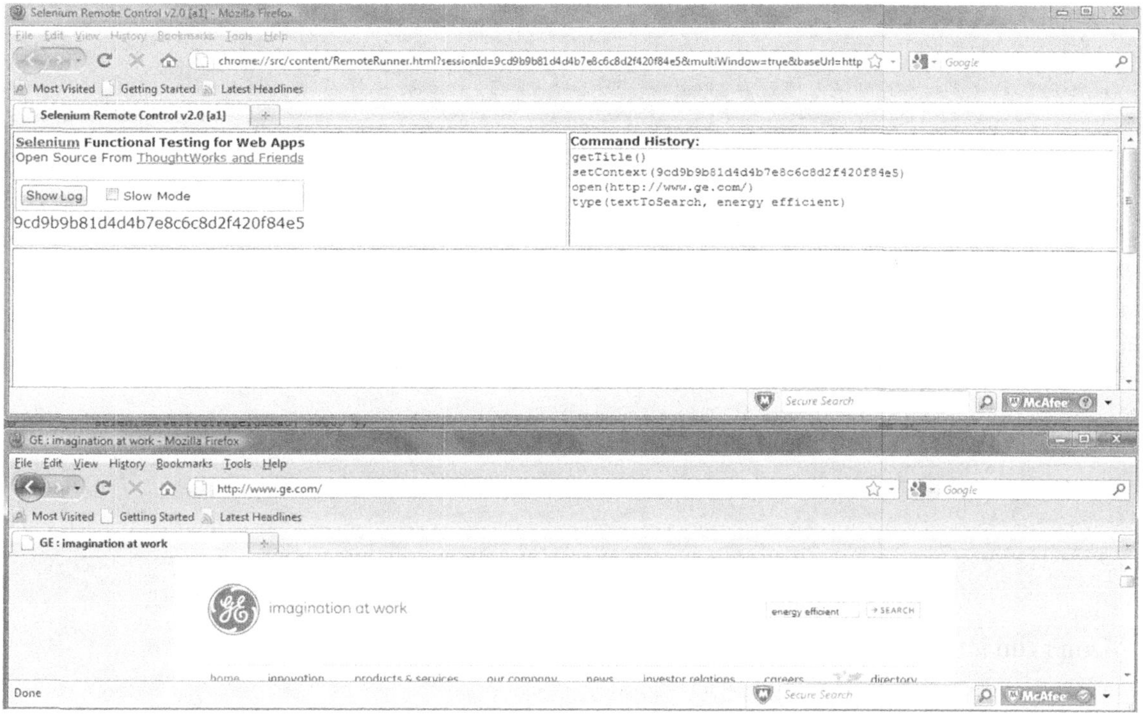

The output of the test would appear in the JUnit log in green color, which indicates successful execution of test.

Check the Results

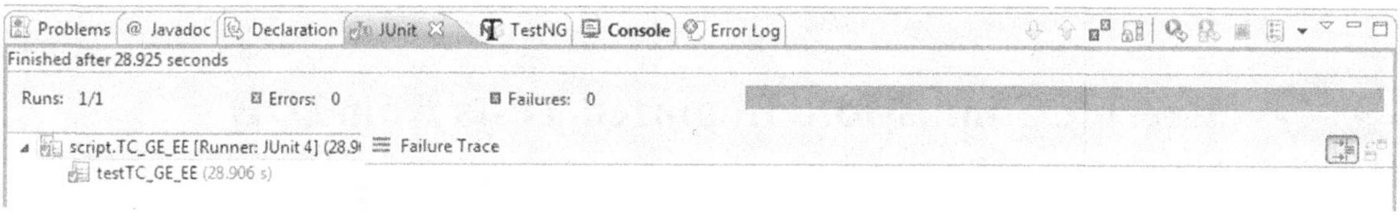

Run the Test in Debug Mode

You can double click on the left frame of the editor window and add the toggle break-point.

TC_GE_EE.java

```
package script;

import com.thoughtworks.selenium.SeleneseTestCase;

public class TC_GE_EE extends SeleneseTestCase {
    public void setUp() throws Exception {
        setUp("http://www.ge.com/", "*chrome");
    }
    public void testTC_GE_EE() throws Exception {
        selenium.open("http://www.ge.com/");
        // Search for any word
        selenium.type("textToSearch", "energy efficient");
        // This is just a comment
        selenium.click("searchSubmit");
        selenium.waitForPageToLoad("30000");
        assertEquals("GE: Search Results", selenium.getTitle());
        assertTrue(selenium.isTextPresent("energy efficient"));
    }
}
```

Don't run it this time, debug it using the menu option Debug As → JUnit Test.

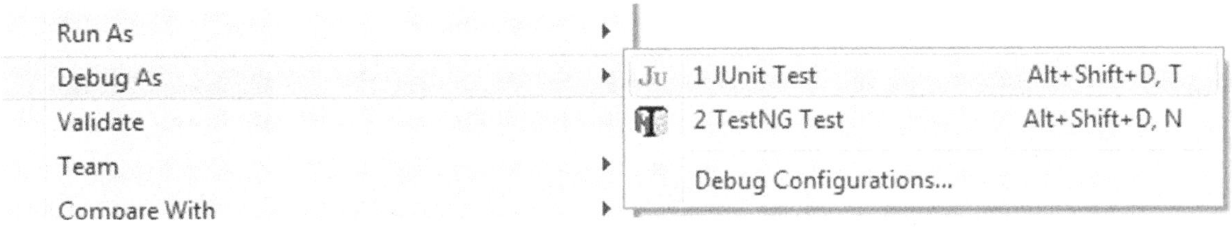

Execute Some More Imported Tests from IDE

Similarly import few earlier test cases that you have created and execute them using JUnit.

EXERCISES

1. What is JUnit, how is it different from Java class?
2. Is Selenium RC server needs to be running while running JUnit script?
3. How do you distinguish between compilation errors and warnings/
4. How do you know whether your JUnit code has run or failed?
5. Which option needs to be enabled to change the format of IDE code?

18

Running a Test Using the TestNG Export from Selenium-IDE

Setting up TestNG in Eclipse

Go to URL http://testng.org/doc/download.html

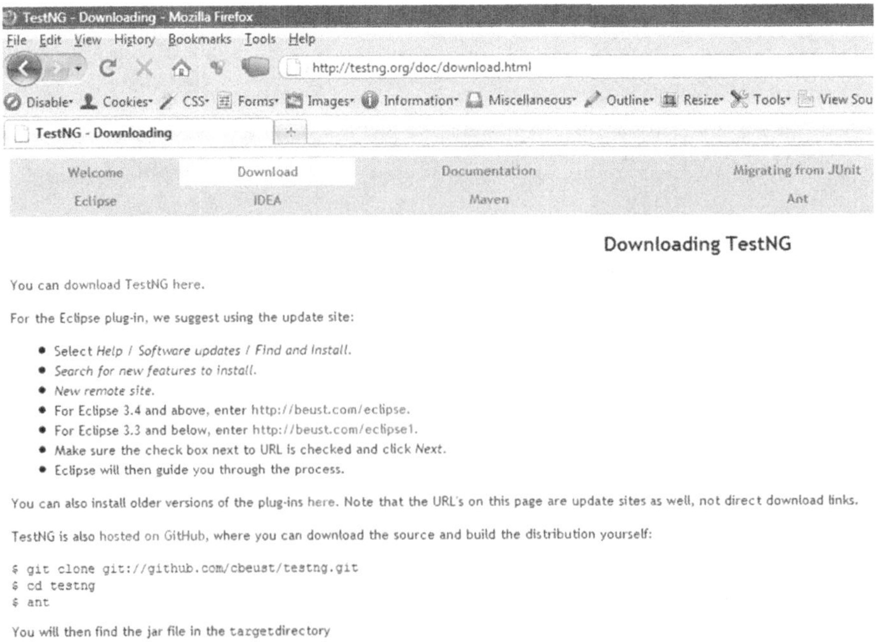

Installing TestNG JAR file

As first, we can download the latest testNG zip file from the link #1 and install it manually.

Unzip the testng-xxxx.zip (in this case testng-6.0.1.zip)

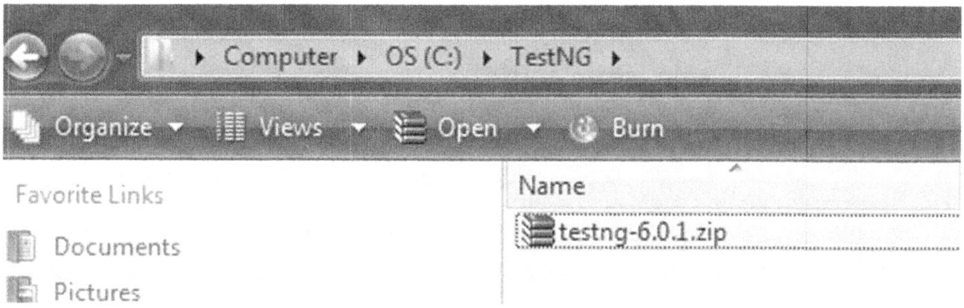

Navigate through the zipped folders to find testng-6.0.1.jar file.

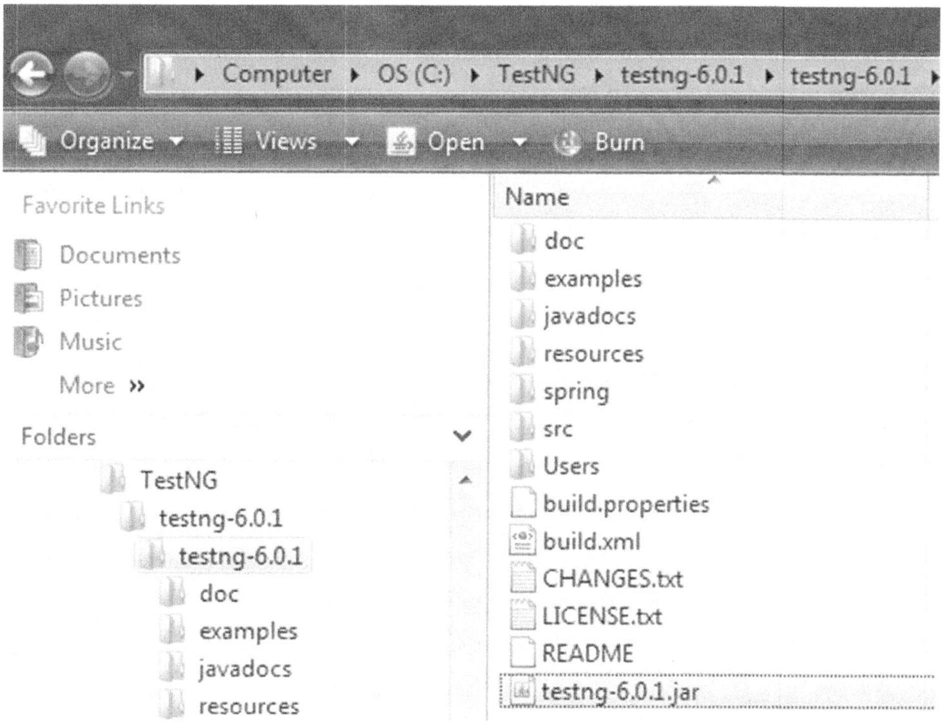

Copy this file in the 'lib' folder of your Eclipse Workspace.

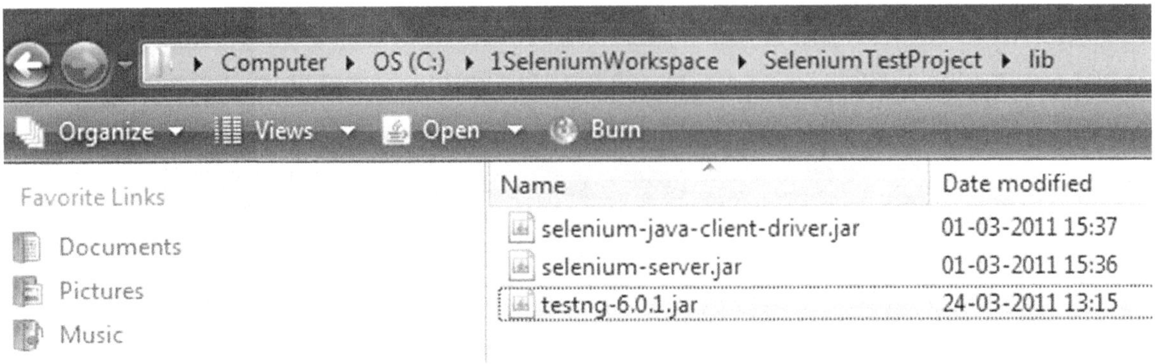

Now go to Eclipse and right click on the Project to select properties, select Java Build Path option.

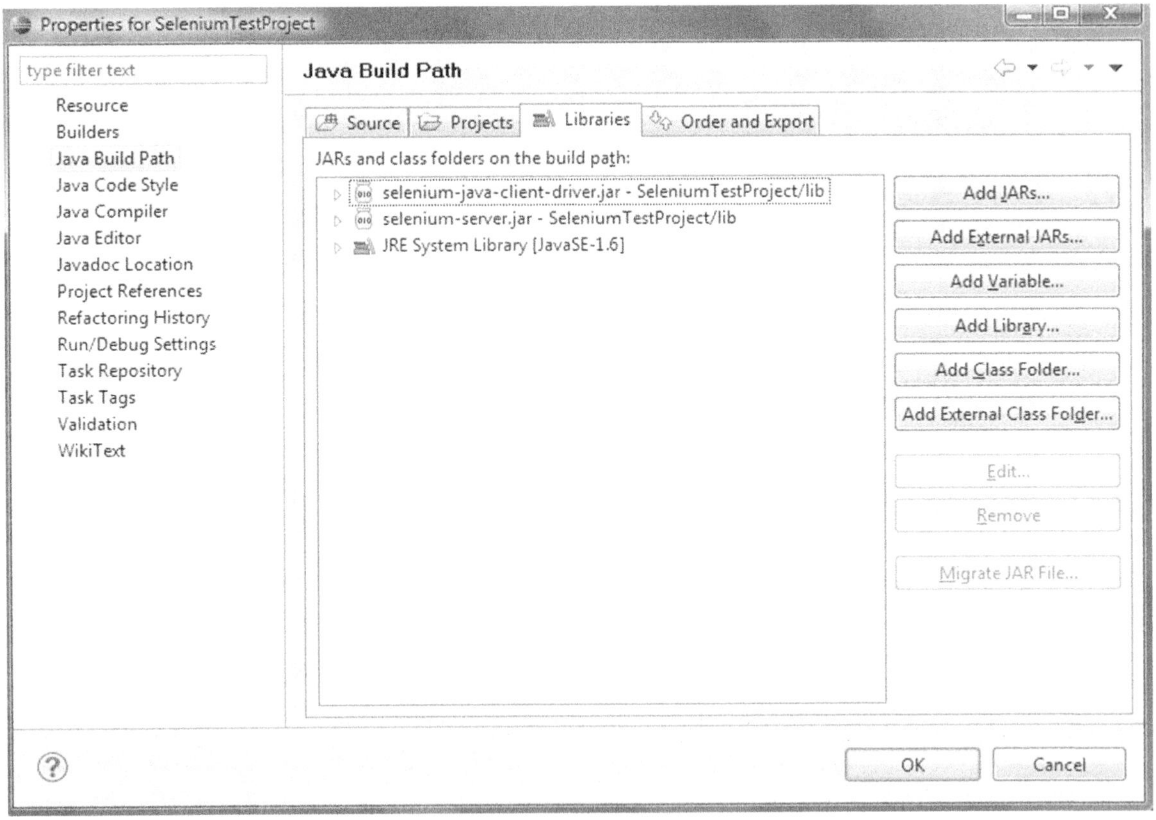

Click on "Add JARs..." option, in the opened window expand the 'lib' folder and select the newly added jar for TestNG. Click on OK-OK to return to Eclispe workspace.

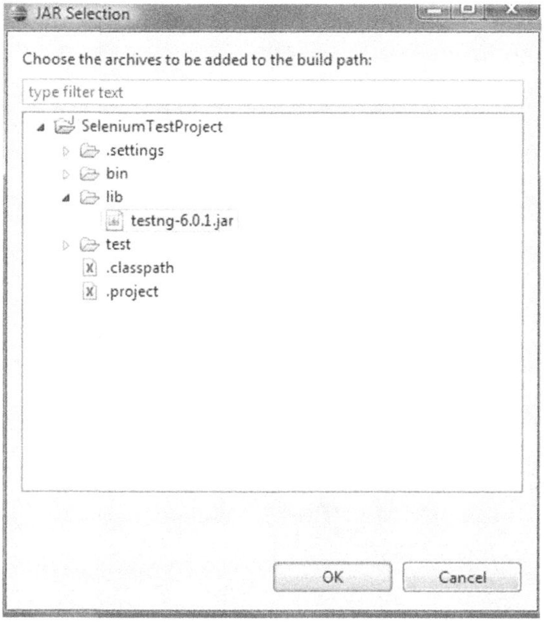

TestNG Plug-in for Eclispe

For Eclipse plug-in and to ensure seamless integration with Eclipse, we will use the link #2. As we are using the higher version of Eclipse, we will use http://beust.com/eclipse , copy this URL.

Launch Eclipse and select menu option Help → Install New Software…

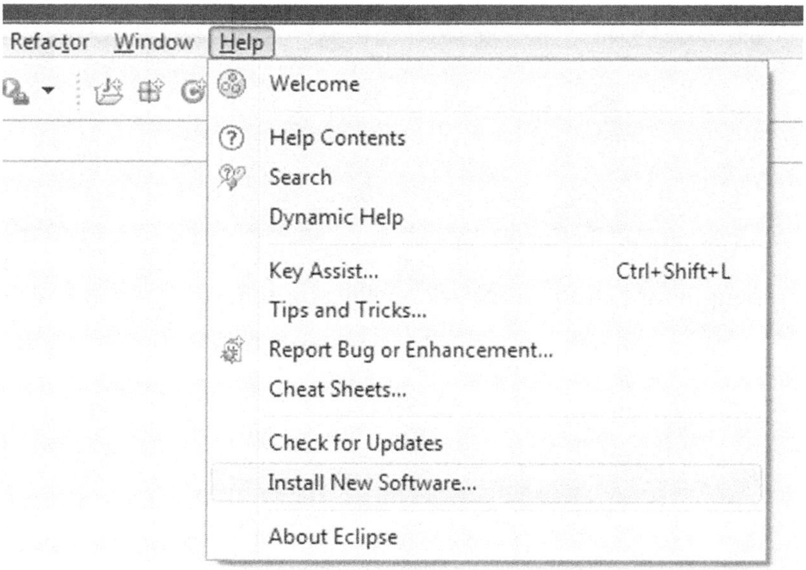

Paste the URL copies in the above step and wait for "TestNG" to appear in the list. Select the checkbox and click on Next button.

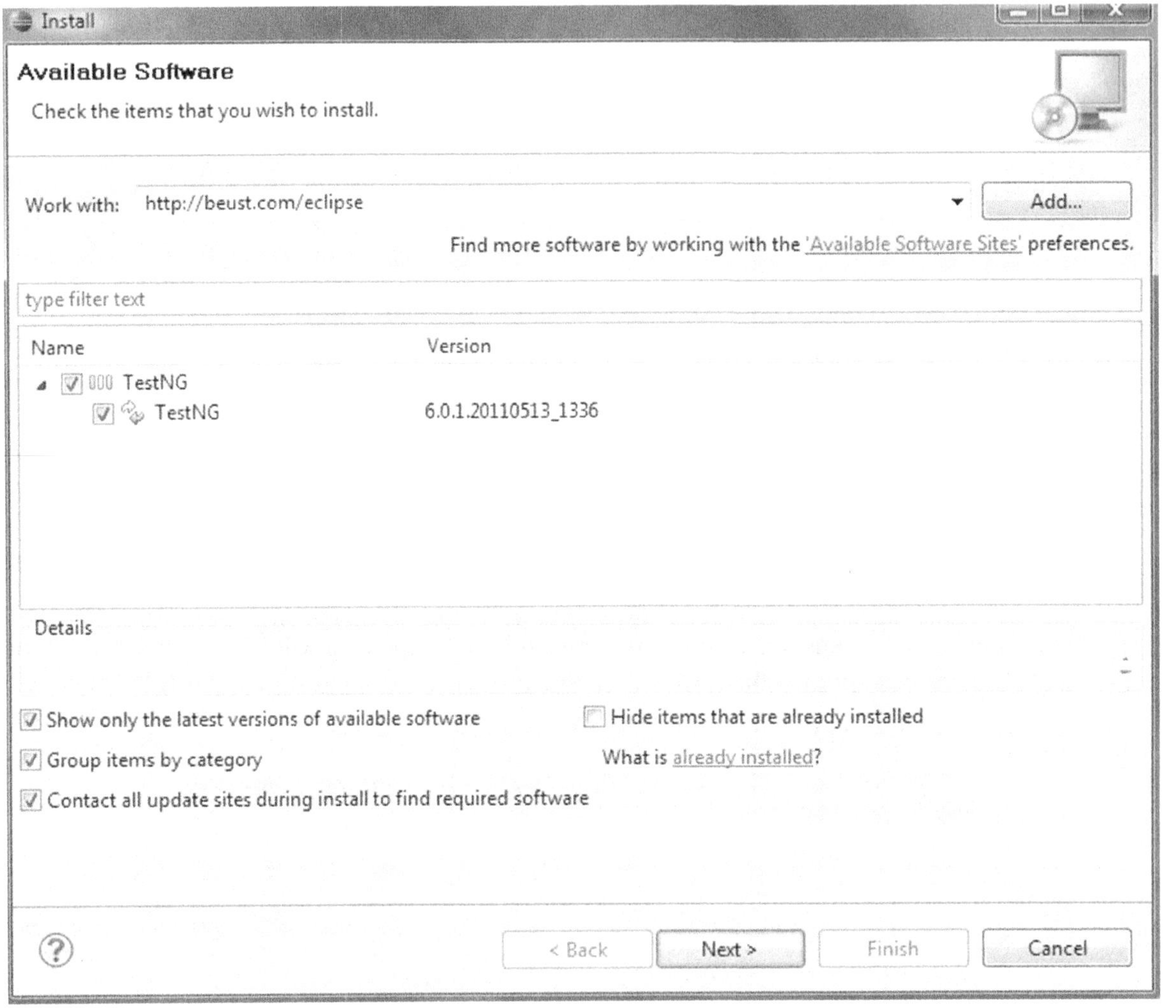

Select TestNG (plug-in for Eclipse) and click on Next button.

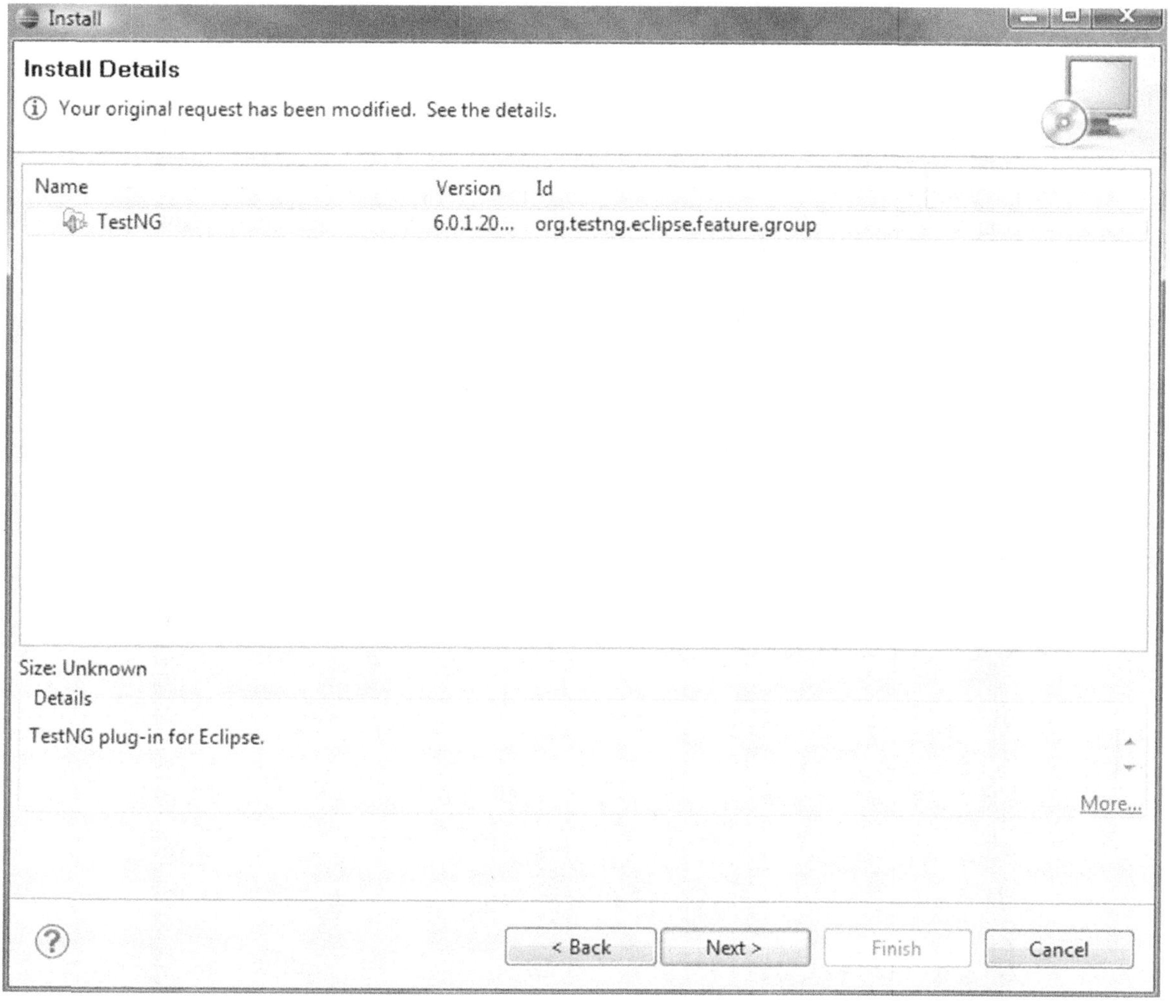

Read and accept the License and click on Finish.

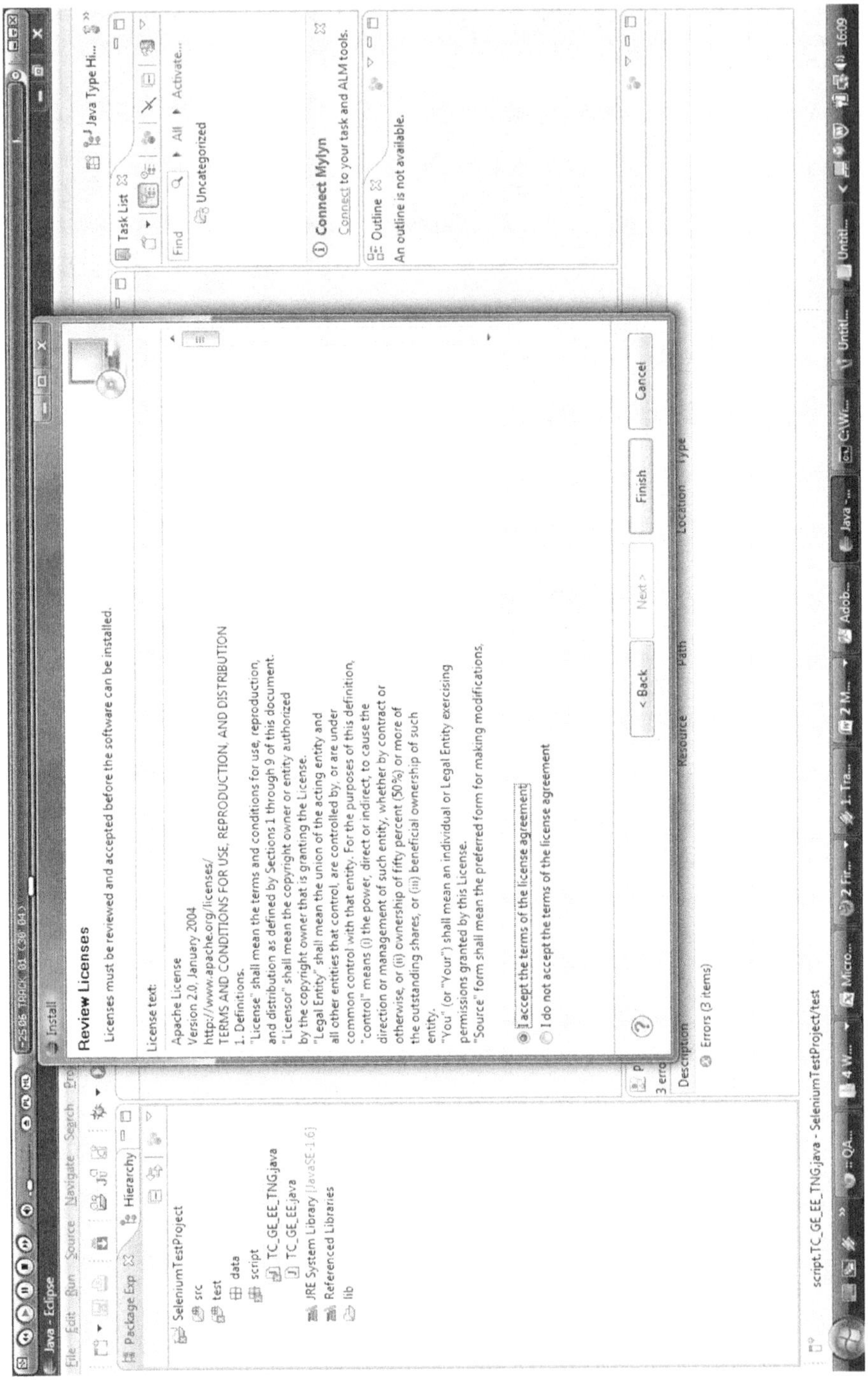
Install
Review Licenses
Licenses must be reviewed and accepted before the software can be installed.
License text:
Apache License
Version 2.0, January 2004
http://www.apache.org/licenses/
TERMS AND CONDITIONS FOR USE, REPRODUCTION, AND DISTRIBUTION
I accept the terms of the license agreement
I do not accept the terms of the license agreement
< Back
Next >
Finish
Cancel
Task List
Connect Mylyn
Outline
An outline is not available.
SeleniumTestProject
script.TC_GE_EE_TNG.java - SeleniumTestProject/test

Installation would start, let it continue

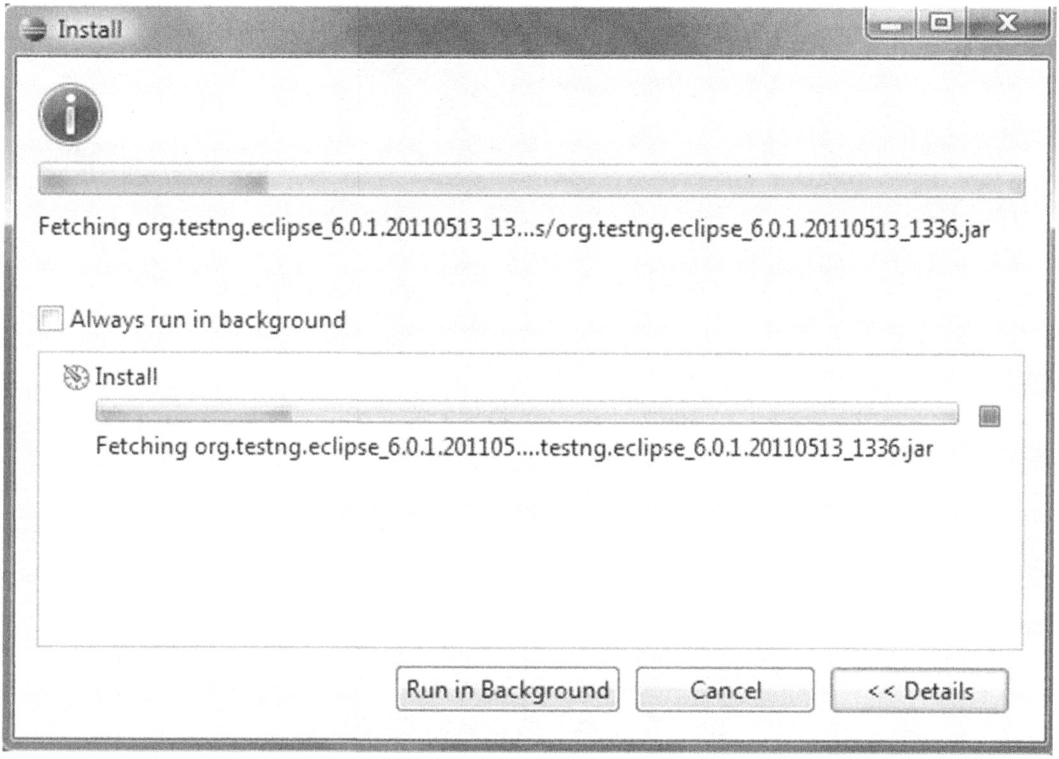

You might get warning like one below, click OK to continue

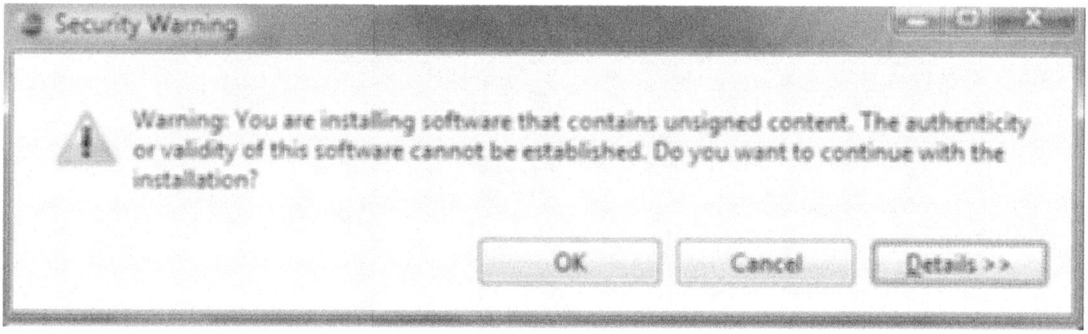

At the end of installation, you will get the following message, click on Yes to restart Eclipse.

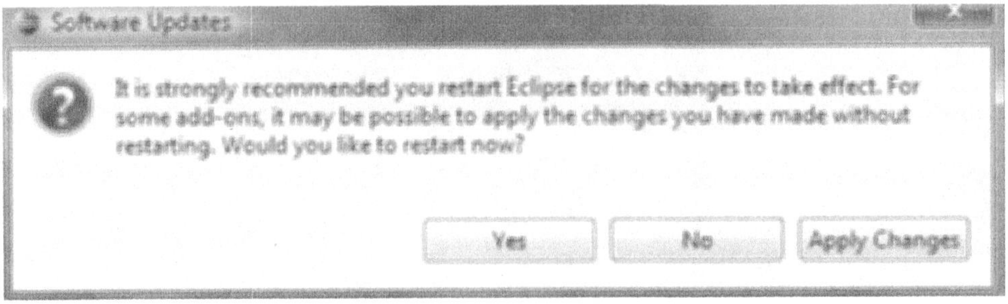

Now, we are ready to run Tests in TestNg format in Eclispe. Let's try one.

Import IDE Tests In Testng Format

Similar to JUnit in the previous Chapter, we will Open the script that we want to run in RC in Selenium IDE first.

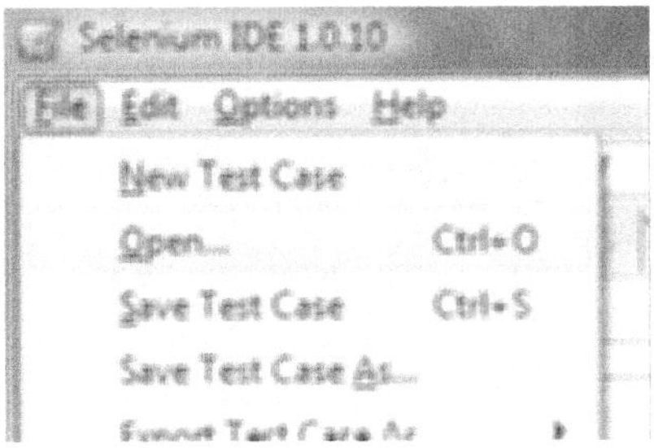

Select TC_GE_EE.html and it will be loaded as below

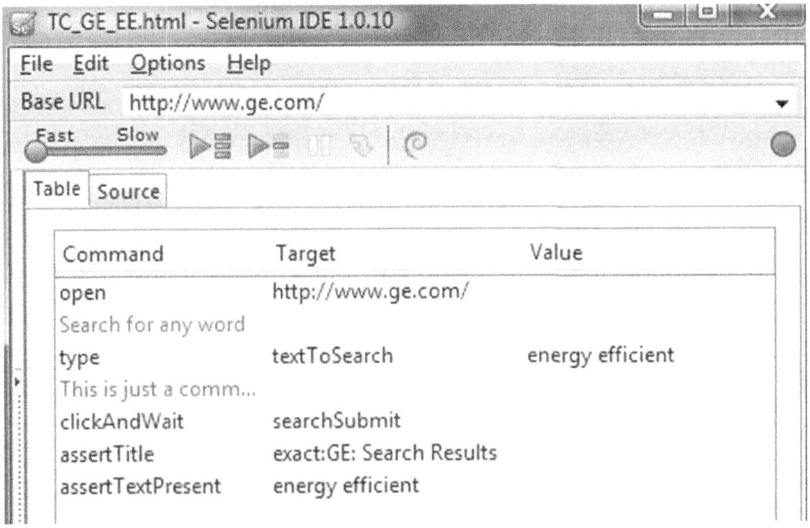

Change the format of the script to TestNG

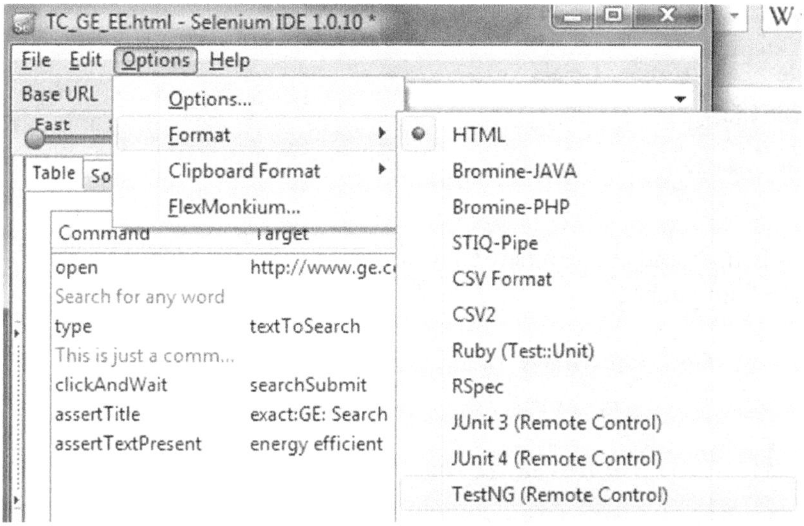

This would open the source tab with converted code in TestNG. Copy the code on clipboard.

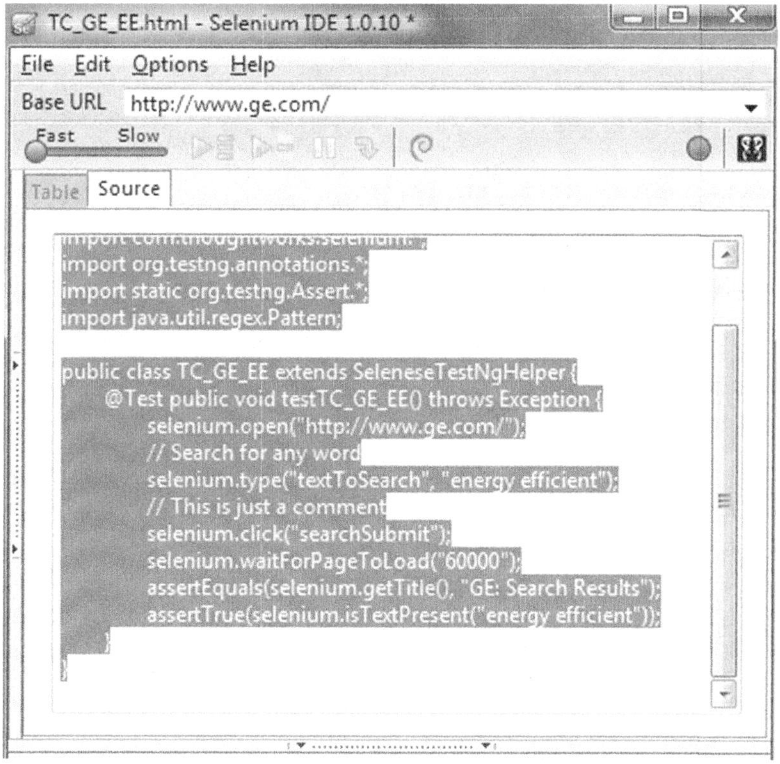

Note: As a good practice, it is always advisable to switch back the format to HTML

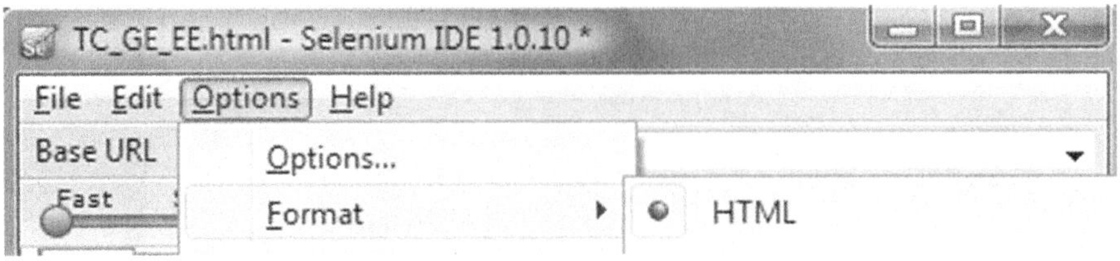

Now switch to Eclipse and create a new Class for this test as 'TC_GE_EE_TNG'. This will give a blank class with default package.

TC_GE_EE_TNG.java

```
package script;

public class TC_GE_EE_TNG {

}
```

Paste the TestNG code that you copied from IDE.

*TC_GE_EE_TNG.java

```
package com.example.tests;

import com.thoughtworks.selenium.*;
import org.testng.annotations.*;
import static org.testng.Assert.*;
import java.util.regex.Pattern;

public class TC_GE_EE extends SeleneseTestNgHelper {
    @Test public void testTC_GE_EE() throws Exception {
        selenium.open("http://www.ge.com/");
        // Search for any word
        selenium.type("textToSearch", "energy efficient");
        // This is just a comment
        selenium.click("searchSubmit");
        selenium.waitForPageToLoad("60000");
        assertEquals(selenium.getTitle(), "GE: Search Results");
        assertTrue(selenium.isTextPresent("energy efficient"));
    }
}
```

Now those are lots of errors, let fix them. Please make following changes to the copied code:

1. Change the package name to the package that you have created 'script'.
2. Change the class name to match the file name 'TC_GE_EE_TNG'
3. Change the class extension from 'SeleneseTestNgHelper' to 'SeleneseTestCase'

This should remove all the errors and you might be left with couple if warnings.

*TC_GE_EE_TNG.java

```
package script;

import com.thoughtworks.selenium.*;
import org.testng.annotations.*;
import static org.testng.Assert.*;
import java.util.regex.Pattern;

public class TC_GE_EE_TNG extends SeleneseTestCase {
    @Test public void testTC_GE_EE() throws Exception {
        selenium.open("http://www.ge.com/");
        // Search for any word
        selenium.type("textToSearch", "energy efficient");
        // This is just a comment
        selenium.click("searchSubmit");
        selenium.waitForPageToLoad("60000");
        assertEquals(selenium.getTitle(), "GE: Search Results");
        assertTrue(selenium.isTextPresent("energy efficient"));
    }
}
```

You can leave the warnings to comment those line to get rid of them.

TC_GE_EE_TNG.java

```
package script;

import com.thoughtworks.selenium.*;
import org.testng.annotations.*;
//import static org.testng.Assert.*;
//import java.util.regex.Pattern;

public class TC_GE_EE_TNG extends SeleneseTestCase {
    @Test public void testTC_GE_EE() throws Exception {
        selenium.open("http://www.ge.com/");
        // Search for any word
        selenium.type("textToSearch", "energy efficient");
        // This is just a comment
        selenium.click("searchSubmit");
        selenium.waitForPageToLoad("60000");
        assertEquals(selenium.getTitle(), "GE: Search Results");
        assertTrue(selenium.isTextPresent("energy efficient"));
    }
}
```

Now we are error free and warnings free as there are no compilation errors, we can save the test case by File – Save or Control + S.

For running the test, right click on the file and select Run As → TestNG Test

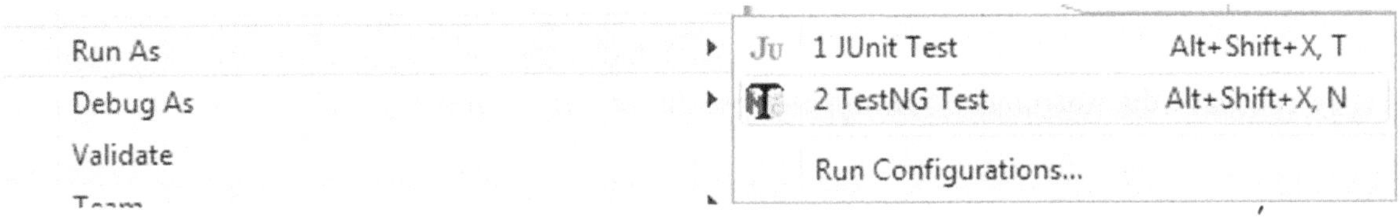

The Test did not run!! What happened? Let's investigate...

Double click on the tab 'Results of running class TC_GE_EE_TNG' to open the results page

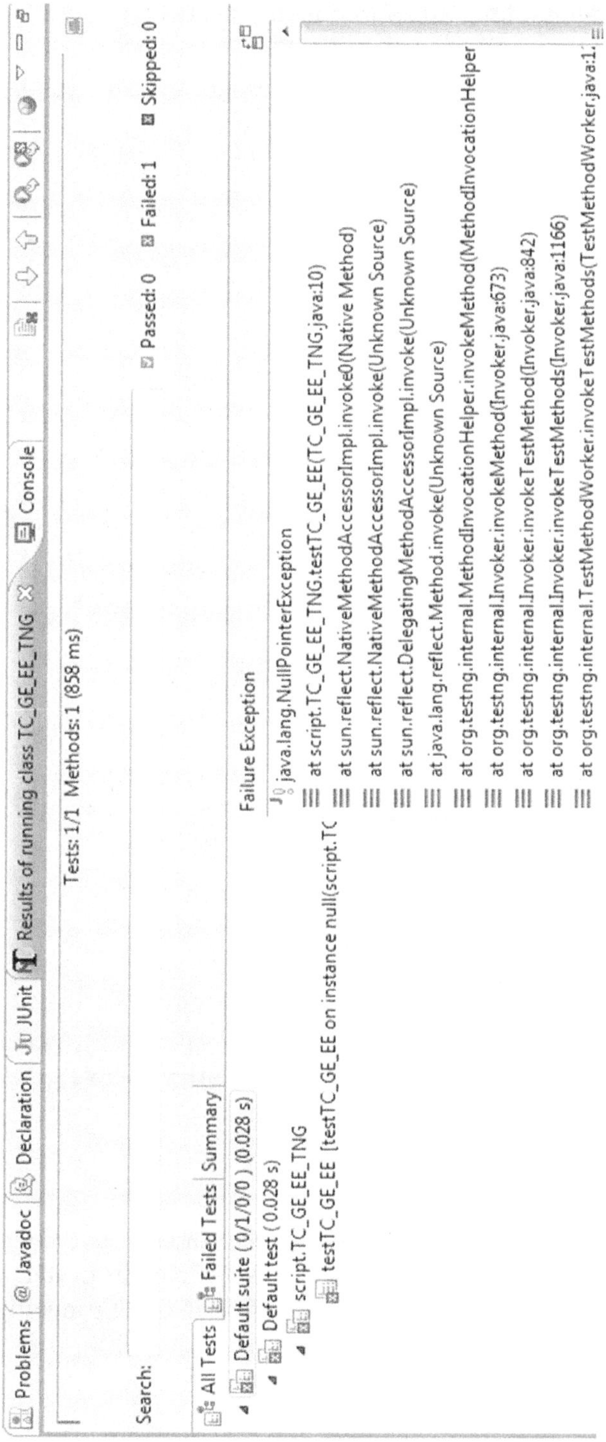
Problems
@ Javadoc
Declaration
JUnit
Results of running class TC_GE_EE_TNG
Console
Tests: 1/1 Methods: 1 (858 ms)
Search:
Passed: 0
Failed: 1
Skipped: 0
All Tests
Failed Tests
Summary
Default suite (0/1/0/0) (0.028 s)
Default test (0.028 s)
script.TC_GE_EE_TNG
testTC_GE_EE [testTC_GE_EE on instance null(script.TC
Failure Exception
java.lang.NullPointerException
at script.TC_GE_EE_TNG.testTC_GE_EE(TC_GE_EE_TNG.java:10)
at sun.reflect.NativeMethodAccessorImpl.invoke0(Native Method)
at sun.reflect.NativeMethodAccessorImpl.invoke(Unknown Source)
at sun.reflect.DelegatingMethodAccessorImpl.invoke(Unknown Source)
at java.lang.reflect.Method.invoke(Unknown Source)
at org.testng.internal.MethodInvocationHelper.invokeMethod(MethodInvocationHelper
at org.testng.internal.Invoker.invokeMethod(Invoker.java:673)
at org.testng.internal.Invoker.invokeTestMethod(Invoker.java:842)
at org.testng.internal.Invoker.invokeTestMethods(Invoker.java:1166)
at org.testng.internal.TestMethodWorker.invokeTestMethods(TestMethodWorker.java:1

It seems we got java "NullPointerException" error, this is a typical run-time error and it doesn't give us much to debug the error.

If you compare with the JUnit test script, you will notice that this TestNG script is missing the setup method. Let's add that

```
public void setUp() throws Exception {
    setUp("http://www.ge.com/", "*firefox");
}
```

TC_GE_EE_TNG.java

```
package script;

import com.thoughtworks.selenium.*;
import org.testng.annotations.*;
//import static org.testng.Assert.*;
//import java.util.regex.Pattern;

public class TC_GE_EE_TNG extends SeleneseTestCase {

    public void setUp() throws Exception {
        setUp("http://www.ge.com/", "*firefox");
    }

    @Test public void testTC_GE_EE() throws Exception {
        selenium.open("http://www.ge.com/");
        // Search for any word
        selenium.type("textToSearch", "energy efficient");
        // This is just a comment
        selenium.click("searchSubmit");
        selenium.waitForPageToLoad("60000");
        assertEquals(selenium.getTitle(), "GE: Search Results");
        assertTrue(selenium.isTextPresent("energy efficient"));
    }
}
```

Let's run again, but the error NullPointerException error persists. We got to be doing something wrong. Notice that gray color *@Test* in the code that we copied from IDE, it was not there in JUnit code. There is our lead, these are called annotation of TestNG, let's investigate further…

What is TestNG?

TestNG is next step towards writing test cases, here 'NG' stands for Next Generation. TestNG is a testing framework derived from JUnit and NUnit and it has taken the best from both and also addressed their shortcomings. Here are certain features of TestNG:

- Annotations. Basically instructions for the defined set of code.
- Test that your code is multithread safe.
- Using XML do Flexible test configuration.
- Support for data-driven testing (with @DataProvider).
- Powerful execution model (no more TestSuite).
- Dependent methods for application server testing.
- Supported ignore, time, parameters, Suite and exception Test.
- Supported by Eclipse, IDEA, Ant, Maven, Netbean, Hudson and so on.
- Test that your source code is multithread-safe.
- Never superfluous code, No required extend specified class.
- Easy to Migrate from JUnit

We need to focus on the Annotations feature of TestNG, let's have a closer look.

What are Annotations?

As mentioned before Annotations are kind of an instruction for the set of code. A TestNG test can be configured by @BeforeXXX and @AfterXXX annotations which allows to perform some Java logic before and after a certain point.

Following is the list of all the annotations with a brief explanation. This will give you an idea of the various functionalities offered by TestNG:

- @BeforeSuite: The annotated method will be run before all tests in this suite have run.
- @AfterSuite: The annotated method will be run after all tests in this suite have run.
- @BeforeTest: The annotated method will be run before any test method belonging to the classes inside the <test> tag is run.
- @AfterTest: The annotated method will be run after all the test methods belonging to the classes inside the <test> tag have run.
- @BeforeGroups: The list of groups that this configuration method will run before. This method is guaranteed to run shortly before the first test method that belongs to any of these groups is invoked.

- @AfterGroups: The list of groups that this configuration method will run after. This method is guaranteed to run shortly after the last test method that belongs to any of these groups is invoked.
- @BeforeClass: The annotated method will be run before the first test method in the current class is invoked.
- @AfterClass: The annotated method will be run after all the test methods in the current class have been run.
- @BeforeMethod: The annotated method will be run before each test method.
- @AfterMethod: The annotated method will be run after each test method.

Other important Annotations are:

@DataProvider(name = "XYX") Marks a method as supplying data for a test method. The annotated method must return an Object[][] where each Object[] can be assigned the parameter list of the test method. The @Test method that wants to receive data from this DataProvider needs to use a dataProvider name equals to the name of this annotation.

name The name of this data provider. If it's not supplied, the name of this data provider will automatically be set to the name of the method.

@Parameters Describes how to pass parameters to a @Test method.

value The list of variables used to fill the parameters of this method.

Updating the Imported Testng Script with Annotations

Let's use the @BeforeXXX and @AfterXXX annotation to fix our imported TestNG script. In this case we will use @BeforeTest and @AfterTest.

As we have learned that @BeforeTest code runs before the actual test code and @AfterTest runs the code after the test. It makes sense to start the Selenium server before running the test, as it is the prerequisite. Also the browser needs to be setup in this section. Also, the browser windows need to be closed after the test has run so we will take care of it in the @AfterTest annotated code. We have incorporated these changes to our imported code.

Please see below for the updated code.

TC_GE_EE_TNG.java

```
package script;

import com.thoughtworks.selenium.*;
import org.openqa.selenium.server.SeleniumServer;
import org.testng.annotations.*;
//import static org.testng.Assert.*;
//import java.util.regex.Pattern;

public class TC_GE_EE_TNG extends SeleneseTestCase {
    @BeforeTest
    public void setUp() throws Exception {
        SeleniumServer seleniumserver=new SeleniumServer();
        seleniumserver.boot();
        seleniumserver.start();
        setUp("http://www.ge.com/", "*firefox");
        selenium.open("/");
        selenium.windowMaximize();
        selenium.windowFocus();
    }

    @Test public void testTC_GE_EE() throws Exception {
        selenium.open("http://www.ge.com/");
        // Search for any word
        selenium.type("textToSearch", "energy efficient");
        // This is just a comment
        selenium.click("searchSubmit");
        selenium.waitForPageToLoad("60000");
        assertEquals(selenium.getTitle(), "GE: Search Results");
        assertTrue(selenium.isTextPresent("energy efficient"));
    }

    @AfterTest
    public void tearDown(){
        selenium.close();
        selenium.stop();
    }
}
```

Now, let's run the test. The Results will be displayed in the appropriate tab as below:

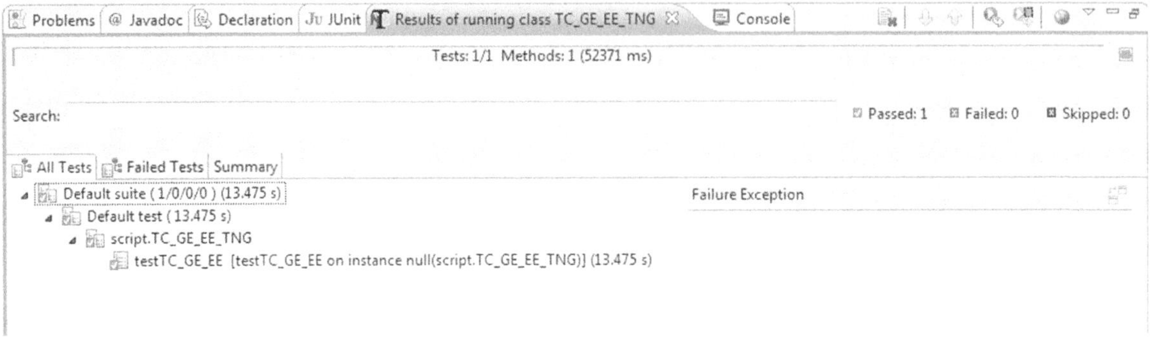

What is Testng xml Configuration File?

A configuration file, testng.xml needs to be created for every TestNG script, in Eclipse it is created by default. You can typically find it under test-output folder. If you wish to run the TestNG script from commands line then you will need this file. The format of this configuration file is as below:

```
<?xml version="1.0" encoding="UTF-8"?>
<!DOCTYPE suite SYSTEM "http://testng.org/testng-1.0.dtd">
<suite verbose="0" name="Default suite">
<test verbose="2" name="Default test" preserve-order="false">
<classes>
<class name="script.TC_GE_EE_TNG"/>
</classes>
</test>
</suite>
```

To run the test, please compile the class TC_GE_EE_TNG and then invoke TestNG with the following command:

```
java -ea -classpath .; testng-6.0.1.jar org.testng.TestNG testng.xml
```

Parallel Testing Using Testng

As testing projects progress and the requirements are added, it is not uncommon to see organizations running thousands of tests. Not all these tests are similar in complexity and some of these tests take a long time to run. In terms of code optimization one can not do much about it because they just happen to test code that takes a long time to execute. This can become a potential bottleneck and jeopardize the testing project.

TestNG's parallel mode comes in handy in those situations, but on a larger scale, you need distributed testing. You can run your test cases in parallel by using the parallel attribute for Test Suite.

The parallel attribute on the <suite> tag can take one of following values:

```
<suite name="My suite" parallel="methods" thread-count="5">
<suite name="My suite" parallel="tests" thread-count="5">
<suite name="My suite" parallel="classes" thread-count="5">
```

- parallel="methods": TestNG will run all your test methods in separate threads. Dependent methods will also run in separate threads but they will respect the order that you specified.
- parallel="tests": TestNG will run all the methods in the same <test> tag in the same thread, but each <test> tag will be in a separate thread. This allows you to group all your classes that are not thread safe in the same <test> and guarantee they will all run in the same thread while taking advantage of TestNG using as many threads as possible to run your tests.
- parallel="classes": TestNG will run all the methods in the same class in the same thread, but each class will be run in a separate thread.

Additionally, the attribute thread-count allows you to specify how many threads should be allocated for this execution.

Note: the @Test attribute timeOut works in both parallel and non-parallel mode.

You can also specify that a @Test method should be invoked from different threads. You can use the attribute threadPoolSize to achieve this result:

```
@Test(threadPoolSize = 3, invocationCount = 10,  timeOut = 10000)
public void testServer() {
```

In this example, the function testServer will be invoked ten times from three different threads. Additionally, a time-out of ten seconds guarantees that none of the threads will block on this thread forever.

EXERCISES

1. What does TestNG name signifies?
2. In order to run TestNG scripts in Eclipse, what else do we need to do in addition to adding TestNGxxx.jar file?

3. What are annotations in TestNG?
4. Can I write @BeforeTest annotation after @Test code block?
5. Where is testing.xml file is created? Can you edit that?
6. What would be ideal code as part of @BeforeTest and @AfterTest annotations?

19

Data Driven Testing Using TestNG

What is Data Driven Testing?

Test Data is one of the most important aspect of testing, be it manual or automation. There are several testing techniques that focus on preparing test data set for e.g. equivalence partitioning, boundary value analysis. Test data can be said to be ideal if for the minimum size of data set all the application errors get identified. Try to prepare test data that will incorporate all application functionality, but not exceeding cost and time constraint for preparing test data and running tests.

When we record a test case it is for one set of data identified for the application workflow. We can record/update the same test and run it again for a different set of data. However when the combination of this data grows it calls for data driven testing. In Data Driven Testing we can generate multiple test scenarios with different data set using the same test.

For example suppose you want to create an account in yahoo for 1000 people, we can put all the user information an excel file and use a single script to do exactly the same action on yahoo website.

Advantages of TestNG Framework in Data driven testing

Selenium does not provide any out of box solution or framework for data driven testing. TestNG makes it easy to implement data driven testing in Selenium. The @DataProvider annotation in TestNG provides the basic engine for this. The data listed or retrieved in the DataProvider feeds the data to the test method. So effectively the method in Test annotation runs for each data set in DataProvider.

For e.g.

//The following method will provide data to any test method that declares that it's Data Provider. This is named "dp1"

```
@DataProvider(name = "dp1")
public Object[][] createData() {
 return new Object[][] {
   { "Ashish", new Integer(10) },
   { "Aditya", new Integer(11)},
 };
}
```

//The following test method declares that its data should be supplied by the Data Provider named as "dp1"

```
@Test(dataProvider = "dp1")
public void verifyData(String n1, Integer n2) {
 System.out.println("The data for test is: " + n1 + " and " + n2);
}
```

This will print:

The data for test is Ashish and 10

The data for test is Aditya and 11

In the above example we have hard-coded the data in the createData() method which returns two dimensional array of string and integer data. The test method verfyData() is linked to the data provider by the parameter dataProvider="dp1".

However in the practical scenarios data set will be large and it might not be a good idea to hard-code values in the dataProvider class. Anyways, in order to have flexibility in our automation it would be better to keep the test data separate than the test automation code. The test data can be stored in a simple spreadsheet or XML or it can be stored in some back-end database.

Test Automation Scenario for Data Driven Testing

Let's try to automate the following:

1. Open website http://www.flipkart.com
2. Search for Book titled as "The Time Of My Life"

3. On the result page, click on the matching book's title to open the book details.

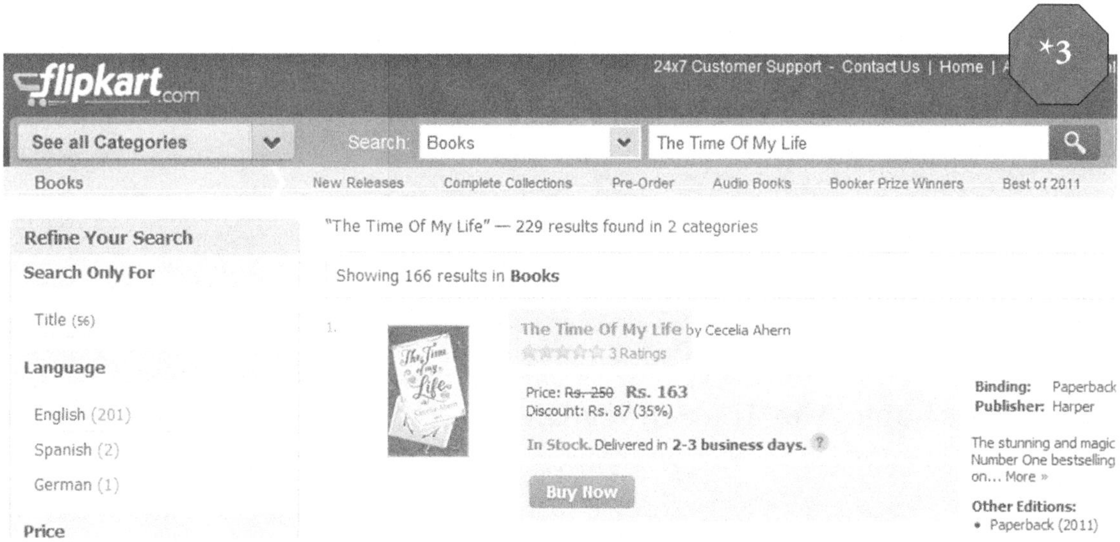

4. On the book details page, confirm the following:
   a. The Author name is "Cecelia Ahern"
   b. The ISBN-13 Number is "9780007463305"
   c. The Book summary is "The stunning and magical new novel from the Number One bestselling author"

flipkart.com
24x7 Customer Supp
*4a
See all Categories
Search: Books
Search for items
Books
New Releases
Complete Collections
Pre-Order
Audio Books
Booker Priz
Home > Books > Literature & Fiction > Literary Collections > Literary > The Time Of My Life
The Time Of My Life (Paperback)
by Cecelia Ahern
3 Ratings
Publisher: Harper
Price: Rs. 250 Rs. 163
Discount: Rs. 87 35% Off
(Prices are inclusive of all taxes)
In Stock.
Delivered in 2-3 business days.
See Details
*4b
Book Summary of The Time Of My Life
The stunning and magical new novel from the Number One bestselling author
Lying on Lucy Silchester s carpet one day when she returns from work is a gold envelope. Inside is an invitation to a meeting with Life. Her life. It turns out she s been ignoring it and it needs to meet with her
*4c
Details of Book: The Time Of My Life
Book: The Time Of My Life
Author: Cecelia Ahern
ISBN: 0007463308
ISBN-13: 9780007463305, 978-0007463305
Binding: Paperback
Publisher: Harper
Language: English
Format: A

Recorded IDE Script

The equivalent IDE script would be as below:

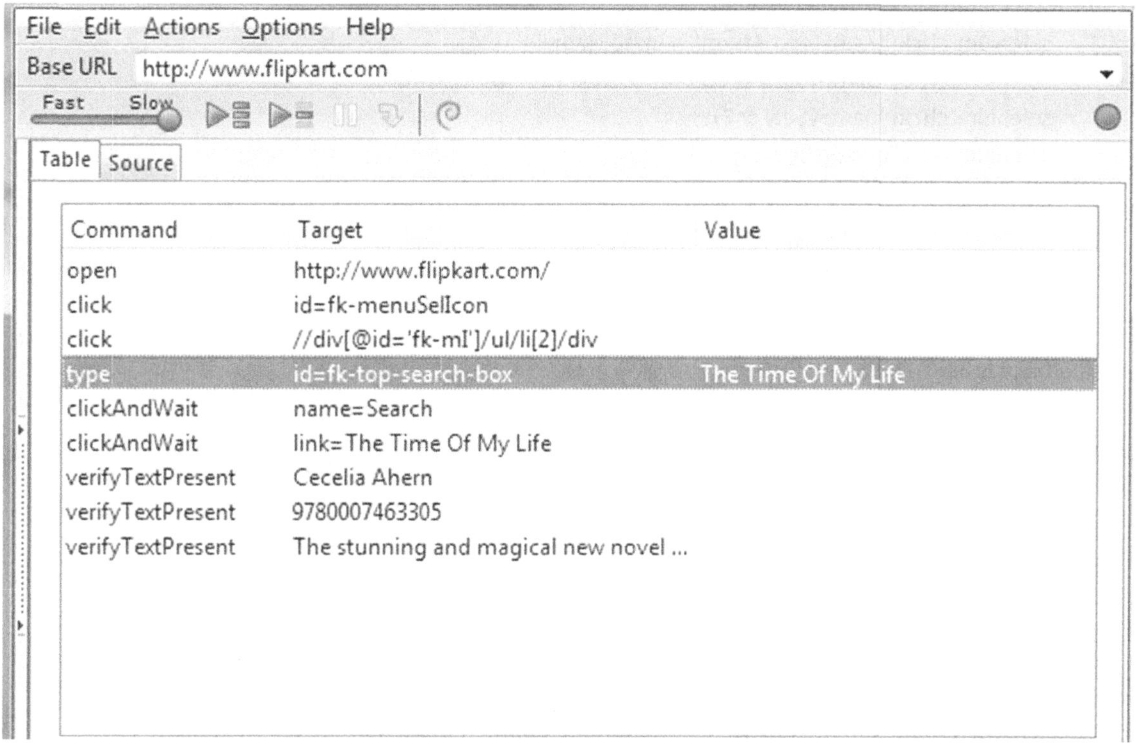

If we were to run this script for different set of data then we will have to record and playback the same test for that data set. It would definitely not be good use of IDE and of our time. If we need to loop then we should work on Java (or other high level languages).

Converted Java (TestNG) Code

The TestNG format code for the above IDE script would be as below:

```
package com.example.tests;

import com.thoughtworks.selenium.*;
import org.testng.annotations.*;
import static org.testng.Assert.*;
import java.util.regex.Pattern;
```

```
public class Flipkart extends SeleneseTestNgHelper {
@Test public void testFlipkart() throws Exception {
        selenium.open("http://www.flipkart.com/");
        selenium.click("id=fk-menuSellcon");
        selenium.click("//div[@id='fk-ml']/ul/li[2]/div");
        selenium.type("id=fk-top-search-box", "The Time Of My Life");
        selenium.click("name=Search");
        selenium.waitForPageToLoad("30000");
        selenium.click("link=The Time Of My Life");
        selenium.waitForPageToLoad("30000");
        verifyTrue(selenium.isTextPresent("Cecelia Ahern"));
        verifyTrue(selenium.isTextPresent("9780007463305"));
        verifyTrue(selenium.isTextPresent("The stunning and magical new novel from the Number One
bestselling author"));
    }
}
```

Please refer to the previous chapters to see the changes needed in order to run this code successfully in Eclipse.

The Data Set

We would like to run our test for the following data set:

bookTitle	*authorName*	*bookSummary*	*isbnNumber*
The Time Of My Life	Cecelia Ahern	The stunning and magical new novel from the Number One bestselling author	9780007463305
New Moon	Stephenie Meyer	I stuck my finger under the edge of the paper and jerked it under the tape. 'Shoot,' I muttered when the paper sliced my finger.	9781904233886
A Dance With Dragons	George R R Martin	The future of the Seven Kingdoms hangs in the balance.	9780007455997
Code Name God	Mani Bhaumick	The split between man and maker has long been widening, and many acknowledge that the wedge is science	9780144001033
The Passionate Programmer	Chad Fowler	Success in today's IT environment requires you to view your career as a business endeavor. In this book, you'll learn how to become an entrepreneur, driving your career in the direction of your choosing.	9789350234310

If we store this data in MS-Excel, it would look as below:

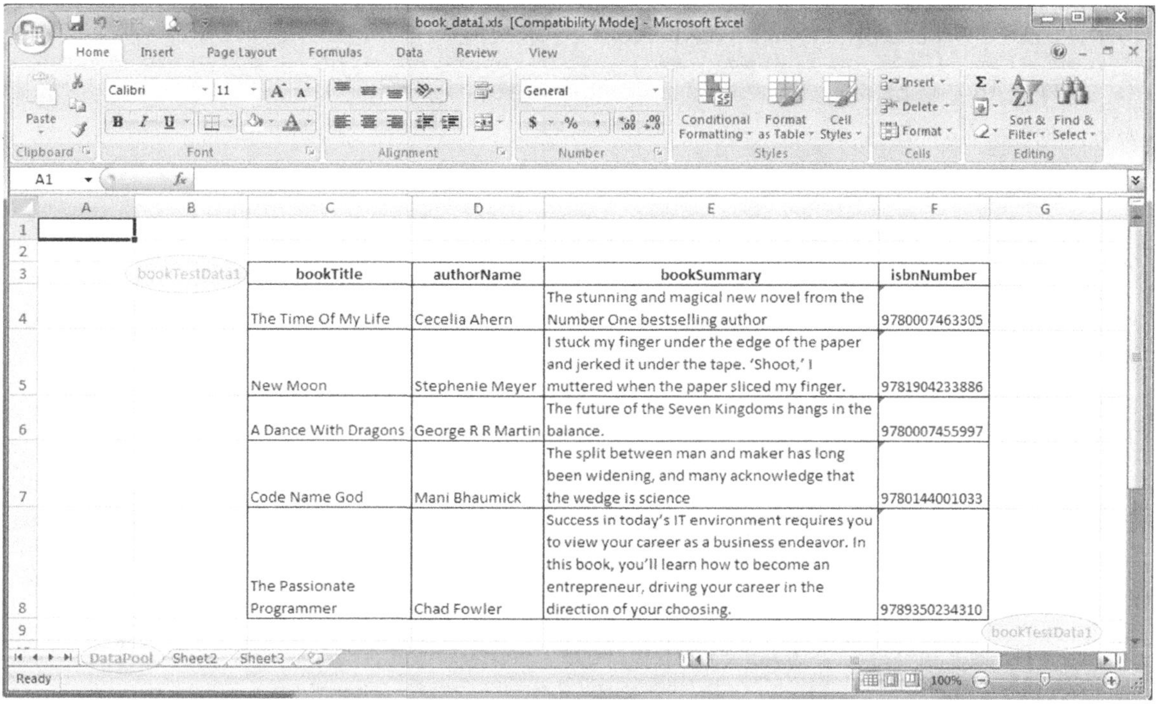

bookTitle	authorName	bookSummary	isbnNumber
The Time Of My Life	Cecelia Ahern	The stunning and magical new novel from the Number One bestselling author	9780007463305
New Moon	Stephenie Meyer	I stuck my finger under the edge of the paper and jerked it under the tape. 'Shoot,' I muttered when the paper sliced my finger.	9781904233886
A Dance With Dragons	George R R Martin	The future of the Seven Kingdoms hangs in the balance.	9780007455997
Code Name God	Mani Bhaumick	The split between man and maker has long been widening, and many acknowledge that the wedge is science	9780144001033
The Passionate Programmer	Chad Fowler	Success in today's IT environment requires you to view your career as a business endeavor. In this book, you'll learn how to become an entrepreneur, driving your career in the direction of your choosing.	9789350234310

Please note that the file name is "book_data1.xls" and the sheet name is "DataPool". Also we have two cells in addition to the data labeled "bookTestData1". These cells are to enable us to identify the test data without hard coding on the number of rows and columns, simply by moving around these labels we can change the scope of Test data.

Fetching the data

We will need to incorporate some way to fetch this data to our DataProvider annotation method which will be passed to the Test annotation method (as described in TestNg section above)

Here we plan to use Java Excel API (http://jexcelapi.sourceforge.net/) to fetch this data. We will get jxl.jar library for this and will get access to the MS Excel related methods such as:

```
Workbook.getWorkbook(new File(fileName));
workbook.getSheet(sheetName);
sheet.findCell(labelName);
```

This will help us traverse through the MS Excel file and fetch the data. The entire code is as below:

```
// The method will accept following 3 parameters;

// 1. xlFilePath - the path of XL file/workbook containing the data, the
// path is relative to java project
// 2. sheetName- name of the xl sheet that contains the table
// 3. labelName- Name of the label between which you wish to fetch the
// data
// The function returns a String type array of array, 2-dimentional
// array. The in-line comments below for explanation of the code.
public String[][] getTableArray(String xlFilePath, String sheetName, String labelName){
// Initialize the array as NULL
    String[][] tabArray=null;
// Put the code in try-catch block to trap any exceptions
    try{
// The workbook object will hold the handle to the Excel file path/name
        Workbook workbook = Workbook.getWorkbook(new File(xlFilePath));
// The sheet object will get handle to the Excel sheet from worksbook handle
        Sheet sheet = workbook.getSheet(sheetName);
// The cell object will find the first cell within the sheet with mentioned label
        Cell tableStart=sheet.findCell(labelName);
// Initialize the counters
        int startRow,startCol, endRow, endCol,ci,cj;

// As we have the first cell bookTestData1, we can get the start row/column
        startRow=tableStart.getRow();
        startCol=tableStart.getColumn();
// Same approach for finding out the last cell with label
// findCell(java.lang.String contents, int firstCol, int firstRow, int lastCol, int lastRow, boolean reverse)
        Cell tableEnd= sheet.findCell(labelName, startCol+1,startRow+1, 100, 64000, false);
// This will give us the last row and last column
        endRow=tableEnd.getRow();
        endCol=tableEnd.getColumn();
// As now we have start row/column and end row/column, we can get size of the array declared in line one
        tabArray=new String[endRow-startRow-1][endCol-startCol-1];
```

```
// Initialize the counter for rows
        ci=0;
// Outer for loop for traversing through the rows
        for (int i=startRow+1;i<endRow;i++,ci++){
// Initialize the counter for column
           cj=0;
// Inner for loop for traversing through the columns

           for (int j=startCol+1;j<endCol;j++,cj++){
// Populate the array element with the data for the row/column combination
              tabArray[ci][cj]=sheet.getCell(j,i).getContents();
           }
        }
     }
     catch (Exception e)   {
// Catch and print the exception
        System.out.println("error in getTableArray()" + e.getMessage() );
     }
// Return the populated array to the calling function
     return(tabArray);
  }
```

The Required Jars

1. testng.jar should be in the class path. (http://testng.org/doc/download.html)
2. testng eclipse plug-in must be installed. Refer to previous chapter to install this plug-in.
3. jxl.jar should be in the class path Java Excel API. Download the jexcelapi.zip, unzip to get the jxl.jar (http://sourceforge.net/projects/jexcelapi/files/jexcelapi/)
4. Selenium-server.jar and selenium-java-client-driver.jar (As part of the Selenium RC installation)
5. junit.jar (selenium classes need junit) files must in class path. (https://github.com/KentBeck/junit/downloads)

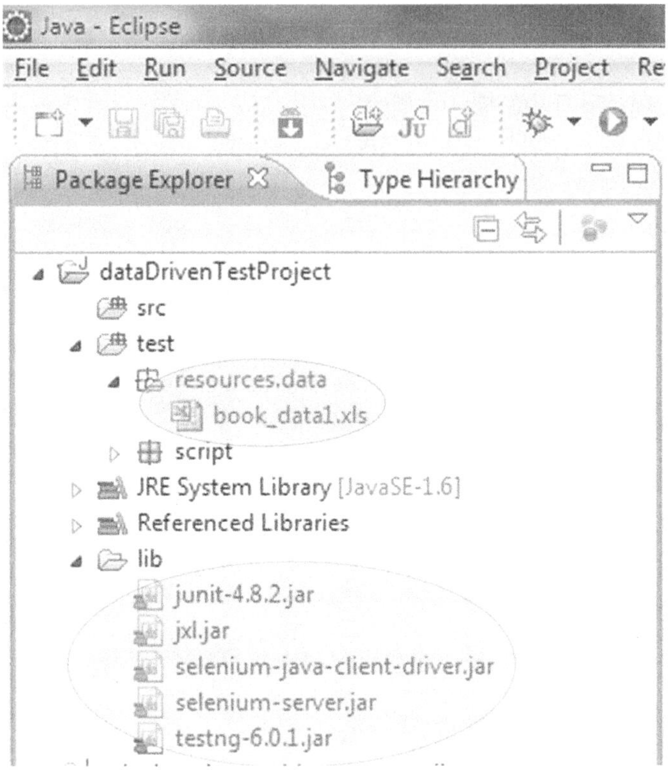

The data file book_data1.xls should be kept at test\\resources\\data\\book_data1.xls

The path mentioned is relative to the project.

Parametrizing the Test Code

Now we need to prepare the Test code which will accept the data from the excel file. The fastest and ideal approach is that we record the test for one set of data in IDE and get the TestNG format converted code. We already did this in the steps above. We need to remove the hard-coded values and parameterize our code. Please note that we need to maintain the order of the variables that we use to match the data in the Excel file. Let's see how we do that as below:

```
//@Test public void testFlipkart() throws Exception {
@Test public void testFlipkart(String bookTitle, String authorName, String bookSummary, String isbnNumber) throws Exception {

        selenium.open("http://www.flipkart.com/");
```

```
        selenium.click("id=fk-menuSellcon");
        selenium.click("//div[@id='fk-ml']/ul/li[2]/div");
//      selenium.type("id=fk-top-search-box", "The Time Of My Life");
        selenium.type("id=fk-top-search-box", bookTitle);
        selenium.click("name=Search");
        selenium.waitForPageToLoad("30000");
//      selenium.click("link=The Time Of My Life");
        selenium.click("link="+bookTitle);
        selenium.waitForPageToLoad("30000");
//      verifyTrue(selenium.isTextPresent("Cecelia Ahern"));
        verifyTrue(selenium.isTextPresent(authorName));
//      verifyTrue(selenium.isTextPresent("The stunning and magical new novel from the Number One
bestselling author"));
        verifyTrue(selenium.isTextPresent(bookSummary));
//      verifyTrue(selenium.isTextPresent("9780007463305"));
        verifyTrue(selenium.isTextPresent(isbnNumber));
    }
```

The end-to-end Code

When we put together all this along with the configuration of Eclipse for the jar files, we get the following code.

```
//Data Driven Test Framework using Selenium and TestNG
//This Test performs search for the books and looks for the attributes on the result page
//Data is read from the Excel SS - book_data1.xls

package script;

import com.thoughtworks.selenium.*;

import org.openqa.selenium.server.SeleniumServer;
import org.testng.annotations.*;

import java.io.File;
import jxl.*;

public class DDTFlipkart extends SeleneseTestCase{
```

```
@BeforeTest
public void setUp() throws Exception {
   SeleniumServer seleniumserver=new SeleniumServer();
   seleniumserver.boot();
   seleniumserver.start();

   Integer port = 4444;
String browserString= "*firefox";
String url = "http://www.flipkart.com";
selenium = new DefaultSelenium("localhost",port,browserString,url) {
public void open(String url) { commandProcessor.doCommand("open", new String[] {url,"true"});};
};
selenium.start();

   selenium.setTimeout("120000");
   selenium.open("/");
   selenium.windowMaximize();
   selenium.windowFocus();
}

@DataProvider(name = "DP1")
public Object[][] createData1() {
   Object[][] retObjArr=getTableArray("test\\resources\\data\\book_data1.xls",
         "DataPool", "bookTestData1");
   return(retObjArr);
}

@Test (dataProvider = "DP1")
public void testFlipkart(String bookTitle,
         String authorName, String bookSummary, String isbnNumber) throws Exception {
      selenium.open("/");
      selenium.click("id=fk-menuSellIcon");
      selenium.click("//div[@id='fk-ml']/ul/li[2]/div");
      selenium.type("id=fk-top-search-box", bookTitle);
      selenium.click("name=Search");
      selenium.waitForPageToLoad("120000");
      selenium.click("link="+bookTitle);
      selenium.waitForPageToLoad("120000");
      verifyTrue(selenium.isTextPresent(authorName));
```

```
        verifyTrue(selenium.isTextPresent(bookSummary));
        verifyTrue(selenium.isTextPresent(isbnNumber));
    }


@AfterClass
public void tearDown(){
    selenium.close();
    selenium.stop();
}

public String[][] getTableArray(String xlFilePath, String sheetName, String tableName){
    String[][] tabArray=null;
    try{
        Workbook workbook = Workbook.getWorkbook(new File(xlFilePath));
        Sheet sheet = workbook.getSheet(sheetName);
        Cell tableStart=sheet.findCell(tableName);
        int startRow,startCol, endRow, endCol,ci,cj;
        startRow=tableStart.getRow();
        startCol=tableStart.getColumn();

        Cell tableEnd= sheet.findCell(tableName, startCol+1,startRow+1, 100, 64000,  false);

        endRow=tableEnd.getRow();
        endCol=tableEnd.getColumn();

        tabArray=new String[endRow-startRow-1][endCol-startCol-1];
        ci=0;

        for (int i=startRow+1;i<endRow;i++,ci++){
            cj=0;
            for (int j=startCol+1;j<endCol;j++,cj++){
                tabArray[ci][cj]=sheet.getCell(j,i).getContents();
            }
        }
    }
    catch (Exception e)   {
        System.out.println("error in getTableArray()" + e.getMessage());
```

```
        }
        return(tabArray);
    }

}//end of class
```

The output result will be displayed as below:

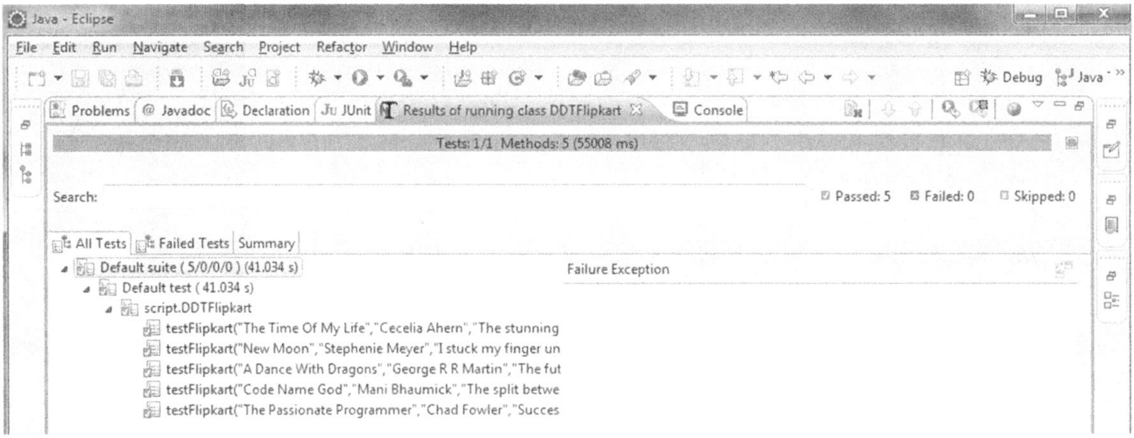

EXERCISES

1. What is need for data driven testing?
2. Where can the data for testing be stored?
3. Which annotation of TestNG support data driven testing?
4. How can we avoid hard-coding of rows/columns of data file?
5. How can IDE help in data driven considering it will be an RC (TestNG) code?

20

SELENIUM GRID

What is Grid Computing

Grid Computing is an age old computer engineering concept, its classic definition can be "grid computing is a form of distributed computing in which an organisation (business, university, etc.) uses its existing computers (desktop and/or cluster nodes) to handle its own long-running computational tasks."

The above concept has been extended to create Selenium Grid, which is nothing, but topology of various RCs controlled by a HUB RC.

Need for Selenium Grid

As our test suite grows in size and complexity, it demands more power from the RC server and also the execution time grows considerably. Depending upon our hardware configuration and stability we can be certain to some extent that our RC server will not freeze or hang (however that can happen).

Even though we might be certain about stability of RC server, we might want to divide our run time across multiple RCs, another requirement could be that of parallel running the same tests for various combination of operating systems/browsers.So Selenium Grid extends Selenium RC by running tests on different servers in parallel. It reduces the time, and subsequently the cost, for testing in various browsers under multiple operation systems.

In Grid topology, various copies of Selenium RC servers are controlled by a central HUB. The HUB and Spoke architecture conceptually displays as below:

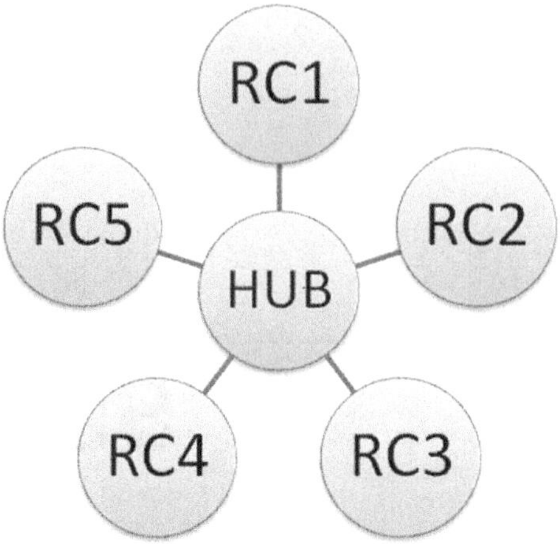

Selenium Grid architecture:

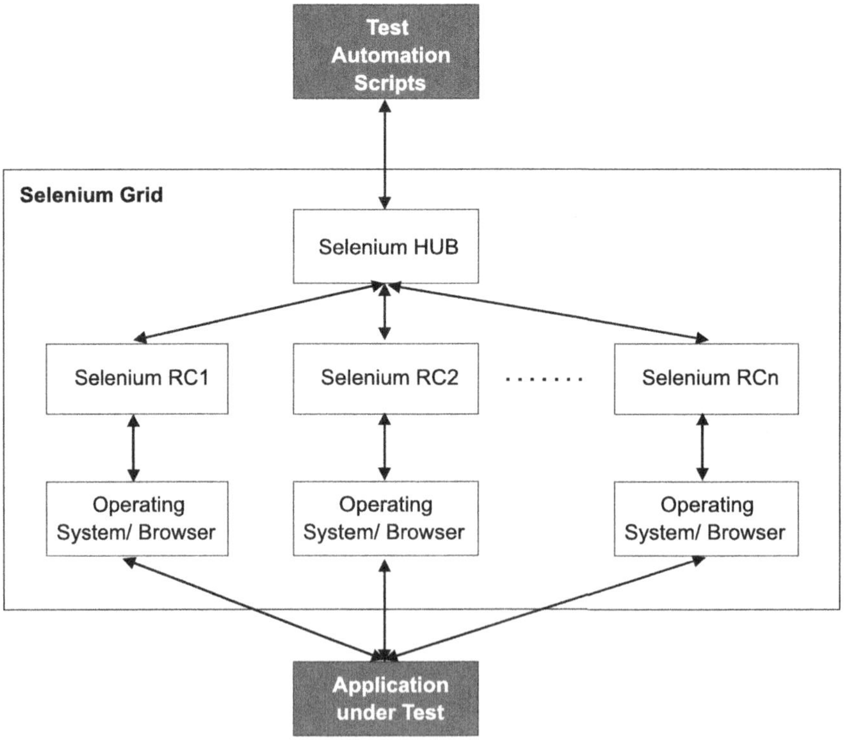

The testers who write the test automation scripts need not worry about the underlying architecture of the Grid. So, if testers can write and run automation scripts on RC then they don't need to learn the intricacies of Selenium Grid, which in fact is nothing but network topology of various RCs. However, Selenium Grid itself does not provide a parallel running strategy. If you want to take advantage of Selenium Grid, you need to write your selenium tests in parallel mode.

TestNg Configuration for Parallel Execution

We are using TestNG as the scripting language and test framework as TestNG is designed to simplify a broad range of testing needs and to extend the JUnit. Example of a simple TestNG configuration file is shown as below:

```
<!DOCTYPE suite SYSTEM "http://testng.org/testng-1.0.dtd">
<suite name="Suite1"  parallel="methods" thread-count="2">
<test name="Testcase" >
      <classes>
         <class name="com.test.workflow.device.testcase"/>
      </classes>
  </test>
</suite>
```

The <suite> tag can represent one TestNG XML file containing one or more tests. The <test> tag allows a test to contain one or more TestNG classes. The <class> tag signifies that a TestNG class can contain one or more test methods. The test method is defined in Java files, as shown below:

```
@Test
public void testMethod()
{
   ....
}
```

Installing GRID

You need to have Java JDK version 5+ installed on your system. Download from link http://www.java.com/en/download/index.jsp. Please refer to chapter 3 for more details.

To run Grid you need to have Ant (Another Neat Tool from Apache) installed, version 1.7+. Download Ant from Binary distribution link http://ant.apache.org/bindownload.cgi. Follow the steps as below:

1. Download the binary distribution zip file for e.g. apache-ant-1.7.1-bin.zip
2. Unzip the file to your preferred folder where you wish to install Ant for e.g. c:\ant\

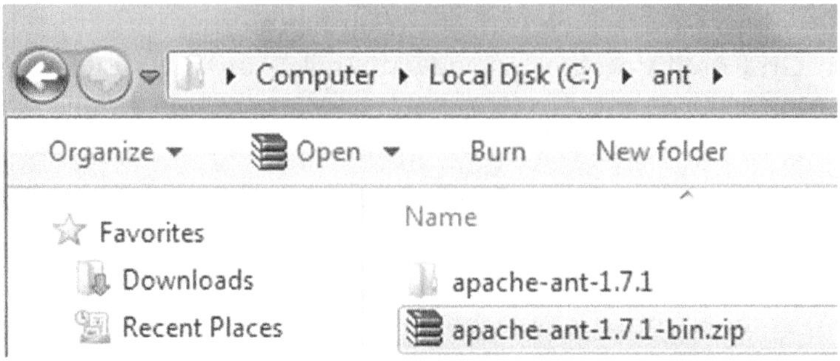

3. Add the 'bin' folder to your environment PATH variable. For e.g. C:\ant\apache-ant-1.7.1\bin\ (Please ensure you have included the trailing '\' in the path, at times it can create problem when not included). Close the command prompt if any.
4. Try command ant –version to see if Ant has been installed properly. You will get message 'Apache Ant version 1.x.x compiled on date'.

Now we are ready to install Grid. Download the latest binary from link http://selenium-grid.seleniumhq.org/download.html for e.g. selenium-grid-1.0.8-bin.zip and unzip the content to the folder in which you would like to install Grid for e.g. c:\selenium-grid-1.0.8

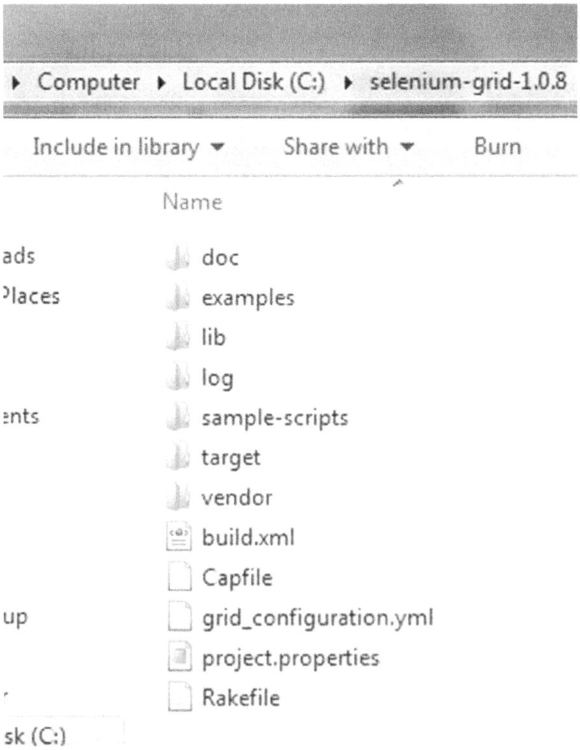

To check whether Grid has been installed properly, go to the Grid installation directory in command prompt and type command "ant sanity-check" and you shall get message conveying that the build was successful.

Configuring GRID

Launching HUB

Open command prompt and go to the Selenium Grid installation directory and type command:

Title HUB

Ant launch-hub

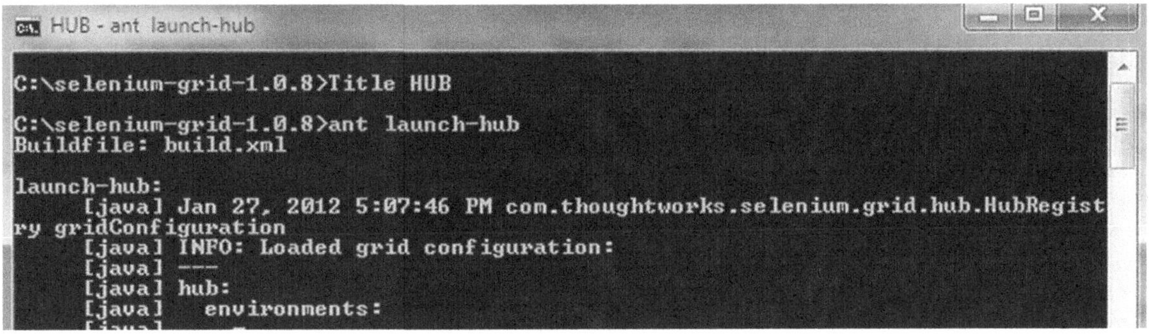

The Title command is to set the Title of the commands prompt to make it easier to identify the window later.

At this point we can view the Grid console on http://localhost:4444/console as below:

As now RCs are available, we will add one.

Launching RC

Open new command prompt and type following commands:

Title RC1

Ant launch-remote-control

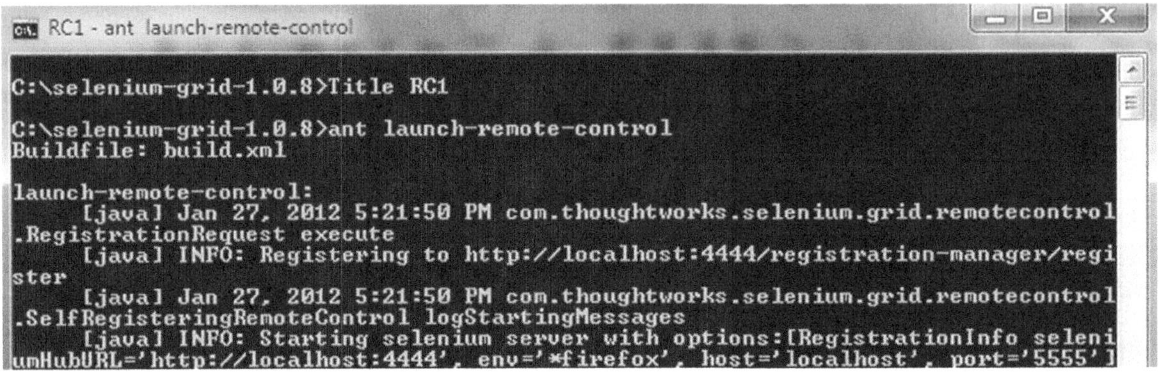

Now check on the Hub Console, we have one Remote Control available:

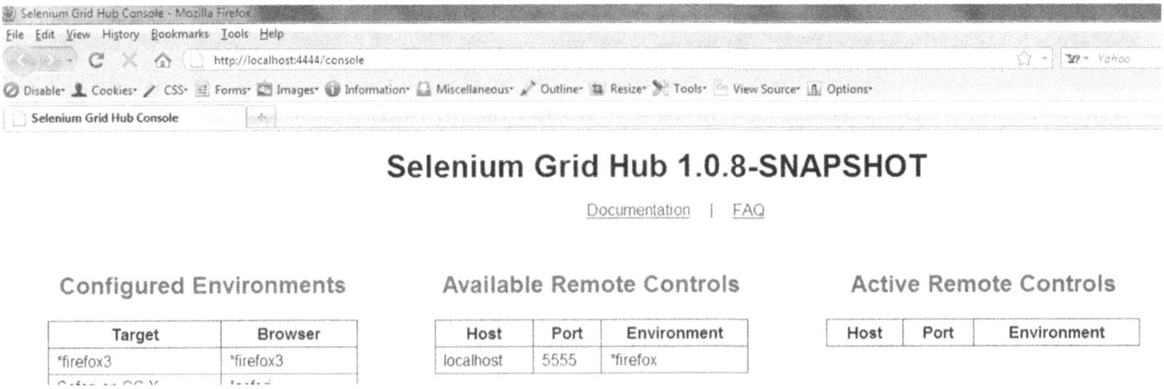

Please note that the RC was launched as default port 5555 and browser *firefox.

If we wish to add more RCs to hub, we can do it one by one as per the required configuration. For e.g. if we want to add a node to the same machine to run Internet Explorer browser then we call following commands in the new commands prompt:

Title RC2_IE

Ant –Dport=5556 –Denvironment=*ieplore launch-remote-control

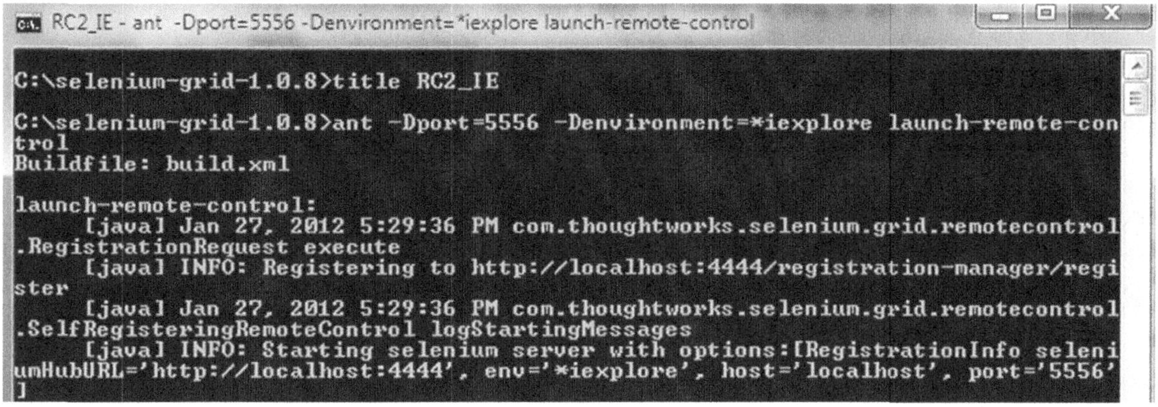

Please note that we have given next port number as 5556 and browser as Internet Explorer.

If you are adding this RC at another machine one LAN then add two more parameters as –Dhost and –DhubURL.

For e.g.

ant -Dhost=192.161.118.106 DhubURL=http://192.161.118.75:4444

-Denvironment=*firefox launch-remote-control

For each remote control, set the port to something different; you can't have two remote controls using the same port.

- Dport is the port that the Hub will use to talk to the remote control. This must be unique.
- Denvironment is the environment you'll be using. Set it to something in the available environments list (check the Hub console in the browser).
- Dhost is the IP address (or name) of the machine that is running the remote control.
- DhubURL is the full URL (including http:// and the port) of the machine that's running the Hub

Now we should have this newly added RC visible in the console as below:

Simply following this process more RCs can be added to the Grid.

If you wish remove some machine from the available RC list then you can stop and shutdown that RC. However if that RC has crashed then you can remove it from your grid by the command below in browser:

http://<hub ip address/machine name>:4444/registration-manager/unregister?host=<node machine>&port=<Port of the frozen RC>&environment=<environment setup>

This will unregister it from the hub. For e.g http://localhost:4444/registration-manager/unregister?host=locahost&port=5556&environment=*iexplore

Running Test on Grid

While creating our tests for Grid we need to ensure that they are independent i.e. suppose if we need to login before filling the registration page then we need to ensure that each of our test (which we plan to run parallel on Grid) has login process before the registration test. We need to instruct the test to run on Grid HUB, this can be done on the @setUp() method in our test as below:

```
@BeforeTest
public void setUp() throws Exception {

 Integer port = 4444;
   String browserString= "*firefox";
   String url = "http://www.qaagility.com";
   selenium = new DefaultSelenium("192.161.118.75",port,browserString,url) {
   public void open(String url) { commandProcessor.doCommand("open", new String[]
{url,"true"});};
   };

   selenium.start();

    selenium.setTimeout("120000");
    selenium.open("/");
    selenium.windowMaximize();
    selenium.windowFocus();
}
```

Where 192.161.118.75 is the IP Address of HUB Machine.

We need to utilize the parallel test execution option of TestNG which can be configured in the TestNG.xml file as below:

```
<suite name="TestEnvSuite" parallel="classes" thread-count="2" verbose="1">
<test name="EETestBase">
 <classes>
 <class name="script.TC_Google_EE"></class>
 <class name="script.TC_Yahoo_EE"></class>
</classes>
</test>
</suite>
```

EXERCISES

1. Why do we need Grid?
2. What is the default port number for the HUB?
3. What is the default port number and browser for the first RC?
4. Where the Grid HUB related information can be saved in the tests?
5. Why the tests that need to be run on grid in parallel needs to be independent?
6. What is the use of TestNG while running tests on Grid?

21

Selenium Test Management Using Bromine

What is Bromine?

Bromine is an open source QA tool that uses selenium RC as its testing engine.

It provides project management, OS/browser specification, test-case creation as well as user management.

Bromine substantially eases the process of creating, maintaining and running Selenium RC tests. The tests are created with the custom Selenium IDE format and uploaded to Bromine. The test can then be run on test machines (we refer to them as nodes) which are configured in Bromine.

Another nice thing about using bromine is now you can run your tests in other languages, not just the Selenium IDE, which is limited to the IDE's generated "Selenese" commands for tests. You can export your IDE into PHP or Java, and then on the bromine server you can change the code as per your requirements.

Its lofty aim is to be the open source alternative to commercial tools (such as HP Quality Center).

Installation

Prerequisites:

- Java

- Selenium RC
- Webserver (eg. Apache)
- MySQL database

By now, you must have got Java and Selenium RC, if not please refer to previous chapters. For Apache webserver and MySQL database, easiest and most efficient option is to use XAMPP server, it gives Apache, MySQL, PHP (and Perl which we won't use here) as a unit. (http://www.apachefriends.org/en/xampp.html)

After you have taken care of these prerequisites, we can proceed with Bromine installation.

Download Bromine

- Download Bromine from http://brominefoundation.org/download.php?f=zipupdate_v1.zip (or http://seleniumhq.org/download)
- Unpack and copy all files to your webroot. Bromine must be served directly from the webroot!
- If you are using XAMPP this is the C:\xammp\htdocs directory. The file structure should be:

  htdocs
  – cake
  – app
  – IDE-Formats
  – vendors
  – .htaccess
  – index.php
  – README

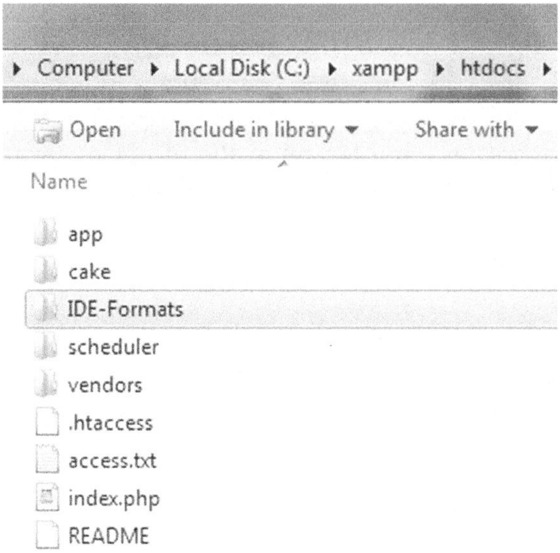

Configure Apache Server and MySQL

➢ From the XAMPP control panel, start the Apache server and MySQL

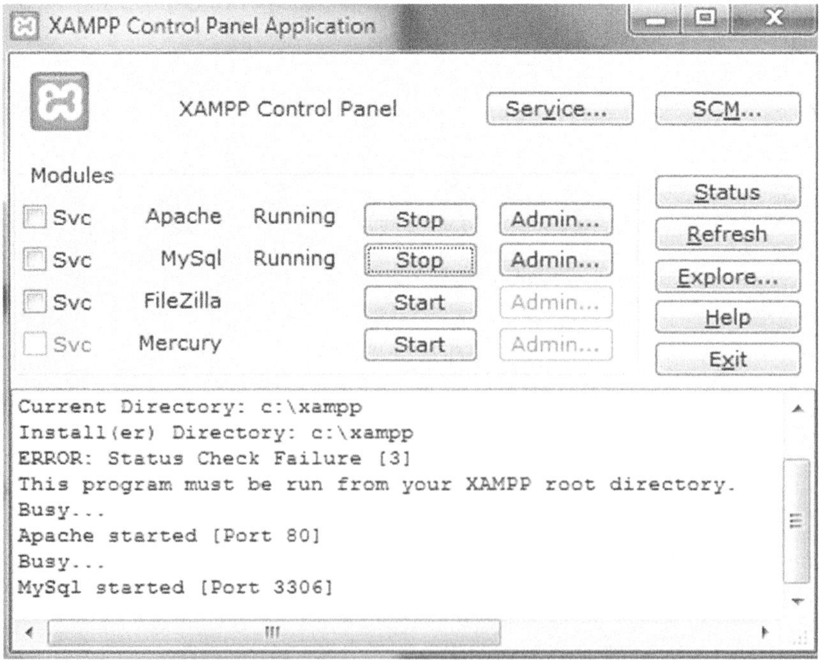

➢ Open http://localhost/phpmyadmin/ in browser, this will point to XAMPP SQL databases, select 'bromine'

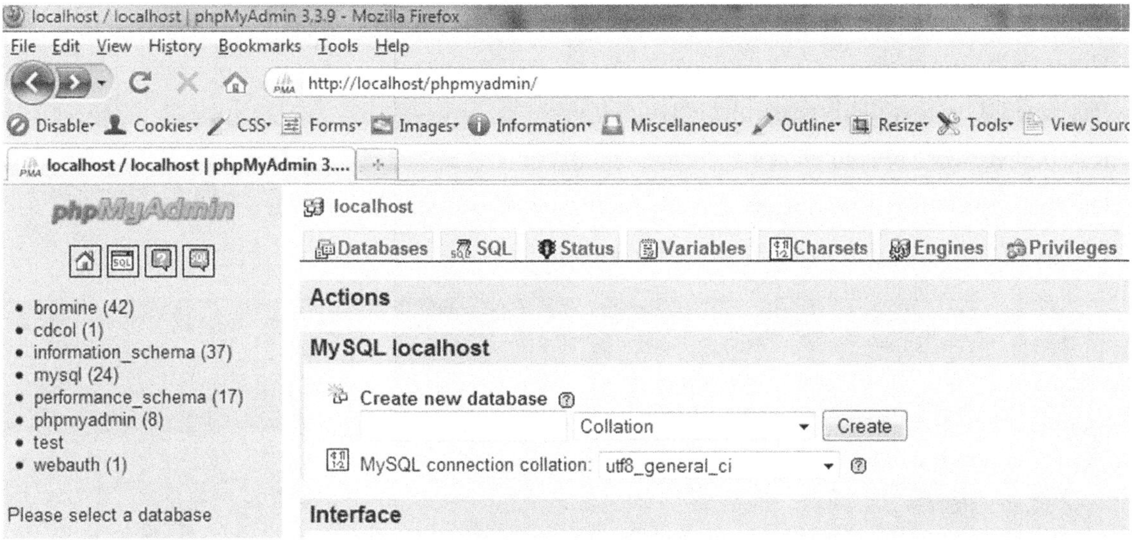

➢ Click on 'Priviledges' tab

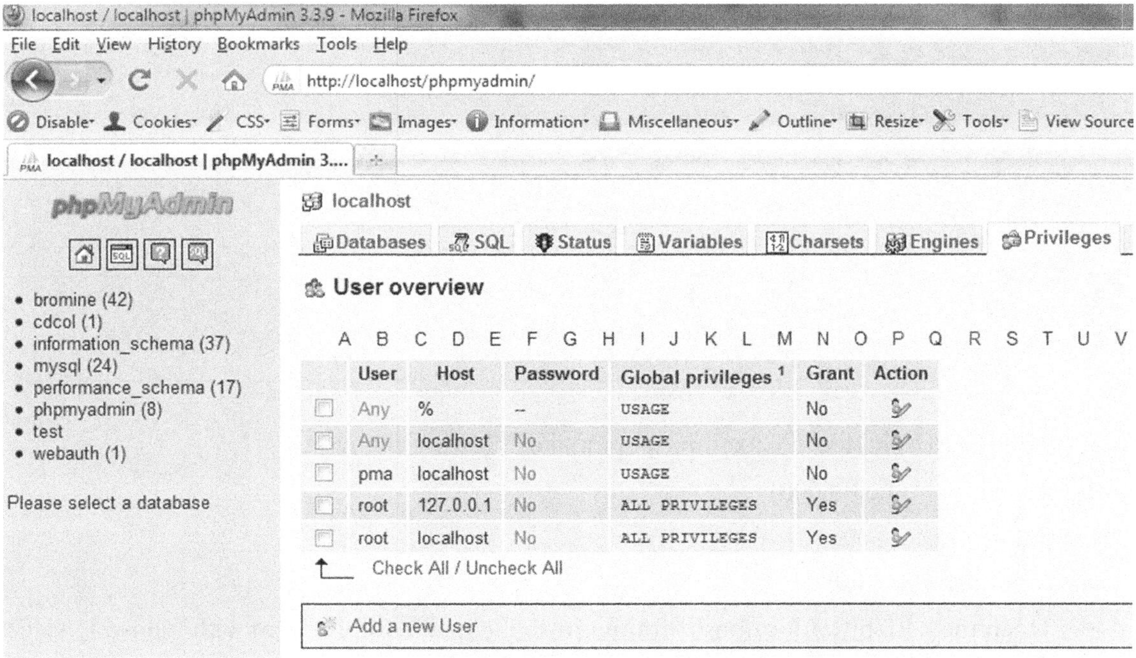

➢ Click on Add a new User

Create new user using following information:

User name: Use test field:/bromine

Host: Local/localhost

Password: Use text field:/*password of your choice*

Retype: *password of your choice*

Database for user: chose option 'Create database with same name and grant all privileges'

Click on 'Go' button at the bottom of the page.

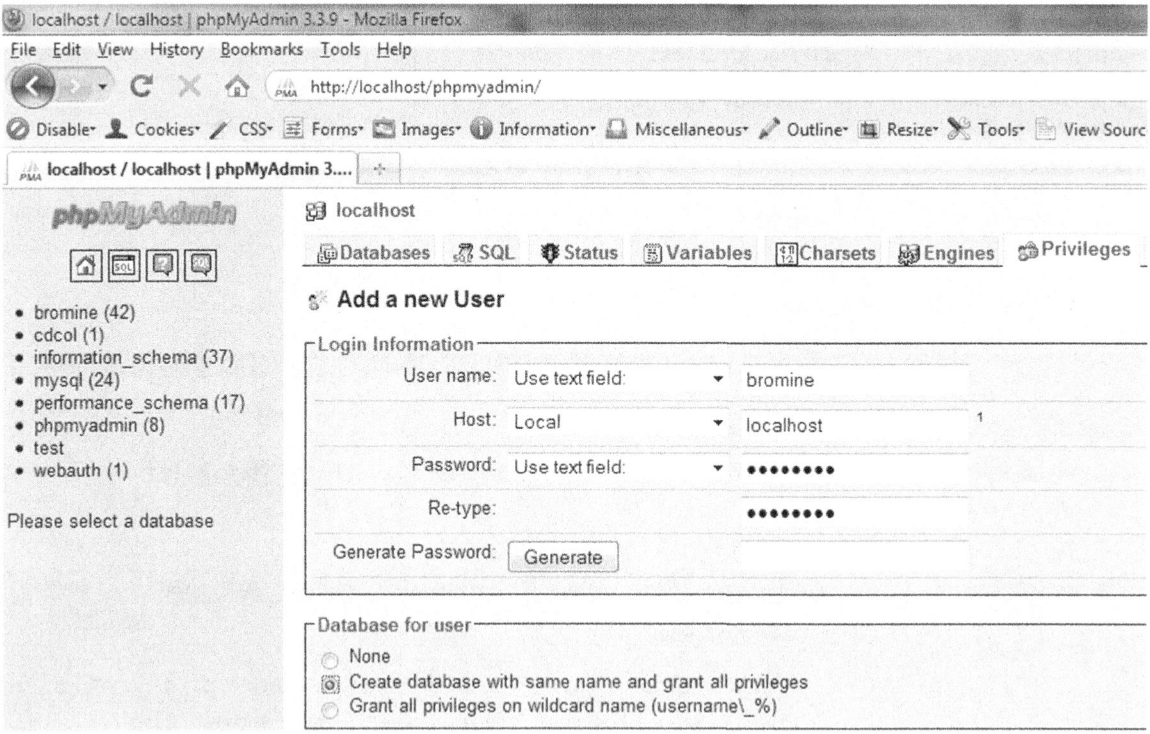

➢ Edit the PHP.ini file at C:\xampp\php, make following changes:

max_execution_time = 60001

max_input_time = 60001

magic_quotes_gpc = Off

➢ Open the URL http://localhost/bromine/install.php and fill the form with following value:

Host: localhost

Username: root

Password: *as you wish*

Database: bromine

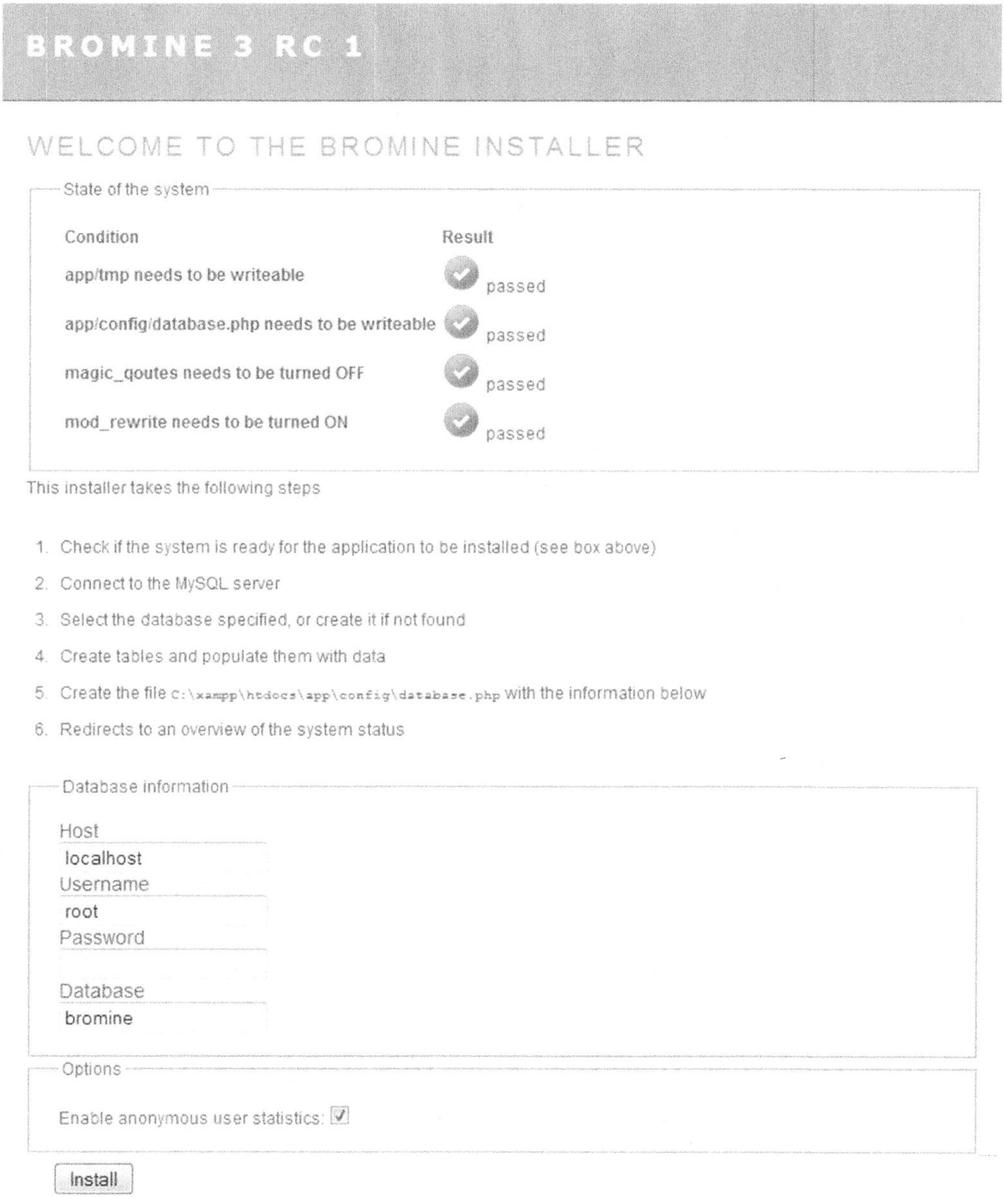

- Click on Install
- You would get message that "Install Complete"

Launching Bromine

➢ Open URL http://localhost/ and enter Name/password to enter Bromine. 'admin'/'admin' as default values.

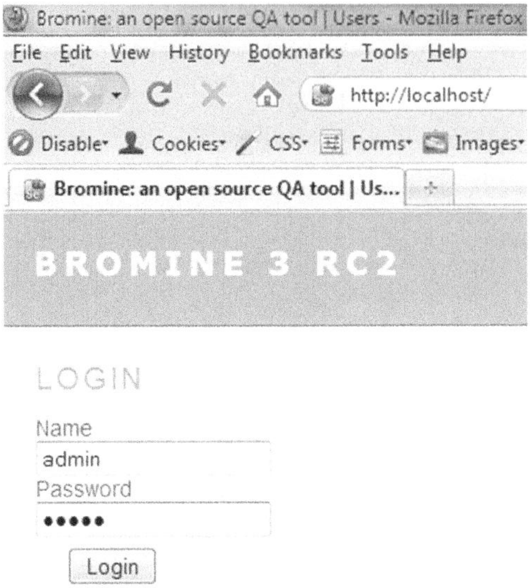

➢ Once login, select default project (optional)

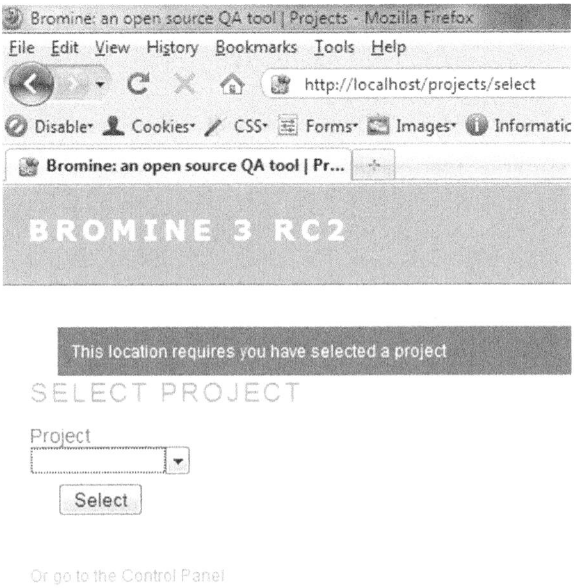

➢ This will take you inside the project and display screen as below:

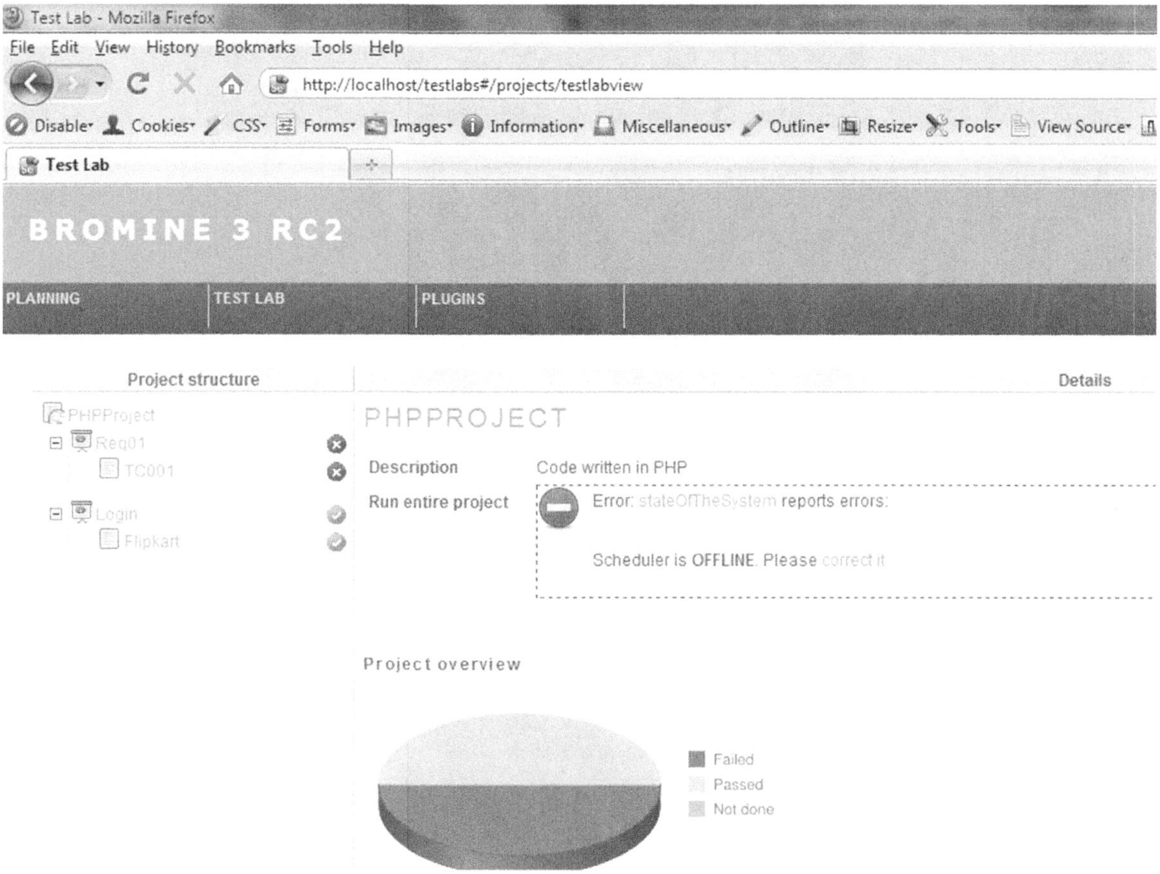

➢ If you don't have a project (when you start there will not be any projects), you need to create one as below:

Control Panel ( ) → Projects → New Project

Click on Submit to save.

➢ Let's look at the Menu option Planning, this is where we can create Requirements and Test Cases for the project

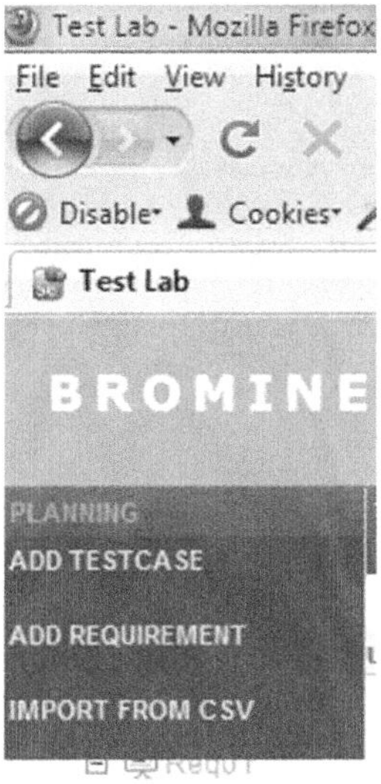

Using this option we can create Requirements and allocate Test Case to them. We can also import Requirements/Test Case from CSV file. Example files as below:

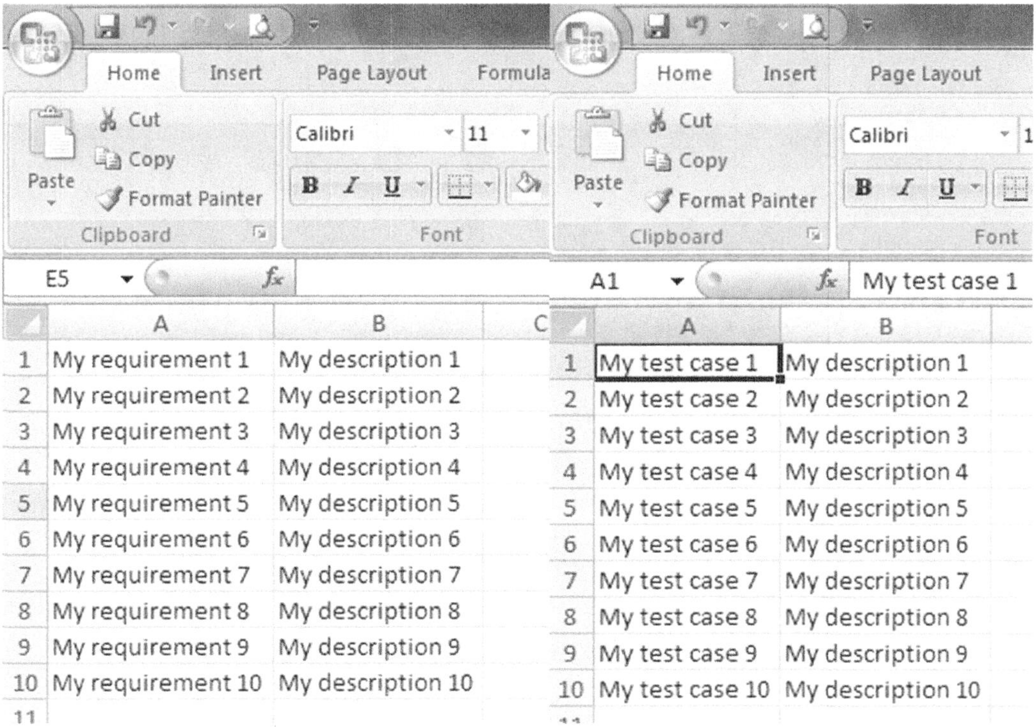

➢ If we need to create Requirement from Menu option then go back to 'Workspace' ()

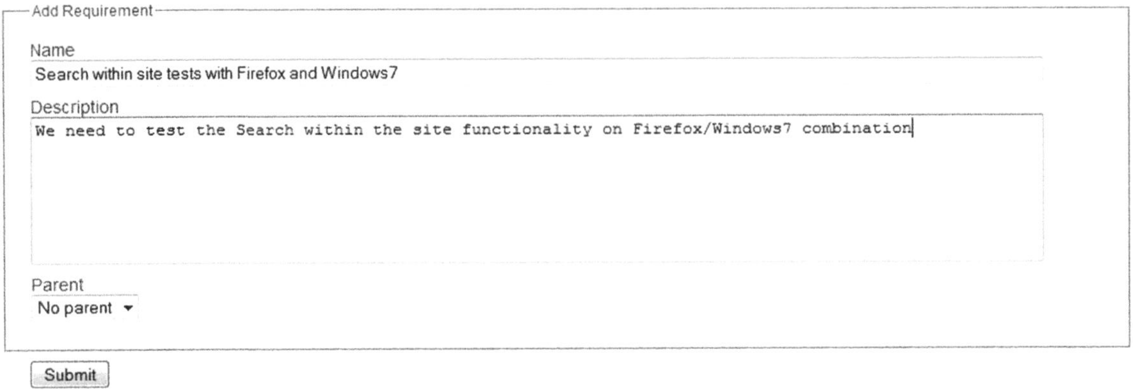

➢ We can then edit to save the O.S./Browser requirement

	Windows Vista	Ubuntu	Windows 2000	Mac OSx	Windows 98	Windows 95	Windows 7
Internet Explorer 7	☐	☐	☐	☐	☐	☐	☐
Internet Explorer 6	☐	☐	☐	☐	☐	☐	☐
Firefox 2	☐	☐	☐	☐	☐	☐	☑
Safari	☐	☐	☐	☐	☐	☐	☐
Firefox 3	☐	☐	☐	☐	☐	☐	☑
Opera	☐	☐	☐	☐	☐	☐	☐
Internet Explorer 8	☐	☐	☐	☐	☐	☐	☐

➢ We can then click on 'Add Testcase' link to add new test cases to this requirement.

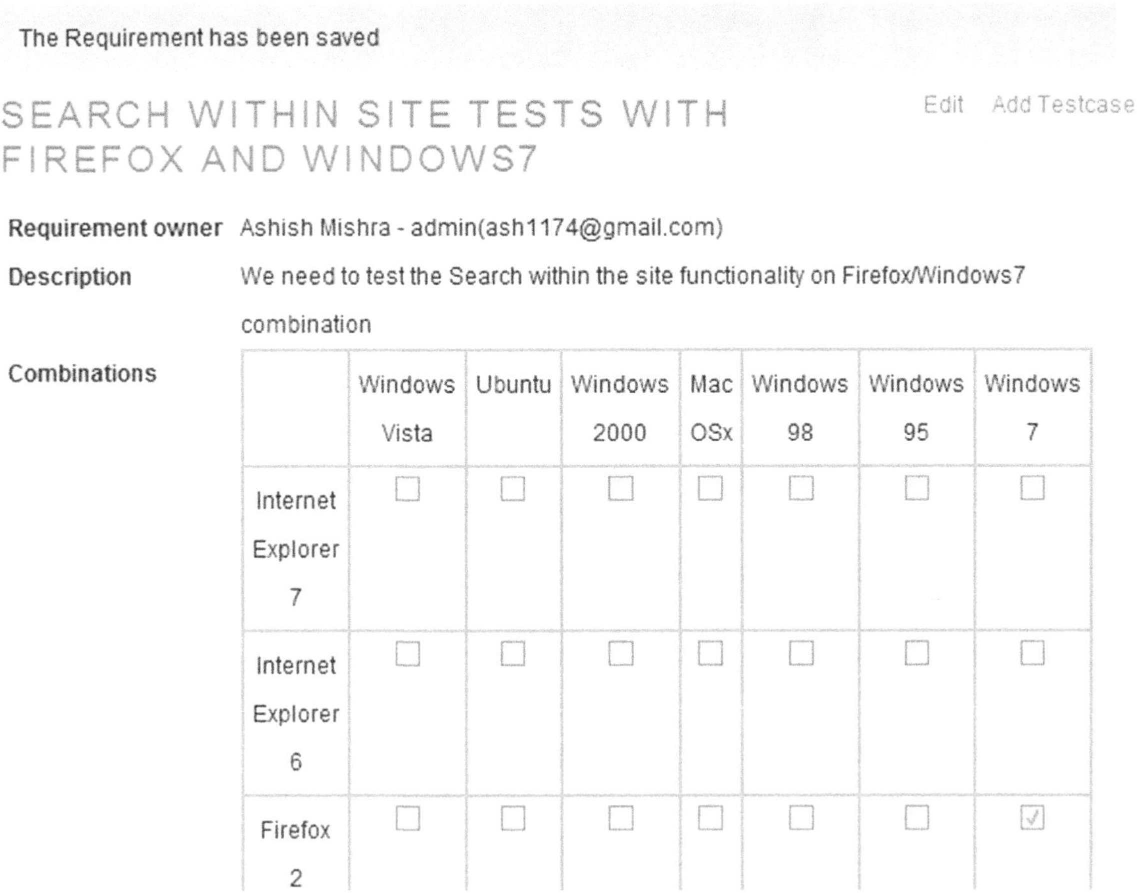

The Requirement has been saved

SEARCH WITHIN SITE TESTS WITH FIREFOX AND WINDOWS7

Edit Add Testcase

Requirement owner Ashish Mishra - admin(ash1174@gmail.com)

Description We need to test the Search within the site functionality on Firefox/Windows7 combination

Combinations

	Windows Vista	Ubuntu	Windows 2000	Mac OSx	Windows 98	Windows 95	Windows 7
Internet Explorer 7	☐	☐	☐	☐	☐	☐	☐
Internet Explorer 6	☐	☐	☐	☐	☐	☐	☐
Firefox 2	☐	☐	☐	☐	☐	☐	☑

➢ We can also create new test case from menu option Planning – Add Testcase and link to Requirement (one or more)

➢ Now we can Edit the Testcase to add Testscript as there is no script uploaded.

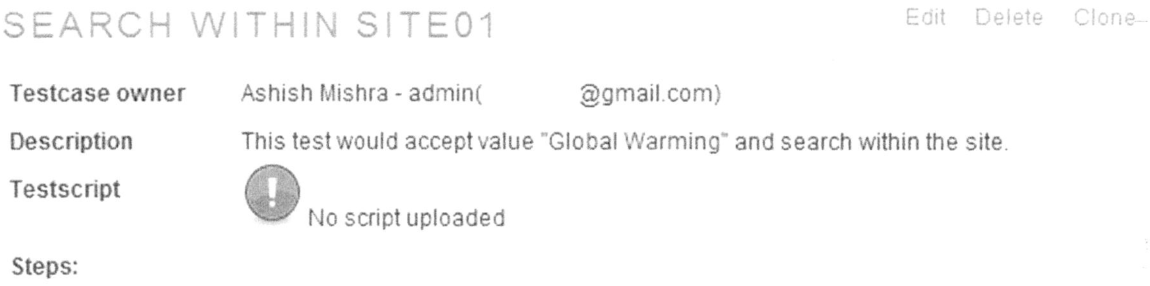

➢ We can add our IDE scripts to this test case, however we need to have them in Bromine format. Refer to Chapter 8 for more details on adding new format to IDE. We will pickup the formats from folder C:\xampp\htdocs\IDE-Formats

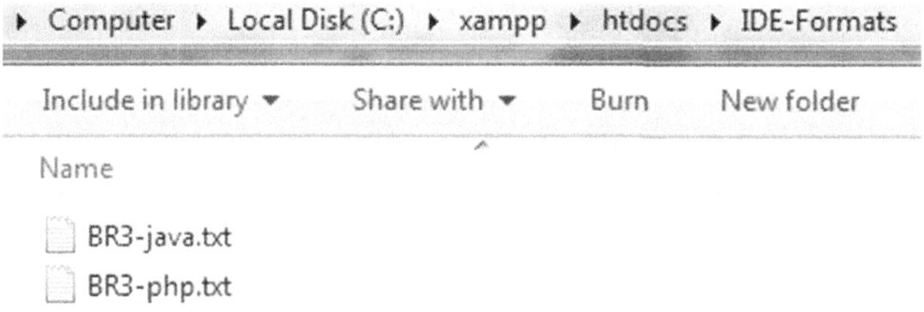

➢ As we need the PHP format, we will use BR3.php.txt code and add that as new format to IDE

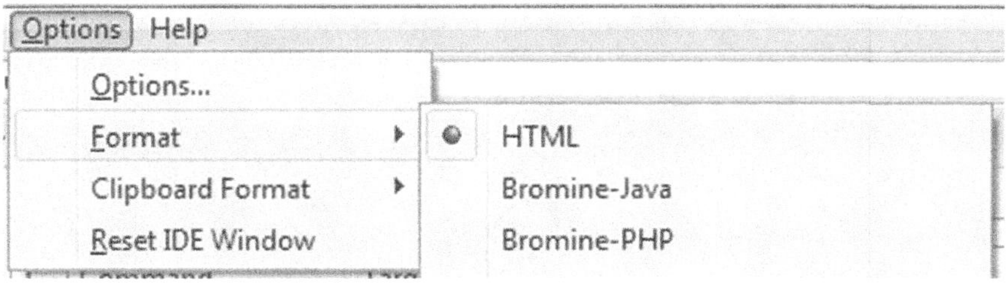

➢ Subsequent to this, we can pick up any recorded script in IDE and convert to Bromine-PHP format. This format code can be loaded to the Test case created in Bromine.

Running Test case in Bromine

After you have converted the IDE script to PHP Code, you can save it to your preferred folder. Edit the Testcase in which you would like to run this script and upload it.

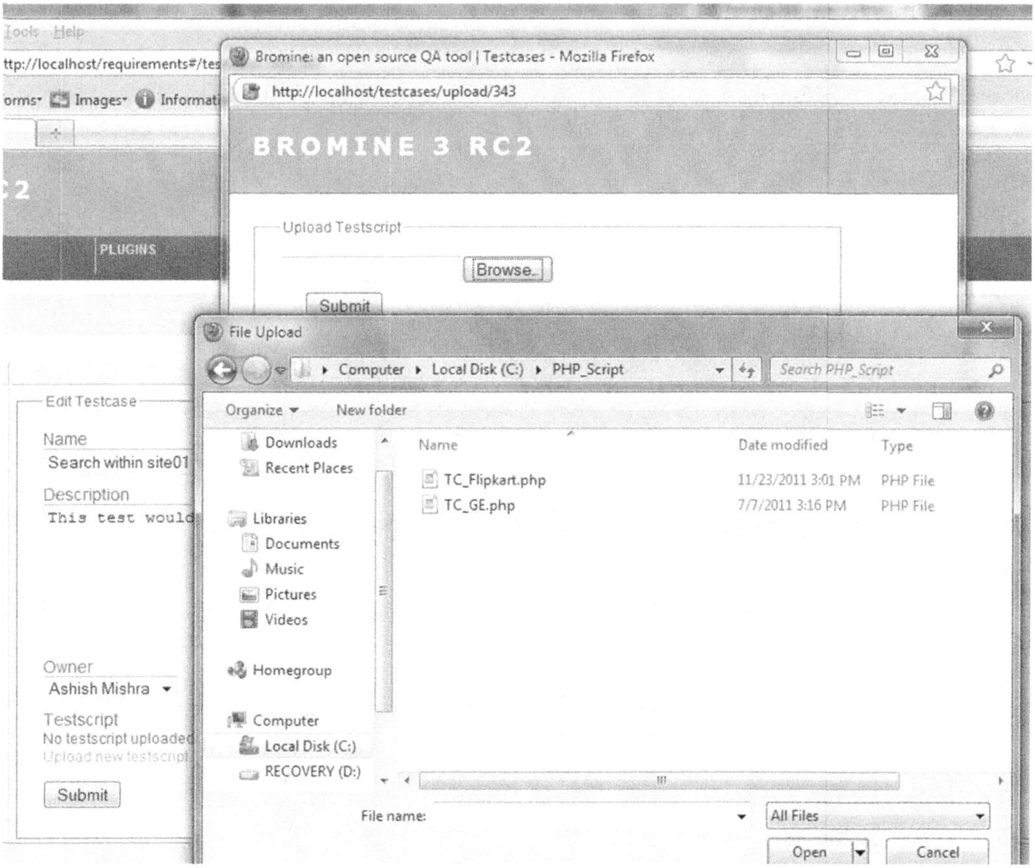

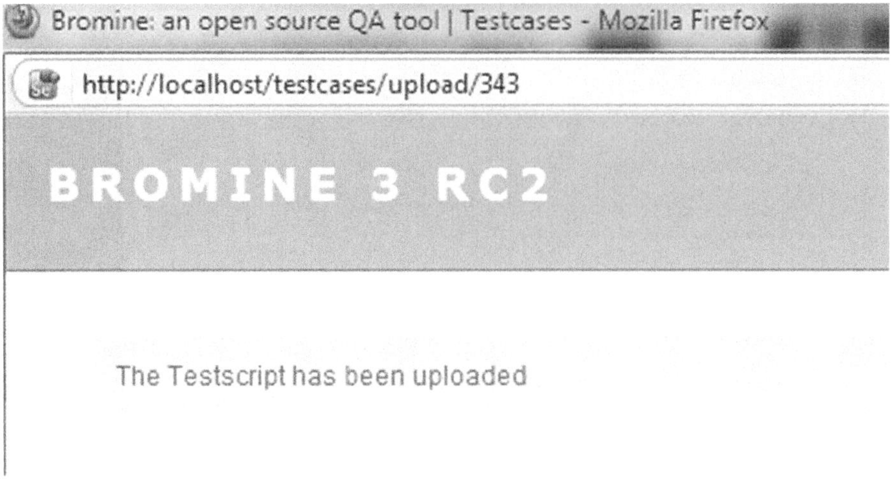

After the PHP Script has been uploaded, it can be viewed using the 'View testscript' link (Please note, you can only view it here, editing is not possible… for editing you need to edit the script at source file and then upload again)

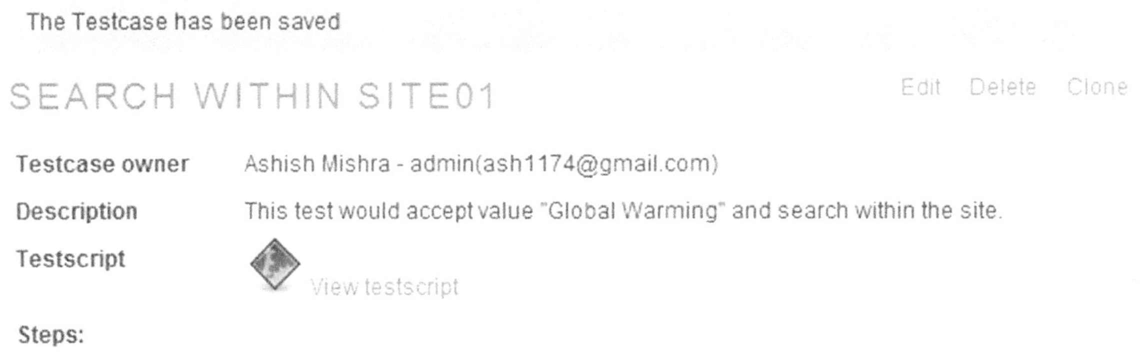

In order to run this script you need to go to the Test Lab menu option. Since there is no RC running, it will give you following screen with error:

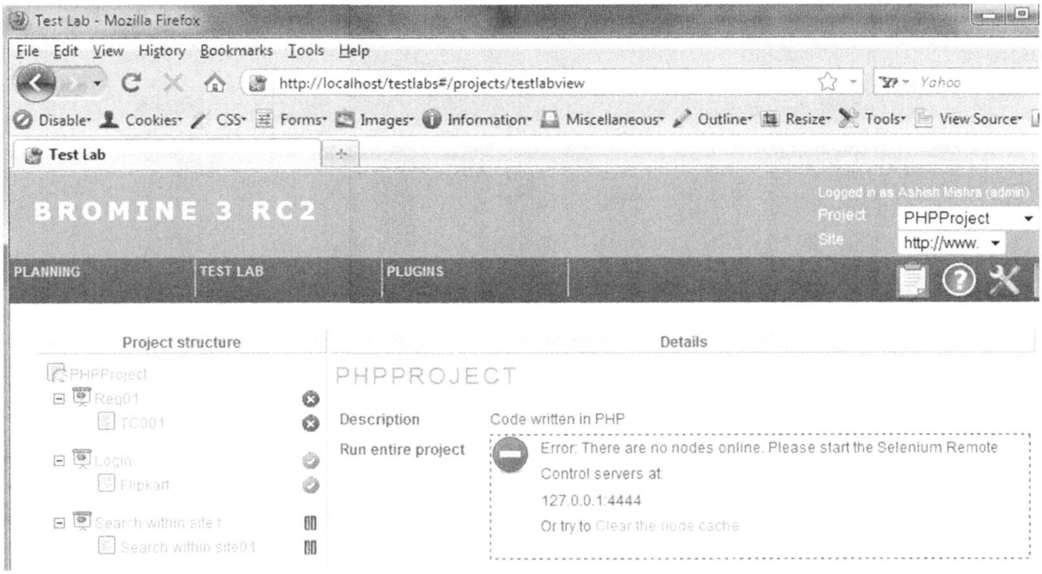

To fix this we need to start the RC. After starting RC on machine, click on link 'Clear the node cache' and the error should go away, however some warnings may remain if certain combination of O.S./Browser that is part of our requirement does not exists.

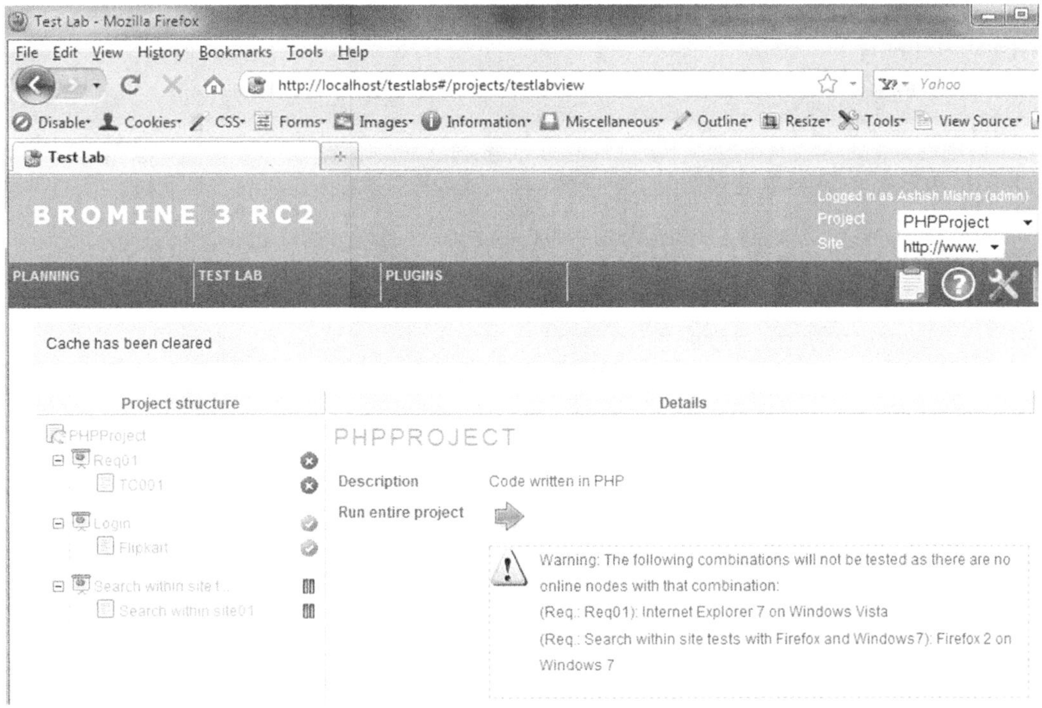

By clicking on the horizontal green arrow, we can run the test. While the tests run we can track its progress.

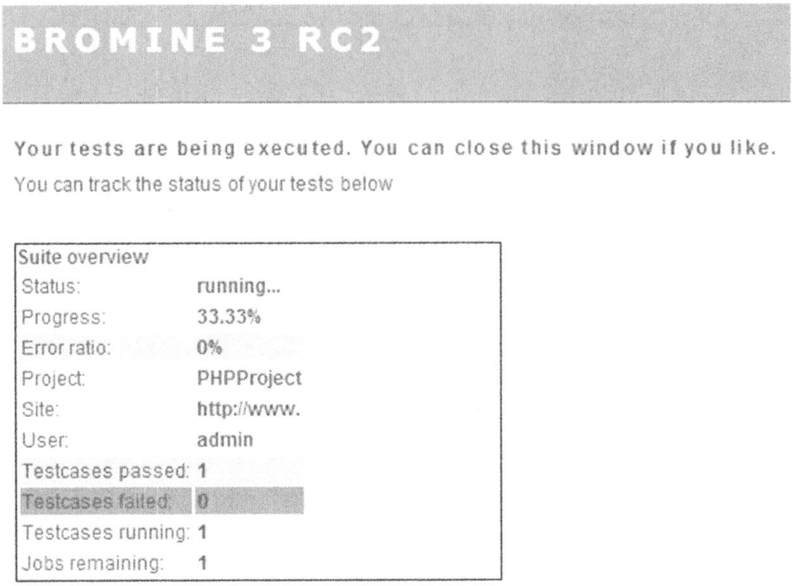

Upon completion, you will get the Dashboard of Tests, error ration and also screenshots of the test steps (IDE like).

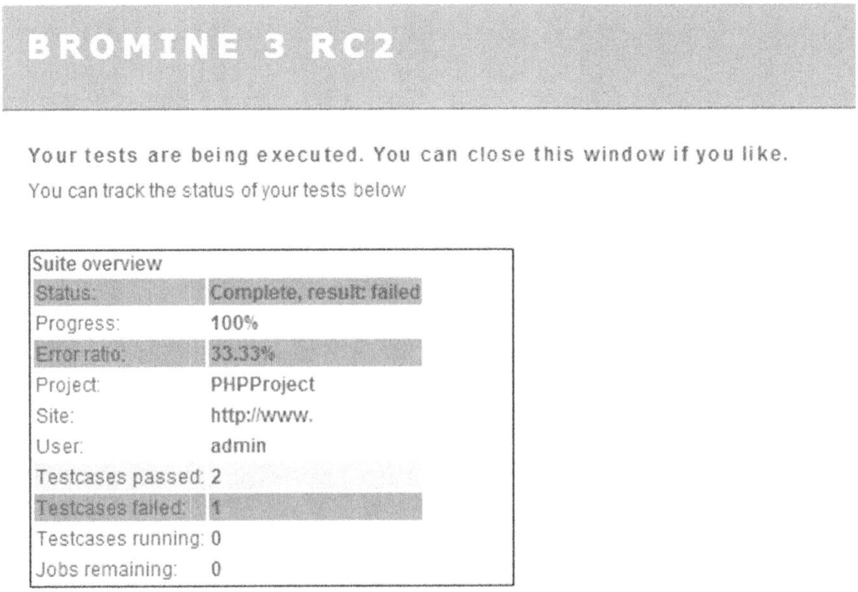

As your test run, the dashboard will show you the Project Overview Pie-chart.

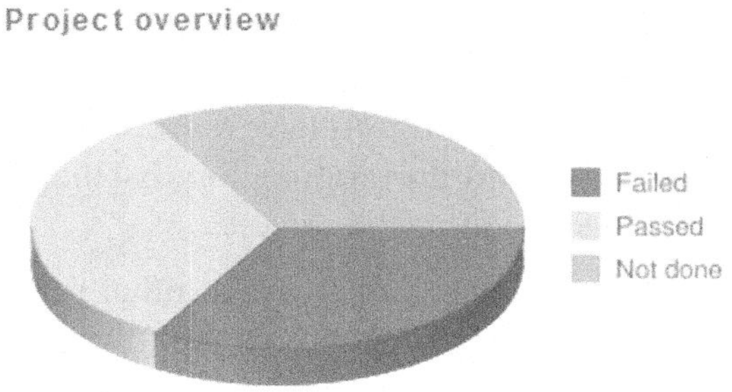

You can run Java test similarly by getting the Java code using the Bromine-Java format and saving it in jar file as Bromine only accepts PHP or Jar files.

Evaluating and managing results

Test Lab view

Testlabs is where you review results and run your test scripts.

Results are always based on the newest run, and a 'parent' will inherit the worst results from it's children, meaning that if a sub-requirement has any failed test cases the parent requirement will be marked as failed.

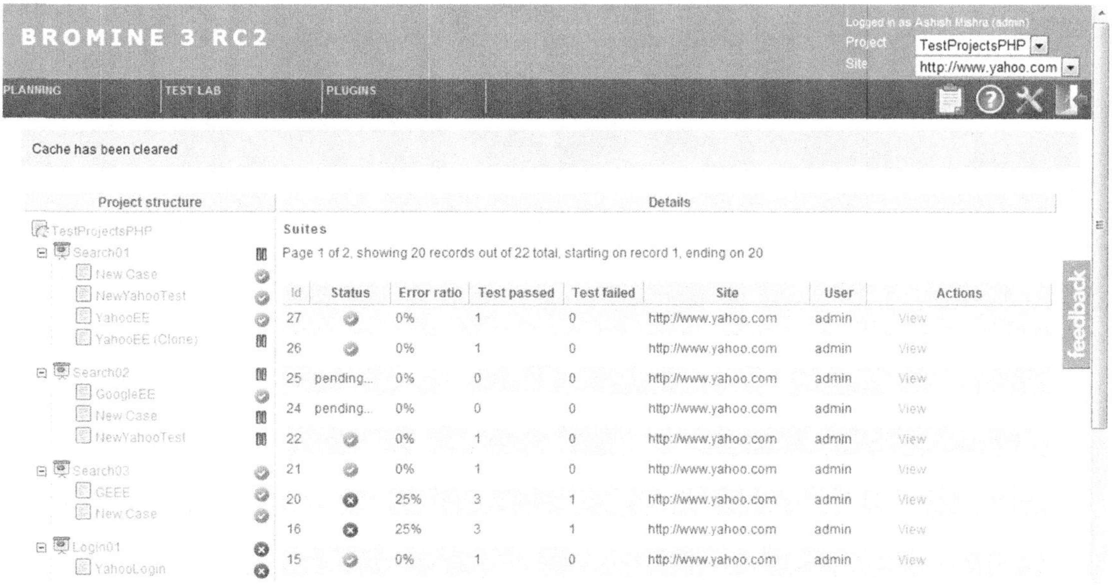

Planning View

Planning is where you plan all your testing activities, meaning you setup your requirements and test cases.

Projects Everything belongs to a project. Projects have multiple users attached to them. Projects have multiple sites attached to them. Sites are the various URLs that the project uses e.g. development/production URLs. Add/edit the sites by editing the project.

Requirements work as containers for test cases as well as other sub-requirements. You can add requirements from the Planning menu. Requirements contain the OS/browser combinations that contained test cases will be run in.

A test case can have a single test script attached to it. Attach the test script by using the upload test script functionality. Test cases can have steps attached to them. Steps are a step by step description of the test, e.g. open google.com, google.com opens. Test cases must be linked to a requirement. A single test case can be linked to multiple requirements.

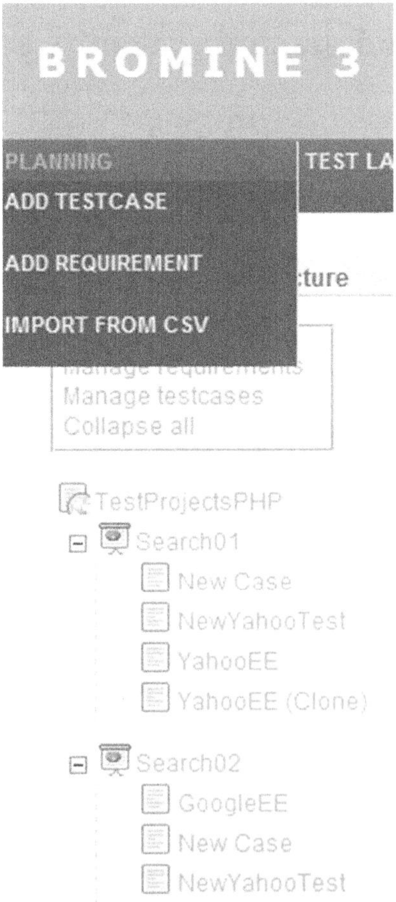

Control Panel View

Control panel is where you configure Bromine. You shouldn't need to spend much time here once Bromine has been setup.

- Projects add/edit/delete projects- Projects can have many requirements, test cases, users, sites and results.
- Nodes add/edit/delete- Nodes are the RC servers Bromine runs test scripts on. Nodes can have many browsers and has one operating system.
- Browsers add/edit/delete browsers- Name is the humanly readable form, e.g. firefox, path is the selenium command to open the browser, e.g. *firefox
- Operating systems add/edit/delete operating systems- You can use operating systems more loosely if you like to provide more nitty-gritty environment definitions for your tests to be run on. e.g. "XP with service pack. 1" or "Vista quad core" or "XP javascript disabled".
- Users add/edit/delete users- User belongs to group. Groups add/edit/delete groups here. Groups can be used to set permissions on a larger scale than user-specifically. Manage access Use this to set permissions for users/groups.
- State of the system Use this to check for the most common errors when using Bromine, e.g. not having write permissions to various folders and such
- Plugins Install/uninstall, activate/deactivate plugins- Installed and activated plugins can be accessed from a plugins menu.

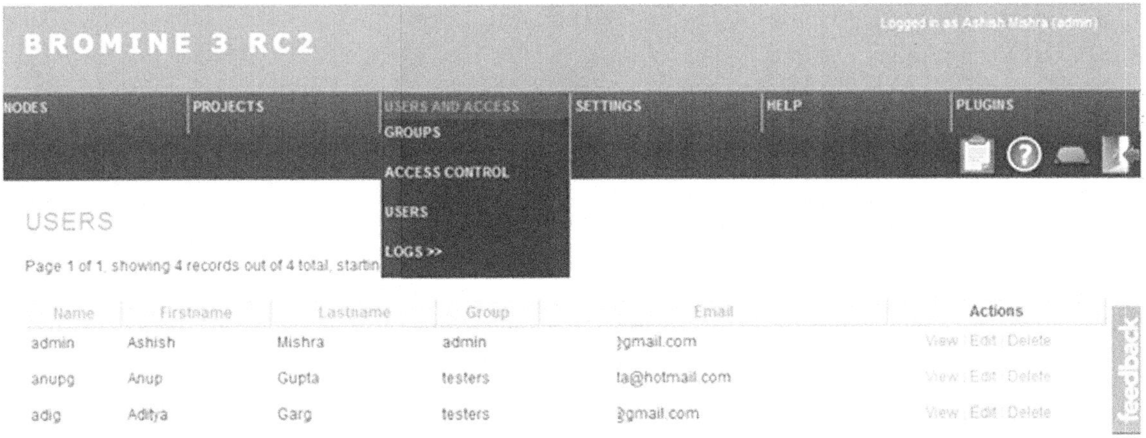

EXERCISES

1. What is the purpose of Bromine?
2. Can Bromine run without IDE?
3. Can Bromine run without RC?
4. Can we run IDE test cases directly in Bromine?
5. Which two languages Bromine supports?
6. Where can we find the two formats of Bromine?
7. What is a Node in Bromine?
8. What language Bromine built by?
9. What does XAMPP stand for?

22

Selenium 2.0 – Future of Test Automation

Selenium 2.0 and Webdriver Project

Webdriver has been integrated with Selenium to give Selenium 2.0 (more precisely Selenium 2.x). How does this impact Selenium as a tool?

Webdriver definition:

Shorter version: A developer-focused tool for the automated testing of webapps.

Longer version: WebDriver is a tool for automating testing web applications, and in particular to verify that they work as expected. It aims to provide a friendly API that's easy to explore and understand, which will help make your tests easier to read and maintain. It's not tied to any particular test framework, so it can be used equally well with JUnit, TestNG or from a plain old "main" method.

Comparsions to Selenium

Selenium 2 is a next-generation web testing framework that does a better job of controlling browsers than Selenium 1. Selenium 2 includes a brand-new remote protocol for driving browsers across a network. Sauce OnDemand leverages this new protocol to help you run your Selenium 2 tests in the cloud.

Selenium, a popular and well established testing framework is a wonderful tool that provides a handy unified interface that works with a large number of browsers, and allows you to write your tests in almost every language you can imagine (from Java or C# through PHP to Erlang!). It was one of the first Open Source projects to bring browser-based testing to the masses, and because it's written in JavaScript it's possible to quickly add support for new browsers that might be released.

Like every large project, it's not perfect. Selenium is written in JavaScript which causes a significant weakness: browsers impose a pretty strict security model on any JavaScript that they execute in order to protect a user from malicious scripts. Examples of where this security model makes testing harder are when trying to upload a file (IE prevents JavaScript from changing the value of an INPUT file element) and when trying to navigate between domains (because of the single host origin policy problem).

WebDriver takes a different approach to solve the same problem as Selenium. Rather than being a JavaScript application running within the browser, it uses whichever mechanism is most appropriate to control the browser. For Firefox, this means that WebDriver is implemented as an extension. For IE, WebDriver makes use of IE's Automation controls. By changing the mechanism used to control the browser, we can circumvent the restrictions placed on the browser by the JavaScript security model.

In those cases where automation through the browser isn't enough, WebDriver can make use of facilities offered by the Operating System. For example, on Windows we simulate typing at the OS level, which means we are more closely modeling how the user interacts with the browser, and that we can type into "file" input elements.

Additionally, being a mature product, the API for Selenium RC has grown over time, and as it has done so it has become harder to understand how best to use it. For example, it's not immediately obvious whether you should be using "type" instead of "typeKeys" to enter text into a form control. Although it's a question of aesthetics, some find the large API intimidating and difficult to navigate.

With Selenium you need to start a server to execute the integration tests, but with WebDriver you only need to pick a driver and you are good to go. You basically just create a unit test without any dependencies of a server.

One of the other advantages of WebDriver is the clear API. In the next sections I will explain how the API of WebDriver works.

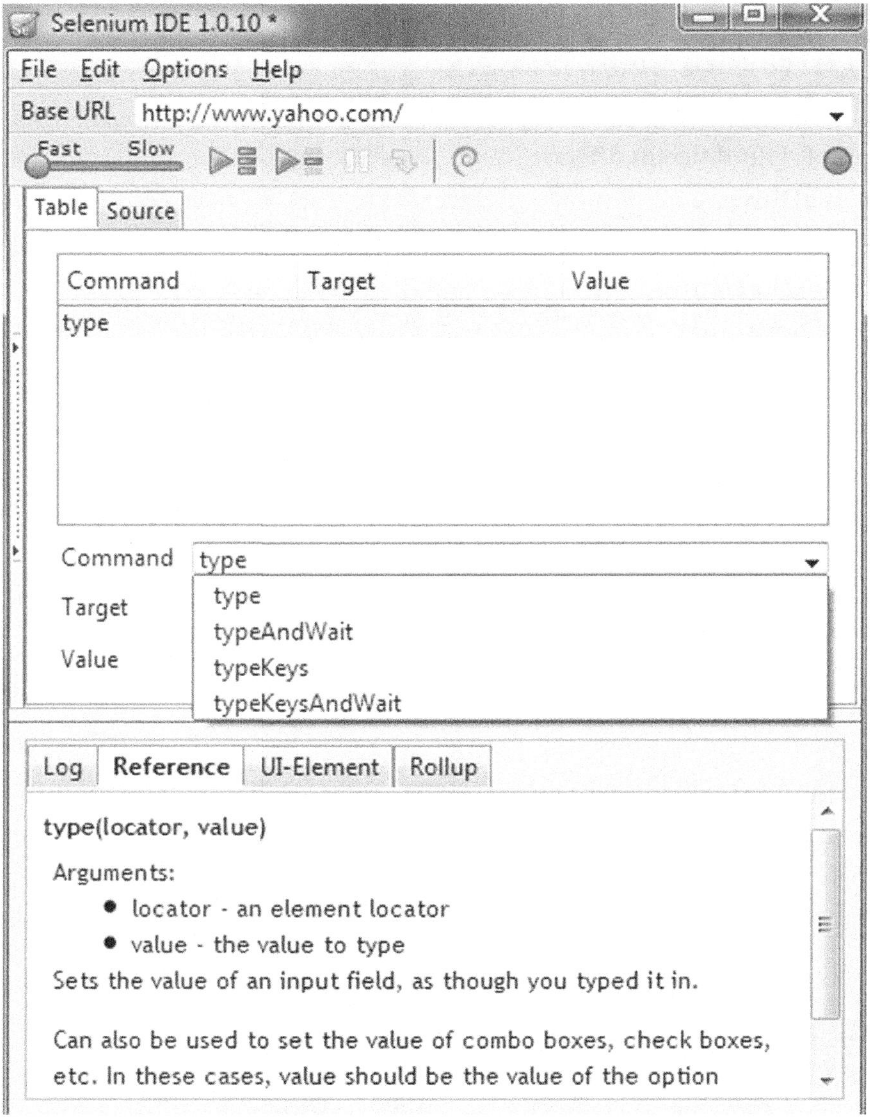
Selenium IDE 1.0.10 *
File Edit Options Help
Base URL http://www.yahoo.com/
Fast Slow
Table Source
Command Target Value
type
Command type
Target
Value
type
typeAndWait
typeKeys
typeKeysAndWait
Log Reference UI-Element Rollup
type(locator, value)
Arguments:
locator - an element locator
value - the value to type
Sets the value of an input field, as though you typed it in.
Can also be used to set the value of combo boxes, check boxes,
etc. In these cases, value should be the value of the option

Drivers in Selenium 2.x

When you start with WebDriver you have to make a choice which driver you want to use. WebDriver currently supports four different drivers:

- HtmlUnitDriver
- FirefoxDriver
- InternetExplorerDriver
- ChromeDriver

HTMLUnit Driver

This is currently the fastest and most lightweight implementation of WebDriver. As the name suggests, this is based on HtmlUnit.

- Pros
  - Fastest implementation of WebDriver
  - A pure Java solution and so it is platform independent.
  - Supports Javascript
- Cons
  - Emulates other browser's JS behaviour

The HtmlUnitDriver is really fast, but does not allow you to see what is actually happening._This can become interesting when you just want to execute the test and get an overview of the results.

So when you want to display the steps that are executed you have to chose one of the other three drivers.

Emulating a Specific Browser

Notwithstanding other considerations above, it is possible to get HtmlUnitDriver to emulate a specific browser. You should not really be doing this, as web-applications are better coded to be neutral of which reasonably recent browser you are using. There are two more constructors for HtmlUnitDriver that take allow us to indicate a browser to emulate. One takes a browser version directly:

HtmlUnitDriver driver = new HtmlUnitDriver(BrowserVersion.FIREFOX_3);

The other uses a broader capabilities mechanism:

HtmlUnitDriver driver = new HtmlUnitDriver(capabilities);

Firefox Driver

- Pros
  - Runs in a real browser and supports Javascript
  - Faster than the InternetExplorerDriver
- Cons
  - Slower than the HtmlUnitDriver

Firefox Driver Installation

The FirefoxDriver contains everything it needs in the JAR file. If you're just interested in using this driver, then all you need to do is put the webdriver-firefox.jar or webdriver-all.jar on your CLASSPATH, and WebDriver will do everything else for you.

Important System Properties:

The following system properties (read using System.getProperty() and set using System.setProperty() in Java code or the "-DpropertyName=value" command line flag) are used by the FirefoxDriver:

Property	*What it means*
webdriver.firefox.bin	The location of the binary used to control firefox.
webdriver.firefox.profile	The name of the profile to use when starting firefox. This defaults to webdriver creating an anonymous profile
webdriver.reap_profile	Should be "true" if temporary files and profiles should not be deleted
webdriver.firefox.useExisting	Never use in production Use a running instance of firefox if one is present
webdriver.development	Never use in production Indicates that we're in development mode.

Normally the Firefox binary is assumed to be in the default location for your particular operating system:

OS	*Expected Location of Firefox*
Linux	firefox (found using "which")
Mac	/Applications/Firefox.app/Contents/MacOS/firefox
Windows	%PROGRAMFILES%\Mozilla Firefox\firefox.exe

By default, the Firefox driver creates an anonymous profile

InternetExporer Driver

This driver has been tested with IE 6, 7 and 8 on XP, but should also work with IE 5.5. It has also been successfully tested on Vista.

➢ Installing

Simply add the webdriver-all.jar or webdriver-ie.jar to your CLASSPATH. You do not need to run an installer before using the InternetExplorerDriver, though some configuration is required.

➢ Pros
- Runs in a real browser and supports Javascript

➢ Cons
- The InternetExplorerDriver will only work on Windows
- Comparatively slow (though still pretty snappy :)

➢ Required Configuration

* Add every site you intend to visit to your "Trusted Sites" If you do not do this, then you will not be able to interact with the page.

ChromeDriver

Note that ChromeDriver is one of the newest drivers. Please report any problems through the mailing list/issue tracker.

➢ Installation

The ChromeDriver contains everything it needs in the JAR file. If you're just interested in using this driver, then all you need to do is put the webdriver-chrome.jar or webdriver-all.jar on your CLASSPATH, and WebDriver will do everything else for you.

The ChromeDriver works with any version of Google Chrome >= 4.0.

➢ Pros
- Runs in a real browser and supports Javascript
- Because Chrome is a Webkit-based browser, the ChromeDriver may allow you to verify that your site works in Safari. Note that since Chrome uses its own V8 javascript engine rather than Safari's Nitro engine, javascript execution may differ.

➢ Cons
- Slower than the HtmlUnitDriver

Emulating Selenium RC

The Java version of WebDriver provides an implementation of the Selenium RC API.

➢ Pros:

- Allows for the WebDriver and Selenium APIs to live side-by-side
- Provides a simple mechanism for a managed migration from the Selenium RC API to WebDriver's
- Does not require the standalone Selenium RC server to be run

➢ Cons:
- Does not implement every method
- More advanced Selenium usage (using "browserbot" or other built-in JavaScript methods from Selenium Core) may not work
- Some methods may be slower due to underlying implementation differences

Which Implementation to Use

Name of driver	*Available on which OS?*	*Class to instantiate*
HtmlUnitDriver	All	org.openqa.selenium.htmlunit.HtmlUnitDriver
FirefoxDriver	All	org.openqa.selenium.firefox.FirefoxDriver
InternetExplorerDriver	Windows	org.openqa.selenium.ie.InternetExplorerDriver
ChromeDriver	All	org.openqa.selenium.chrome.ChromeDriver

For sheer speed, the HtmlUnitDriver is great, but it's not graphical, which means that you can't watch what's happening. As a developer, you may be comfortable with this, but sometimes it's good to be able to test using a real browser, especially when you're showing a demo of your application (or running the tests) for an audience. Often, this idea is referred to as "safety", and it falls into two parts.

Firstly, there's "actual safety", which refers to whether or not the tests works as they should. This can be measured and quantified. Secondly, there's "perceived safety", which refers to whether or not an observer believes the tests work as they should. This varies from person to person, and will depend on their familiarity with the application under test, WebDriver and your testing framework.

To support higher "perceived safety", you may wish to choose a driver such as the FirefoxDriver. This has the added advantage that this driver actually renders content to a screen, and so can be used to detect information such as the position of an element on a page, or the CSS properties that apply to it. However, this additional flexibility comes at the cost of slower overall speed. By writing your tests against the WebDriver interface, it is possible to pick the most appropriate driver for a given test.

Migrating from Selenium RC to Webdriver

You can use the underlying WebDriver technology using the Selenium-RC API. This is primarily provided for backwards compatibility. It allows those who have existing test suites using the Selenium-RC API to use WebDriver under the covers.

Download latest Selenium 2.x (referred as Selenium Server) files from the URL http://seleniumhq.org/download/

For e.g. For version 2.19.0, selenium-server-standalone-2.19.0.jar and selenium-java-2.19.0.zip (selenium-java-2.19.0.jar)

Keep these two jar files in the classpath of your project in Eclipse. Now we need to change our RC code to make it Selenium 2.x compatible.

Using WebdriverBackedSelenium:

Replace:

Selenium selenium = **new** DefaultSelenium("localhost", **4444**, "*firefox", "http://www.yoursite.com");

selenium.start();

With:

WebDriver driver = **new** FirefoxDriver();

Selenium selenium = **new** WebDriverBackedSelenium(driver, "http://www.yoursite.com");

And keep your test script block as it is.

Exceptions

Not every script from RC works with WebdriverBackedSelenium. For e.g.

The javascript evaluations

Replace:

String title = selenium.getEval("browserbot.getCurrentWindow().document.title");

With:

((JavascriptExecutor) driver).executeScript("return document.title;");

Selenium 2 continues to be a moving target with its API, so you'll want to keep up to date.

For e.g. Recently, we found that the toggle() and select() commands have not only been deprecated but removed completely from the implementation. If you try to issue these commands, the Selenium server simply doesn't recognize the commands and WebDriverExceptions are raised.

Selenium 1 users will find that is_text_present() and wait_for_condition() commands no longer exist, and are replaced by a more DOM-driven approach of selecting the element first before firing click() events or retrieving attribute values through get_attribute().

You no longer have to have wait_for_condition() for page loads. Instead, you set implicitly_wait() to a certain timeout limit to rely on find_element_by_id() to wait for the presence of DOM elements to appear to between page loads.

Limitations

Selenium 2.0 has some known issues while playback.

- Explicit waits for Ajax calls are highly recommended.
- While playing back with Firefox 4.x, if you get error like this.getWindow() is null you can get around the problem with the following code fragment, before the line of script that raises this error.

  browser.switchTo().defaultContent()
- Because of browser security reasons, while recording file uploads, WebDriver is able to access only the name of the file being uploaded and not the absolute path. You have to go and edit the path in the recorded script.
- Selenium 2 (WebDriver) requires users to either enable or disable all protection modes under IE security settings. Check here for more details.

EXERCISES

1. What is the relation between Selenium 2.x and Webdriver?
2. Can Selenium RC script run in Selenium 2.x?
3. What are the available driver implementations in Selenium 2.x?
4. What is the use of HTMLUnit driver? What is so peculiar about it's test execution?

AUTHORS' PROFILES

Ashish Mishra is the founder director at QAAgility Technologies and has worked with Selenium as consultant and trainer for various clients. He deals with the ground realities of the test automation requirements and challenges in projects of varied sizes and complexities. Ashish is a big movie aficionado and is fascinated by art of movie making.

Aditya Garg is the founder director at QAAgility Technologies and has led and setup large testing organizations. Aditya loves testing and trainings on the testing topics. Aditya is a bollywood fan and also loves eating and cooking Indian food.

Made in the USA
Coppell, TX
05 November 2026

11314454R00149